FINANCIAL FOUNDING FATHERS

ROBERT E. WRIGHT & DAVID J. COWEN

FINANCIAL
founding fathers

THE MEN WHO MADE AMERICA RICH

THE UNIVERSITY OF CHICAGO PRESS *Chicago & London*

ROBERT E. WRIGHT is clinical associate professor of economics at the Leonard N. Stern School of Business at New York University. He is the author of numerous works, most recently *The First Wall Street: Chestnut Street, Philadelphia, and the Birth of American Finance.*

DAVID J. COWEN is a Wall Street veteran and independent scholar in New York City. He is the author of *The Origins and Economic Impact of the First Bank of the United States, 1791–1797.*

The University of Chicago Press, Chicago 60637
The University of Chicago Press, Ltd., London
© 2006 by Robert E. Wright and David J. Cowen
All rights reserved. Published 2006
Printed in the United States of America
15 14 13 12 11 10 09 08 07 06   5 4 3 2 1

ISBN (cloth): 0-226-91068-7

Library of Congress Cataloging-in-Publication Data

Wright, Robert E. (Robert Eric), 1969–
    Financial founding fathers : the men who made America rich / Robert E. Wright and David J. Cowen.
        p.   cm.
    Includes bibliographical references and index.
    ISBN 0-226-91068-7 (cloth : alk. paper)
    1. Capitalists and financiers—United States—Biography.
    2. Businesspeople—United States—Biography.   I. Cowen, David Jack, 1959–   II. Title
    HG172.A2W75   2006
    330.973′05′0922—dc22

                                                    2005026938

For our families:
From David—for Andrew and Beth
From Bob—for Madison, Alexander, Trevor, Stephanie, and Deb
and
For our mentor:
Richard Sylla, Henry Kaufman Professor of the History of
Financial Institutions and Markets, Stern School of Business,
New York University

The book has been a true joint project between the two authors
with each providing an equal share of the input of research
and output of writing. As a result there is no lead author on this book
but rather a blend of two voices into one.

CONTENTS

IN THE BEGINNING

       "Follow the money," the Hollywood version of Deep Throat advised reporters Carl Bernstein and Bob Woodward as the Watergate scandal unfolded. "Show me the money!" fictional athlete Rod Tidwell ordered his agent Jerry Maguire. "Money," we all say at one time or another, "makes the world go round." But we also regularly claim that it is the "root of all evil." Since the nation's founding, Americans have been obsessed with money, or to be more precise, with wealth. In the 1830s, French travelers like Alexis de Tocqueville and Michael Chevalier were particularly repelled by Americans' love of lucre, but their observations were based in fact, not Franco-American animosity. As storied Harvard economist John Kenneth Galbraith once quipped, "everything happens [in America] as if Saint Peter, when receiving souls in heaven to send the ones to Paradise and the others to Hell, asked them only one question: 'What have you done on earth to increase the gross national product?'" Americans were often more concerned with wealth than others because they were better at producing it than most other people were.

    Why they were relatively better at producing wealth, at making money, than others is an open question. This book provides one type of answer, one based on the lives of early America's most important, and in some cases most notorious, financiers. But this is no elitist, top-down story. The real heroes are the American people, the farmers, merchants, manufacturers, and artisans whose interactions with the financial system, and with the government institutions and policies that supported that system, ensured that the economy remained highly meritocratic, that it dispersed its fruits fairly, if not evenly. We begin and end this book with two critical episodes where the electorate interceded to make matters right once again.

    Hell hath no fury like an artisan scorned. And the artisans definitely felt scorned and furious. Skilled craftsmen who owned their own shops and tools, the artisans who showed up at New York City's polls to elect state legislators in

April 1800 sought sweet revenge against the party in power, the Federalists. In previous elections, the artisans, who represented about a third of the electorate, staunchly supported both the Federalist leadership, including President George Washington and Alexander Hamilton, and Federalist causes, like the adoption of the U.S. Constitution. But now Federalist-inspired policies angered them. At the top of the list were two items that directly impacted their wealth: excise taxes and rejection of their loan applications by the city's two Federalist-controlled banks. A member of the opposition Republican Party,[1] young aristo-crat Aaron Burr, felt the artisans' pain, as cunning politicos do. He won Man-hattan's artisans over to the Republican cause by promising substantial tax relief and by offering them numerous bank loans from his newly formed Manhattan Bank.

This New York story is more than just an interesting sidebar to the presiden-tial election of 1800. That famous election, readers may recall, pitted Burr and Republican planter Thomas Jefferson against the sitting Federalist president, John Adams, and the now obscure Charles C. Pinckney. Adams had defeated Jefferson in the 1796 election but in an ironic twist ended up with his famous op-ponent, the author of the Declaration of Independence and former secretary of state, as his vice president. Most people know the election of 1800 because the same strange Constitutional electoral rule, thankfully long since amended (just imagine John Kerry or Al Gore as second-in-command to George W. Bush), that made Jefferson vice president in 1796 resulted in a tie between Jefferson and Burr in 1800. That unhappy and unexpected result threw the election into the House of Representatives. Rather than bow out gracefully—the deal between the two had been that Burr would be vice president—Burr remained silent. A dead-locked Congress and constitutional crisis ensued.

Most observers, then and now, blame Burr for the electoral controversy. But interestingly, Adams lost his reelection bid due to the efforts and popularity of Burr, not Jefferson. Direct democracy was not the order of the day. State legis-lators, not the citizenry, cast the state's votes for presidential electors. The elec-tion of state legislators in spring 1800, therefore, decided not only which party

---

1. The early Republican Party later metamorphosed into what we today call the Democratic Party (symbolized by a donkey). The modern Republican Party, symbolized by an elephant, arose on the eve of the Civil War. For more details, see the Concordance entry "Republican Party." Readers should note that the Concordance serves as a glossary of terms and guide to in-dividuals mentioned in the book. It also contains a timeline of events important to the financial founding fathers discussed in this book.

would control New York that year but also which party would control New York's votes in the Electoral College that fall. As it turned out, the presidential election was a very close one; New York's votes represented the Republican's margin of victory. Why did the artisans vote Republican in the crucial spring elections? As noted, they did so because Burr swayed them with campaign promises and loans from the Manhattan Bank. Because he brought New York into the Republican fold, and did so months before the other states voted, Burr cost Adams his second term. Burr felt that his pivotal role in the election justified his silence as Congress debated who should be president.

Why isn't this crucial aspect of the election of 1800 taught in high school or college American history classes? Other subject areas are commonly favored at the expense of U.S. economic and financial history. While we now know the role that Indians and debtors played in the coming and winning of the Revolution, the part women played in the Constitution, and the central importance of slavery and its aftermath to all of American history, our history books are largely mute on the contribution of early financial institutions and markets.

That oversight, in and of itself, would be of little consequence were it not for the fact that finance was an absolutely crucial aspect of the nation's early history. Remove the financial system established and extended by certain of the founding fathers and U.S. history would have turned out quite differently, if indeed the United States would have had any history as a nation at all.

Americans are justly proud of the democracy that they forged in the nineteenth century, extended in the twentieth, and seek to protect in the twenty-first. But they forget that democracy comes at a cost, a cost that not all nations can afford to pay. All democracies need the same elixir—economic prosperity. The more resources that a nation's economy can produce, the fewer and more muted will be the discontents and the less venal the government will become.

But from whence springs economic prosperity, this tonic of democracy and political stability? Surely not from veins of gold, deposits of oil, or other natural endowments—at least not alone. China is well endowed with natural resources and Japan by comparison is almost bare. Yet Japan, even after a decade of difficulties, is far wealthier on a per capita basis. England and Holland had but little in the way of natural resources (England at least had coal), yet they each managed to acquire and rule vast empires far richer in the fruits of the earth. Conversely, Spain once had access to the precious metal mines of the New World, but yet grew relatively poorer even as it expropriated those deposits.

Adam Smith had it right. Economic prosperity comes not from the possession of physical valuables like gold and silver but rather from the *ability* to produce goods and services, like the maxim that giving a man a fish will feed him for a day, but teaching him to fish will feed him for a lifetime. The United States enjoyed access to a great wilderness, but so had the Indians, the Canadians, and the Mexicans. Yet America flourished, and the others did, and are still doing, everything they can to integrate their economies with that of the United States.

Consider one significant difference between the early United States and its neighbors: Early Americans knew finance and created the financial institutions and markets necessary to induce economic growth. America had more bridges, factories, and cannons than other countries because Americans had the financial wherewithal to fund the creation of such wonders, to induce the savers among them to entrust their stashes—big and small—to men with potentially profitable plans. Finance, in short, was the horse to the economy's wagon. And sitting in the driver's seat of that wagon were the financial founding fathers, the subject of this book. Our financial founding fathers laid the base that enabled America to become a rich nation.

None of this is to say that the early financial system led to U.S. economic preeminence overnight. The American economy emerged from the Revolution in shambles. At least nine out of ten people worked in agriculture, and per capita income lagged that of Britain, Holland, and probably France too. What early financial firms and markets did was to make the agricultural and commercial sectors, where the nation's initial comparative advantage lay, more efficient. More importantly in the long run, they helped to create the modern part of the economy, the industrial sector. With the aid of insurance, bank credit, and capital markets, U.S. manufacturing grew extremely rapidly. Because it started from such a small base, however, it took decades for American industry to catch the world's attention.

In the simplest terms, the financial founders created the financial system that drove the economic growth that allowed America to become America. Far from causing deep divisions, economic growth tends to smooth out differences and to smooth over conflicts. Economic growth, by which we mean increased real per capita aggregate output, pleases everyone. The benefit of that growth, increased personal wealth, does not fall to everyone equally, but outside of the ivory towers of academe nobody questions it as long as the wealth acquisition "game" is fairly played. If we found a goose that laid golden eggs and you got ten eggs for every egg that I received, I might get a little jealous. But I certainly would not kill the goose. And if you fed the goose ten times as much as I did, I would not even begrudge you your fair take.

At a very fundamental level, early Americans quickly came to understand that financial development was the goose that laid the golden eggs, that it was the key to generating the economic growth that would allow everyone to lead better lives. During the presidential campaign of 1800 there were certainly important issues, like the Kentucky and Virginia Resolutions, splashed across the front pages of newspapers throughout the country. But what did the Republicans do to win election in 1800? They established a bank! That's right, a bank! That bank lent to the opponent's most vulnerable constituency, Manhattan artisans upset over excise taxes and the fact that, after years of ample accommodation, they could no longer obtain loans from either of the Federalist-controlled banks in New York, the Bank of New York or the New York branch of the Bank of the United States.

Readers raised on standard historical fare may wonder: did not debates about the funding system and the national bank nearly tear the nation asunder in the early 1790s? Yes, there were *debates,* but nothing more. Debates do not tear nations apart, the *lack* of debate does. The founders disagreed about many things, including finance. But they allowed the voice of reason to prevail. And that made all the difference. For the record shows that after they took office, Republicans in the federal government used the financial tools developed by Federalist Alexander Hamilton to purchase Louisiana and to fund a war against Great Britain. At the state and local level, Republicans too turned to negotiable bond issues and banks to fund everything from canals to colleges to water works.

Some Republicans, with Thomas Jefferson the visible leader of this camp, had serious misgivings about banks and corporations, but cooler heads, in particular Treasury secretary Albert Gallatin, prevailed. In the end, Republicans ended up creating dozens, then scores, then hundreds of commercial banks. But they did not stop there. They chartered other types of financial institutions, including savings banks and fire, marine, and life insurance companies, in prodigious numbers. Bridges, boat lines, canals, ferries, hotels, ironworks, libraries, salt mines, stock exchanges, textile mills, theaters, trading companies, and sundry utilities also gained corporate privileges and held initial public offerings of stock, and all with the helping hands of Republicans. Most importantly of all, Republicans tied the interest of the state to the success and well-being of all those corporations by imposing moderate taxes on them.

There were certainly differences between the parties. Generally, Federalists backed England and abhorred the violent French Revolution. Republicans, on the other hand, were friends of France and its revolution. Federalists were interested in commerce and large-scale manufacturing, Republicans in agriculture and craft manufacturing. Federalists wanted cities and a vertical social order to predominate. Republicans sought a vast agricultural paradise with a horizontal social order dominated by stout yeoman farmers. But underneath those differences there lay a good degree of common ground, the desire for economic prosperity, and, eventually, a general consensus that financial development was the means to that end.

True, in 1811 Republicans killed the recharter of the Bank of the United States, Hamilton's creation and the nation's first central bank. Yet a few years later, as the financial system lay in shambles, they scrambled to re-create, and of course control, a bigger successor to Hamilton's bank. They learned, however, that a privately owned joint-stock corporation was not terribly amenable to political control. So when the successor came up for renewal, they killed it, replacing it with a coterie of smaller, easier to control commercial banks and a government entity called the national subtreasury system.

What we are suggesting is that there is an underlying continuity to our history in terms of finance. In short, those who bashed banks and bonds were a distinct minority. Granted, some held high positions in government and made a lot of noise. They could and would turn a phrase. Most Americans, however, clearly saw that finance was important to their well-being. If anything, they wanted more of it, especially, as New York's artisans showed in 1800, if they could get more for themselves.

We will demonstrate this point through the public lives of nine men, some famous, some unknown, others misunderstood, all among America's financial founding fathers—Alexander Hamilton, Tench Coxe, Albert Gallatin, Thomas Willing, Robert Morris, William Duer, Stephen Girard, Nicholas Biddle, and Andrew Jackson. Although the emphasis on men rather than events or institutions has its drawbacks, in this case the benefits of biography outweigh the costs. Most readers find stories about people intrinsically more interesting than descriptions of banks or explanations of financial instruments.

Two of our financial founding fathers—Hamilton and Jackson—are household names if only because their portraits adorn the $10 and $20 Federal Reserve notes, respectively. On the back of those notes are emblazoned the words "In God We Trust." Those four words remind us that money, finance, the early nation, and religion are intertwined in ways numerous and deep. In fact, the source most widely cited by the Revolutionaries was not John Locke's *Second Treatise of Government* or Montesquieu's *Spirit of the Laws,* but Deuteronomy, the book of the Old Testament in which Moses, in a series of speeches, sets out the laws for what will be the nation of Israel.

While some early Americans pitted religion against finance, railing against the worship of Mammon (money), most Americans then and to this day have successfully reconciled the two. Finance is merely a tool that people can choose to use for good or evil. The U.S. government certainly seems to think so. In addition to Federal Reserve notes, and despite the separation of church and state, it has for two centuries put phrases like "In God Is Our Trust" on its bonds and coins. In his famous first inaugural speech—the one where he says that Americans have nothing to fear but fear itself—Franklin Delano Roosevelt used a religious analogy to explain both the causes of and the means to end the Great Depression:

> The money changers have fled from their high seats in the temple of our civilization. We may now restore that temple to the ancient truths. The measure of the restoration lies in the extent to which we apply social values more noble than mere monetary profit.

Greedy financiers were the problem, in other words, not the financial system per se. Most Americans apparently agree that the love of lucre is religiously and morally problematic, not the use of stocks, bonds, and banks. We have therefore linked a "religious" motif to each of our financial founding fathers. The motifs pay homage to the very old notion that there *might* be a higher power at work guiding the nation and also clarify each character's role in our story. Moreover, these metaphors were a way to tie our story together around a central theme.

Alexander Hamilton was none other than the metaphorical "creator" of the financial system, the self-made man who turned America into the land of self-made men. Hamilton, of course, was not actually a god. He did not even work alone. Washington had the foresight to appoint him Treasury secretary in 1789 and the good sense to accept his counsel on financial matters. English precedents provided him with the raw materials that he needed to build his financial universe. Moreover, bankers, securities dealers, and other financiers provided the gravity of self-interest that made the whole system work.

Another of Hamilton's major helpers was Tench Coxe, his now obscure but nevertheless brilliant second in command, or Assistant Treasury Secretary. When Hamilton chose Oliver Wolcott to succeed him as Treasury secretary, however, Coxe became indignant and turned into the metaphorical "Judas," abandoning the Federalists for the Republicans. Turncoats were not at all uncommon in the early period, and most changed allegiances due to disputes over "patronage"—appointment to government jobs, in other words. Regardless of his party affiliation, Coxe's contributions were considerable.

Hamilton was not so fortunate in his first choice of Assistant Treasury Secretary, William Duer, who turned out to be a rogue of the first magnitude. Though born in England, Duer became a staunch Patriot during the Revolution. Unfortunately, about the same time he also became the "sinner," a self-interested swindler who ruined the lives of countless people, rich and poor alike. Perhaps worse yet, in 1792 he helped to cause a financial panic that convinced many that Hamilton's financial system was corrupt and had to go. His financial shenanigans provided the Republicans with a rallying cry that maintained its potency for over a decade.

Albert Gallatin, the "savior," is proof positive that continuity characterized early U.S. financial policies. This Swiss-born whiskey rebel served as Jefferson's and Madison's Treasury secretary. In that position, he further solidified Hamilton's financial edifice rather than dismantling it, as Jefferson in his less lucid moments was wont to do. Moreover, after a distinguished stint as a diplomat, he became a successful Wall Street banker. Like a hippie turned CEO, Gallatin began his public life as a troublemaker but ended it as one of the pillars of the establishment and a staunch advocate of financial development.

The next two chapters, "Angels Risen and Fallen" and "The Saint," juxtapose business failure and success. The bigger point of both chapters is that market forces, not political forces or tradition, dictated who partook most of the early economy's growth. Robert Morris, like William Duer, made fabulous riches but then committed several crucial blunders and lost it all back. Stephen Girard and Thomas Willing, in contrast, structured their businesses soundly and were amply and permanently rewarded. Those who best fed the goose, in other words, received the most golden eggs.

Those two chapters also allow us to delve into the functioning of the newly formed capital markets. In other words, they afford us the opportunity to describe, in a general, nontechnical way, how early financial institutions and markets functioned. The early credit markets were magnificent, almost as splendid as today's. Financiers and investors did not directly produce goods, but they certainly produced services, and valuable ones at that. As a group or market, they decided which entrepreneurs got the capital and liquidity necessary to improve their businesses and indirectly the entire economy. Out of self-interest, investors chose those entrepreneurs who were likely to earn the highest profits, or in other words the best, brightest, and most efficient. The entrepreneurs, in turn, employed workers and supplied the market with quality inexpensive wares and services. The process made everyone richer and provided a solid foundation for economic growth.

The final chapter, "Apocalypse No," explains that even the "Bank War" between Andrew Jackson and Nicholas Biddle over the second Bank of the United States did not harm the American economy in the long run. Though the conflict between Jackson and Biddle did jolt the economy and disrupt the financial system, by that time they were robust enough to recuperate from the shock. By the mid-1840s the economy had returned to full strength, not to be cut down again until the Civil War. And by repaying the national debt in full, Jackson actually strengthened the credit of the United States. That made it easier (and cheaper) for the government to borrow in the future to finance its wars against Mexicans and slaveholders.

Like Joseph Ellis in *Founding Brothers,* we begin our story with Hamilton. Unlike Ellis, who first describes Hamilton's tragic death on the dueling grounds of Weehawken, we start with Hamilton at the height of his powers, safely at home in Philadelphia, his wife beside him, and working throughout the night.

Alexander Hamilton (1755–1804)

February 22, 1791, was an ordinary day for the 42,000 or so citizens of Philadelphia, the largest city in the new nation and, for the time being, its capital. But for one unusual man, Secretary of the Treasury Alexander Hamilton, it was an extraordinary day, and a more extraordinary night. Hamilton was at work on a document that would make or break America's nascent financial system. The stakes were enormous. What lay at risk was the centerpiece of Hamilton's financial system, a bank. Not just any bank, but a *Bank of the United States,* with the right to open branches anywhere in a nation then serviced by only four relatively small and localized banks. Hamilton's proposed Bank was to be managed by private businessmen but to include a strong government investment of $2 million, or 20 percent, of the slated $10 million in capital. Though a seeming pittance today, $10 million was a colossal sum for the day, dwarfing as it did the combined capital of all joint-stock companies then in operation in the country. In other words, if the Dow Jones Index then existed, the Bank alone would have comprised over half of it.

Several years earlier, in 1789, Hamilton had been appointed the first ever Secretary of the Treasury. In that post, he directed a monumental undertaking to straighten out the nation's tangled finances. He funded the national debt and even engineered the "assumption" by the new federal government of all the various state debts accrued during the Revolutionary War and its aftermath. That was no mean feat, given that the taxpayers of the fiscally responsible states did not want to pay the debts of their profligate neighbor states. With a little luck and a big dose of political acumen, Hamilton had made federal "assumption" of state debts a reality. With that base in place, the time had come to continue work on the financial system by establishing a national bank, an institution where savers and users of capital could come together, where a paper currency could be created and made acceptable for commerce by its easy convertibility into specie (gold or silver coins), where both entrepreneurs and governments could safeguard their cash and receive loans.

Banks were then highly controversial, but Hamilton was at the apex of his brilliance, guiding his Bank bill through Congress, ably aided by Congressman Fisher Ames of Massachusetts, a nationalist of the most fervent type. Although the Bank bill passed the Senate on January 20, 1791, congressman and *Federalist Papers* co-author James Madison tried to defeat it in the House. On February 8, the diminutive Madison and his allies lost a roll call that counted 39 in favor of the Bank and only 20 opposed. The political fighting had been particularly nasty, causing one senator to state in his diary that "some gentlemen would have been ashamed to have their speeches of this day reflected in the newspapers of tomorrow." The attack by the mostly southern opponents to the Bank was a landmark in American history, marking as it did the birth of the agrarian or Jeffersonian wing of the Republican Party. While this stand was the agrarian Republicans' first, it was certainly not their last; they would not rest in their attempt to destroy the creative work of Hamilton and his funding system.

Although it had passed both houses of Congress, the Bank bill was anything but a done deal. To become law, President George Washington would have to sign it, and do so before February 26, the time limit imposed by the Constitution. While Hamilton's ties to the president were many and deep, forged as they were during the crises and dangers of the Revolutionary War, Virginia's agrarian Republicans, led by Secretary of State Thomas Jefferson, Attorney General Edmund Randolph, and Madison, also had strong ties with Washington. All four gentlemen shared Virginian roots and bore the stain of slaveholding, though some more thoroughly than others. The agrarians were formidable adversaries because they were well-educated men with brilliant minds. Most importantly, their opposition was not so much political as ideological; they vehemently opposed the Bank as unconstitutional and potentially dangerous to republican government. Jefferson and Randolph pressed the president to veto the Bank bill, and Madison's vain attempt to galvanize opposition to the Bank in Congress made it obvious where he stood.

Washington had a decision to make. Dare he veto a bill of such importance passed by both houses of Congress and eagerly submitted by his closest economic advisor? Dare he sign the measure and face the accusation that he had passed a law that was, according to many prominent Virginians, impolitic, poor policy, and, perhaps most damning, clearly unconstitutional? Washington showed Hamilton the arguments against the Bank set forth by Randolph and Jefferson and gave him a week to respond. In essence, he placed in Hamilton's hands the power to save his creation.

It was the sixth day, February 22, and Washington's deadline loomed. As the sun set, thirty-two Philadelphia watchmen who shouted out the hour started their work as each of the 662 lamps that brought light to the seaport's dark thoroughfares were lit. By suppertime that evening, the printing presses of the local newspapers stopped. The door of the Treasury Department at 100 Chestnut Street was locked. City Tavern, the central meeting place for politicians and merchants, served its last meal for the evening at 8 p.m. A few hours after that most of the other hundred or so taverns shut their doors for the night. Perhaps Bishop William White, the revered pastor of Christ Church, reviewed his Sunday Sermon at his residence, 309 Walnut Street, before turning in. By midnight most residents were fast asleep, and one would expect that the home of Robert Morris on Sixth and Market, where President George Washington resided, was quiet, as were the residences of Thomas Jefferson at 274 High Street, Tench Coxe at 126 South Third Street, and his neighbor Oliver Wolcott at 121 South Third Street.

But if anyone that night ventured a little farther down Third Street from the Wolcott house they would have observed the lights on at number 79, the home of Alexander Hamilton. The hour of the walk would not have mattered as Hamilton, with wife Elizabeth assisting, worked all night long to finish the rebuttal. Many years later, Elizabeth Hamilton recalled that night: "I sat up all night with him. . . He made your government. . . . He made your bank. . . . My husband said, 'We must have a Bank.'"

Many observers, however, demurred or remained unconvinced of the necessity of a national bank. Hamilton believed that the long-term viability of his new funding system depended on passage of the law. The pressure to produce a flawless retort weighed heavily on him, and he rose to the challenge. In the first clear articulation of the broad or loose interpretation of the Constitution, Hamilton argued that the Bank, though not explicitly mentioned in the Constitution, was clearly constitutional because "every power vested in a Government is in its nature *sovereign,* and includes by *force* of the *term,* a right to employ all *means* requisite and fairly *applicable* to the attainment of the *ends* of such power."

Hamilton had turned the tables on his opposition. Where Jefferson, Madison, and Randolph argued that the federal government had no power to incorporate a bank because it was not explicitly *allowed* to do so in the Constitution, Hamilton retorted that the government enjoyed all powers necessary to its functioning that were not explicitly *forbidden.* Hamilton's logic was unanswerable. From that day forth the doctrine of "implied powers" increasingly dominated legal interpretation of the Constitution. Hamilton had gained not one but two victories, the establishment of the Bank and the widespread acceptance of the doctrine of implied powers.

Washington signed the bill on February 25. The centerpiece of Hamilton's creation was in place. The creator had once again triumphed. However, the "triumvirate" of Madison, Randolph, and Jefferson was horrified that their fellow Virginian had signed the bill. As one pamphleteer noted, "the great Washington burst from the trammels which had been prepared for him, shook off the bias on which the triumvirate had placed their main dependence, and to the great mortification of their party, fixed his signature on the bill." The agrarian trio would not soon forget.

Quite likely, Washington signed the Bank into law because he knew that the financial system was as yet incomplete and that the country needed a national bank, both to aid the government's fiscal operations and to help unify the nation's credit and capital markets. Moreover, Washington, like Hamilton, wished to expand the role of the federal government. Finally, Washington realized that Madison and Jefferson were being hypocritical. When it suited their purposes, they had implicitly upheld the doctrine of implied powers now explicitly advanced by Hamilton. Reflecting some fifteen months later on the titanic Constitutional struggle, the secretary succinctly explained: "A mighty stand was made on the affair of the Bank. There was much commitment in that case. I prevailed."

Prevail is a word that describes Hamilton perfectly. The ultimate self-made American was most likely born in 1755, not on the mainland but rather in the sticky heat of Nevis, a tiny island in the West Indies. Young Alex learned early to prevail because he had to. He was, as John Adams later claimed, "the bastard brat of a Scottish peddler." Hamilton's father, James Hamilton, was the fourth son of a Scottish aristocrat. With no chance of inheriting his father's property, he traveled the Caribbean seeking his fortune. He did not find it, but he did discover the warm embrace of Rachael Lavien nee Faucitt. That half-French, half-English island beauty had fled from her French husband, who had imprisoned her for what he considered indecent and suspicious behavior.

Rachael and James lived together but could not marry because of Rachael's marriage. Religious and public policy considerations rendered divorce wellnigh impossible for British subjects. Couples often separated, but, because a divorce could only be granted by an act of Parliament, usually only those with political connections or large sums of cash could procure a divorce that would allow legal remarriage. Undaunted, Rachael bore two sons, James and Alexander. The four lived in St. Croix until the feckless James declared bankruptcy and abandoned his family. To supplement the family's income, young Hamilton apprenticed as a clerk in the trading firm of Nicholas Cruger, Cornelius Kortright, and David Beekman. The precocious youth even managed the business when Cruger, the principal based locally, was away.

Hamilton, at the age of 13, had to prevail again when his mother, who had pieced together a livelihood as a retailer, died. He prevailed again when his guardian, a distant relative named Peter Lytton, committed suicide the following year. He prevailed yet again in 1772 when a deadly hurricane struck the West Indies while he was in charge of Cruger's operation. That storm was so severe that Pennsylvania sent provisions to help supply "the unhappy Sufferers." Though one of its victims, the young Hamilton, now just 17, was able to create something positive out of the storm both literally and figuratively: he wrote a letter describing its horrible aftermath and showed it to Dr. Hugh Knox, a local clergymen. Knox was so impressed with the piece that he had it published in a local newspaper. The newspaper story earned Hamilton the respect and admiration of his community and brought forth benefactors—most likely Knox, his employers, and cousin Ann Lytton Venton—who sent him to the mainland for a proper education. Hamilton would never return to his native land.

As a nominal Presbyterian, Hamilton had his heart set on Princeton, then the College of New Jersey. He sailed to the mainland armed with a letter of recommendation from Knox, an alumnus of that college. Princeton, however, would not allow the impoverished orphan to move through the curriculum at his own pace. Columbia, then King's College, was more accommodating. So instead of twiddling away the hours in the wilderness of New Jersey, Hamilton, after living with Elias Boudinot in northern New Jersey as he raced through some preparatory work at a grammar school, settled in the bustling metropolis of Manhattan.

There, Hamilton was quickly drawn to the radical cause bent upon overthrowing British rule. Hamilton, after all, was a college student, and the 1770s were a tumultuous time. He was not a typical radical, though, for he disdained mobs and disorder. So rather than burn effigies or set up Liberty Poles, he penned several widely read polemics. Yet when the real shooting began in 1775, Hamilton zealously enlisted in the patriotic cause. In March 1776 the undergraduate was appointed a captain of the New York artillery, but that at first meant only title without command, as Hamilton, in accordance with the custom of the day, had to provide his own troops and supplies. Eventually, however, he scraped a unit together.

Hamilton and his men fought bravely in several early battles, including the unsuccessful attempt to hold Manhattan from the British. Hamilton and his unit covered Washington's retreat across New Jersey. In the sharpest exchanges,

Hamilton's artillery kept the British at bay while the bulk of the American forces crossed first the Raritan River and later the Delaware. Hamilton also took part in the successful, and famous, counterattacks at Trenton and Princeton in the winter of 1776–77. One wonders if Hamilton took special joy in pouring grapeshot into a Redcoat position in Princeton's Nassau Hall.

Observers marveled at the apparent contradiction of Hamilton's youth and skill, but the early break in Hamilton's military career was due to his administrative skills, which were nothing short of masterful, not his battlefield heroics. General Washington invited the brilliant young Patriot to become one of his several aides-de-camp, positions usually reserved for the "well-bred," not orphaned bastards. But Hamilton could and would prevail on talent alone. Washington recognized that talent, giving ever-increasing responsibility to the young officer, now a lieutenant colonel. During the next few years of fighting, when desertion was all too common, Hamilton stayed loyally by his commander's side. He was there for the frozen winters at Valley Forge and Morristown; the military disasters like the abandonment of New York City in 1776 and the subsequent retreat across New Jersey; the real treacheries of Benedict Arnold, and the perceived treacheries of an impotent Continental Congress; and the failed opportunities like Monmouth, when he was at Washington's side when the Virginia gentleman lambasted General Charles Lee in mid-battle for gross misconduct. And Hamilton was with Washington during the good times, the infrequent victories, and the secret march to trap Cornwallis at Yorktown. There, Hamilton capped his military career with battlefield heroics by charging and capturing an important British redoubt.

"Little Hammy" or the "Little Lion," as he was affectionately known, was, along with other favorites like Generals Nathanael Greene, William Alexander ("Lord Stirling"), and Henry Knox, clearly ensconced in Washington's inner circle. Some believe that Washington was the father figure that Hamilton never had, and perhaps Hamilton was the son that Washington never had. Their special bond, though occasionally strained, lasted a lifetime. Though much younger than Washington, Hamilton would not long outlive the general.

Despite the turbulence of the war years, battle plans were not the only subjects flourishing in Hamilton's fertile mind. Hamilton understood that the rebels' finances were in shambles. In an attempt to improve the situation, he commenced communication with Robert Morris, another self-made man of deep importance to the Patriot cause. It is here we first glimpse Hamilton's creative genius, as he became the architect and chief advocate of a powerful national bank. In 1779, and again in 1781, as the war raged, Hamilton drew up proposals for a national bank. Those recommendations planted seeds for an idea that would take a decade to come to fruition. Central to Hamilton's early plans were several key provisions of what would later be the hallmarks of his financial program: foreign loans, partial government ownership of a national bank, and use of that bank to provide the national government with short-term loans.

A national bank, Hamilton realized as early as 1781, would both stimulate the economy and enhance the government's shaky credit. "In a National Bank alone," he wrote, "we can find the ingredients to constitute a wholesome, solid and beneficial paper credit." He was correct. Acting as Superintendent of Finance, Morris teamed up with private entrepreneurs to establish the rebellious nation's first national bank, the Bank of North America. We will learn more of this episode in "Angels Risen and Fallen." For now, suffice it to say that the Bank of North America, after struggling to its feet, aided both the war effort and the recovery before politics interceded and temporarily stripped the institution of the corporate status granted it by Congress. It continued to function, however, as an important, Philadelphia-based commercial bank.

Hamilton also married during the war, in December 1780. His bride, his little "nut brown maid," was the sweet and petite Elizabeth Schuyler, daughter of New York patroon (manorial baron) General Philip Schuyler. Hamilton clearly loved his "Betsey." Although Hamilton flirted with Betsey's vivacious sister Angelica, we know of nothing more passing between the in-laws than playful letters and the occasional polite kiss. Hamilton did have at least one extramarital affair, with the lovely Maria Reynolds, who was in league with her husband and attempted to blackmail the nation's highest financial officer. Luckily for Hamilton, news of the adultery and failed blackmail attempt did not leak to the public until years later. Hamilton, to his credit, owned up to the whole thing. He remained wedded to Betsey, who bore him eight children.

After the war, Hamilton, young bride in hand, sought training in the law. The young nation had no formal law schools, but obtaining entry into the lucrative field of law was as expensive then as now. A would-be attorney had to pass rigorous examinations in order to begin practice, but only after apprenticing to a practicing lawyer for three years, the apprentice paying for the privilege of doing the lawyer's menial work. Hamilton, as usual, found the requirements too rigid. For the average mind, three years was probably just enough time to learn the rudiments of the law and pass the examinations. But for Hamilton three years was an eternity, a waste of his considerable talents and energy. He therefore jumped at the opportunity presented by a law waiving the three-year apprenticeship rule for young men who had been called away from their legal studies to the war effort.

Hamilton had certainly gone off to war but he had not really been studying law at the time: though later showered with honorary degrees, he never officially graduated from college. The state legislature, however, had passed the law because it wished to give its officers some hope for the future. So the state allowed Hamilton through the loophole, and even widened it by providing him a study extension from the April deadline until October. Still, Hamilton's accomplishment was truly stunning. Between January and October 1782, he qualified himself to practice both office and courtroom law. He did it, interestingly enough, by writing a forty-thousand-word textbook for himself. That textbook, about half the length of this book, was copied, by hand of course, by other attorneys-in-training until it was finally in wide enough demand to be published. That was roughly the equivalent of a Ph.D. student today writing and publishing a scholarly monograph in order to prepare himself for his qualifying exams. Clearly, this was no ordinary man!

Hamilton soon became the greatest of the nation's early lawyers, at least in the estimation of famed New York jurist James Kent. He did it by penetrating to the very root of each issue, concentrating always on first principles. Those qualities we have already seen in his telling opinion on the constitutionality of the Bank of the United States. They showed up in everything that he did.

Because of his constant attention to first principles instead of the meaningless detritus that usually occupies lesser minds, Hamilton's thought was often far in advance of that of most of his contemporaries. This is not to say that he could see the future but rather that he took positions that remained unpopular or misunderstood until well into the nineteenth century. Two episodes in 1784 demonstrate his prescience. First, Hamilton established a private commercial bank. The innovation came not so much from the bank itself, which closely followed the procedures established by its predecessor, the Bank of North America. Rather, the innovation came from the way in which the bank, the very same Bank of New York that still graces Wall Street, found legal life.

The Bank of New York was a joint-stock company, not a partnership, which was a much too cumbersome form of organization for a large firm. In a partnership, the business had to be liquidated and re-formed each time a partner died or sold out his equity in the company. Moreover, when partnerships sued, or were sued, each partner had to be named in the suit. Worse still, each partner was responsible for all of the firm's debts, even those contracted by other partners. Partners therefore had to watch each other like hawks.

Partnerships with more than a handful of principals were simply too un-wieldy. In a joint-stock company, by contrast, owners could buy or sell their equity or shares in the firm without affecting the operation of the business. Moreover, joint-stock companies could sue and be sued as a single "body politic" instead of as the individuals composing it. And those individuals could not be sued in their individual capacities for the company's debts. For big com-panies requiring large amounts of capital and hence many owners, like an urban commercial bank, the joint-stock form was well-nigh essential.

In the Anglo-American tradition, however, it was customary for a company that wished to take the joint-stock form to obtain a legal charter. That meant that the politicians got involved in order to pass a law granting the company explicit corporate privileges. The great British joint-stock companies, like the East In-dia Company and the Bank of England, had each obtained a parliamentary charter. Many of New York's legislators, however, were in no mood to grant a charter to the Bank of New York. Upstate politicians did not see how a bank in New York City would help them, but they could imagine any number of sce-narios where the bank could hurt them, particularly at the polls in the next elec-tion. The New York State legislature, therefore, refused to answer the bank's "prayer," its formal request to incorporate.

After such a rebuff, most would-be incorporators would have given up. But not the Little Lion. He understood that incorporation merely granted a joint-stock company the imprimatur of the state. The most essential advantages of the joint-stock form, negotiable shares, status as a legal entity, and limited liability, could be secured *without* formal legislative approval. So the Bank of New York formed and began business anyway, under private "articles of association" in-stead of a special legislative act. Hamilton used the same technique again with the Merchants' Bank in the early nineteenth century.

The importance of articles of association has largely been lost to history be-cause most joint-stock companies, including the Bank of New York, the Mer-chants' Bank, and the Bank of North America, sought and eventually received formal incorporation. What has been missed is that many joint-stock companies used Hamilton-style articles of association to begin business before receiving formal sanction to do so. Even when faced with a recalcitrant legislature, any new company that so desired could enjoy most of the benefits of the corporate form. The mere option of forming without a charter gave companies great lever-age to force the legislature to come to terms. If a particular legislature would not deal, the company could simply begin business and wait until favorable election results made formal incorporation possible. Hamilton, in short, had greatly reduced the barriers to entry into large-scale enterprises. Because of the loophole Hamilton found and exploited, state legislatures eventually gave up trying to limit the number of corporations and established administrative procedures for incorporation. Not surprisingly, one of the first states to do so, in both manufacturing and banking, was New York.

The other 1784 episode that demonstrated Hamilton's prescience sprang from the case of *Rutgers v. Waddington,* which underscored the importance of the concept of judicial review. New Yorker Elizabeth Rutgers, a well-to-do elderly widow who fled the British army in 1776, sued Joshua Waddington for £8,000 in damages caused by Waddington's use of her brewery during the British occupation. Rutgers brought her action under the terms of the Trespass Act, a radical piece of legislation that flouted established principles of common and international law. Serving as counsel to the defense, Hamilton shredded the law as essentially illegal and won a ten-fold reduction in the damage claim.

Rutgers v. Waddington did not establish the principle that courts could strike down a law as unconstitutional. But it planted the seeds that later grew into that check or block against abuse of legislative power. For Hamilton, as for most Americans, government was bound to act according to the rules set down in the federal or state constitutions. Yet the constitution would be meaningless if any legislature could pass a law inimical to it and force the courts to execute that law. Judicial review has grown into one of the most important ways by which the government is prevented from growing too venal, too set upon satiating its own ends instead of those of the people.

The *Rutgers* case applied to New York's 1777 state constitution. Though created and passed in the early days of the war, as the state legislature fled the approaching British, New York's first constitution was a successful one. New York attorney John Jay was responsible for it. Jay clearly understood the "agency problem" inherent in government—the tendency, that is, for government officials (the "agents") to act in their own interests rather than in the interest of the people who elected them. Jay made provisions, including a special council of revision to review the constitutionality of laws, to counter it. In that relatively stable constitutional and legal environment, Hamilton thrived. Soon, therefore, he could turn his attention to the establishment of a new federal constitution.

As far as anyone has been able to ascertain, Hamilton's role in the Constitutional Convention proper was relatively minor. His efforts before and after the Convention, by contrast, were crucial. Hamilton was the most ardent of the nationalists, that group of men who sought the creation of a more powerful national government, because he had no ties to any particular state. He had lived in New Jersey and Pennsylvania as well as New York. As an opponent of slavery, he was not comfortable in the southern states with their heavy concentrations of slaves. Commercial New England was more to his liking. But as a native of the West Indies, he thought in terms of "America" rather than any one of the several states.

Accordingly, Hamilton set out to replace the Articles of Confederation, a weak national frame of government established during the Revolution. He first came to despise the impotent Articles during the conflict because they proved unequal to the task of properly provisioning the Continental Army. His hatred solidified during his stints as a Continental congressman and a confederation tax collector as he saw the futility of the instrument firsthand, and even in peacetime. So in 1786 Hamilton jumped at the chance to represent New York at an interstate trade convention in Annapolis, Maryland. Hamilton steered the convention to release a report that solemnly declared that the nation faced a grave crisis that transcended mere trade disputes. That same report urged the states to send delegates to a general convention in Philadelphia in May of the following year.

That meeting, of course, was the one of lore that led to the Constitution. But the mere creation of that document did not make it the law of the land. Before it could take effect, nine states would have to ratify it. Its ultimate adoption, therefore, was by no means assured. Little states with no real future on their own, like Delaware, quickly signed on. (Rhode Island, with its strong streak of independence, was the exception to this rule.) But sentiment in larger states like Massachusetts, New York, Pennsylvania, and Virginia was mixed. Urban and commercial men typically supported adoption because they realized that the new government would be good for trade. Moreover, such men understood that the document contained numerous checks and balances against government venality that would prevent government officials from usurping their liberties and properties. Many inland farmers, on the other hand, did not see much in the proposed Constitution to benefit them. Moreover, they saw much to fear. Had they not just suffered gravely to establish their independence? Would their sacrifices—farmers had won the war, of course, or so they believed—simply go to create a new tyrant that would aid everyone but themselves?

In fact, were it not for the efforts of Hamilton, James Madison, and, to a lesser extent, John Jay, the Constitutional Convention might have become a mere footnote in world history. Those three men penned the famous *Federalist Papers*, hundreds of pages of closely reasoned exposition on the merits of the proposed frame of government. Those essays, which appeared in key newspapers throughout the country, persuaded many fence sitters that the Constitution was sound. The Constitution was not submitted to a plebiscite. Rather, the decision for adoption was delegated to special constitutional conventions in each state. We shall never know what percentage of the American electorate wished to see adoption, but we do know what happened in each state convention, and that Hamilton was the leader of the victorious pro-Constitutional forces in New York's ratifying convention. In the late eighteenth and early nineteenth centuries, legislative gatherings tended to be boisterous, all-out affairs filled with bribery, violence, intrigue, and dastardly parliamentary tricks. Indeed, Pennsylvania and Massachusetts both ratified thanks to deft maneuvering and outright chicanery on the part of nationalist forces.

When New Hampshire became the ninth state to ratify, the Constitution went into effect. When Virginia followed suit on June 25, 1788, the remaining holdouts—Rhode Island, North Carolina, and New York—took on the appearance of rogue states. Nevertheless, the prospect of New York joining the new union at first looked dim. Most of the delegates to the ratifying convention were chosen by upstate farmers and hence were opposed to adoption. To win, Hamilton and Jay spread rumors that New York City was prepared to secede from the state and join the new nation on its own. That outcome would have landlocked upstate New York. (The St. Lawrence River was not a reliable international thoroughfare until the construction of the St. Lawrence Seaway in the twentieth century, and of course the Great Lakes and Mississippi basin were not yet open to American commerce.) The upstate forces capitulated, as did the other holdout states.

On April 30, 1789, the new government commenced in earnest; President Washington was sworn in on the steps of Federal Hall on Wall Street in Manhattan, the temporary national capital. Soon after Congress created the Treasury Department in September 1789, Washington offered Hamilton the post of Treasury secretary, and the Senate concurred. Hamilton accepted the position, not for the pay, which was far inferior to what he was earning in private practice, but rather because it provided him a platform from which he could remake the American economy and the financial system.

Today, the Departments of State, Treasury, Commerce, and Defense are all massive. There was no such parity in 1789; the Treasury was the focal point of the entire executive branch of government. From the outset, the department's influence was marked by its sheer size and scope of affairs. Its initial headcount, thirty-nine, ballooned to fifty-three within a year. Compare that with the staff of five at State under Jefferson, and three at Henry Knox's War Department. Total salaries for each department also demonstrate Treasury's dominance: Treasury, $43,000; State, $6,250; War, $6,500. Hamilton alone among all the cabinet officers had an assistant, or vice-secretary. Most impressively, or ominously depending on one's perspective, Treasury maintained a comprehensive network of agents throughout the country.

The other cabinet members had additional reasons for jealousy. Congress continually asked Hamilton, and Hamilton alone, for strategic guidance. More alarming still, Hamilton responded to such requests with alacrity. The secretary presented several monumental state papers that, when combined with the entrepreneurial talents and self-interested desires of thousands of Americans, forged a national financial system: *The Report on Public Credit* (January 9, 1790), *The Report on the Bank* (December 13, 1790), *The Establishment of a Mint* (January 28, 1791), and *The Report on Manufactures* (December 5, 1791). Taken together, Hamilton's reports were nothing short of a strategic outline for the establishment of a thriving economy rooted solidly in the bedrock of sound fiscal management, a stable monetary system, extensive short-term commercial credit, and long-term development capital. On the grandest scale, the secretary's policies helped to solidify the new government by creating incentives for wealthy individuals to invest in it, directly through ownership of its bonds and indirectly through ownership of shares in the Bank of the United States. He surmised, correctly as it turned out, that the financial system would be "the powerful cement of our Union."

In the *Report on Public Credit,* his first and arguably most famous report, Hamilton proposed that the new national government take responsibility for all state and national debts left over from the war. This was a truly revolutionary concept. Those $75-odd millions of obligations, which took literally scores of different forms, traded at just fractions of their face value. Few expected payments on those decade-old obligations. So why did Hamilton argue that the national government should "service" this debt? Would it not be better simply to default on it, as so many countries had done before (and since)? The fledgling United States certainly did not appear to be in a position to pay its debts. But herein lies the genius of Hamilton. Where others saw a problem, he saw opportunity. While others viewed the national debt as a threat to republican government, Hamilton believed it was "a national blessing." In addition to aligning the interests of the wealthy with those of the government, his funding plan would increase the nation's credit overseas, making it cheaper and easier for both the government and private enterprises to obtain foreign financing. Finally, funding would create a form of liquid capital that would help the economy to allocate resources more efficiently.

Making a proposal was one thing. Getting it through Congress was quite another. Americans were generally agreed that the portion of the national debt owed to foreigners, the foreign national debt, should be paid in full. They differed, however, on the best way to service or pay off those debts. The question of the national debt owed to citizens, the domestic national debt, was even stickier. Some, including Madison, wanted to discriminate against most public creditors by compensating the original holders of the debt in lieu of the current owners. Much of the national debt was composed of promissory notes given by field officers to soldiers and by commissary officers to farmers. The soldiers and farmers had often immediately sold the notes at steep discounts for cash or goods. Madison wanted to make the soldiers and farmers whole, at the expense of those who subsequently purchased the notes.

Hamilton eventually crushed the discrimination argument with his usual barrage of logic and first principles. The debt instruments were simply a species of property, the value of which fluctuated with the government's fortunes and interest rates. They were, moreover, fully negotiable instruments. In other words, exchanging them was perfectly legal. The original holders had not been coerced into selling and had received a valuable consideration for the ownership of the obligations. Only the current owners of the bonds, Hamilton concluded, could be compensated. For those who could not follow his reasoning, Hamilton offered the Continental Congressional resolution of April 26, 1783, authored ironically enough by Madison, that solemnly pledged that there would be no discrimination against those who obtained government debt in the secondary market.

Assumption of state debts, turning debts owed by the state governments into an obligation of the new federal government, proved a tougher nut to crack. Several states, notably Virginia, had demonstrated fiscal responsibility with respect to their war debts and were therefore reluctant to assume the debts of more profligate states like South Carolina and Massachusetts. More vexing still, Thomas Jefferson and James Madison led Virginia's contingent in Congress. The two men were remarkably similar but yet nothing alike. Both had been born and raised in central Virginia, just a few miles from each other in fact, within sight of the magnificent Blue Ridge. Both were uneasy slaveholders but too wrapped up in politics and theorizing to gain the wealth that would have enabled them to afford to free their slaves. Jefferson and Madison worked as a team. Alone, each would have been a formidable adversary. Together, they were almost unstoppable, as their later iron grip on the presidency proved. But the pair had one great weakness, their blind love of the Old Dominion. They fervently desired the national capital to be permanently located in their native state. Hamilton realized this, and used it to his advantage.

Herein lies one of the great deals in American political history, cut between Hamilton and the two Virginians at a dinner party. The Virginians horse-traded votes for assumption of state debts in return for removal of the capital to the shores of the Potomac in ten years time. This was a truly stunning trade made possible only by the fact that the Virginians did not know that Hamilton too sought a southern capital. (He believed that it would assist in keeping southern states in the Union.) The southerners, for their part, vowed never to trade with Hamilton again because they felt that the Treasury secretary had gotten the better of them. But they too gained from the deal. In addition to the nation enjoying a stronger economy due to assumption, three Virginia presidents, who served a total of twenty-four years, enjoyed a relatively short trip from their central Virginia plantations to the Potomac capital.

Hamilton also secured the votes of Pennsylvania's representatives by having the capital moved to Philadelphia from New York for an interim period of ten years. (The Philadelphians wistfully believed that the government would never leave their beautiful city.) According to one contemporary, the opposition to assumption was so "slight and feeble" that it would have easily passed had not southerners decided to hold it up to give them a bargaining chip for a southern national capital. The Residence Bill, therefore, was "the offspring of a political cohabitation (for it cannot be called a marriage) between Pennsylvania and Virginia." "Begotten in darkness," the bill "forced its way through the Senate . . . where it underwent the solemn farce of a discussion—a phalanx of well-disciplined troops were placed to guard it."

The positive effects of funding and assumption of the debt upon not only the country's credit standing but also its commerce were felt almost immediately. Writing from Hartford in 1791, Noah Webster, the "schoolmaster of America," boasted about the era of prosperity brought on by assumption. "The establishment of funds to maintain public credit," he noted, "has an amazing effect upon the face of business and the country." "Commerce," he continued, "revives and the country is full of provision. Manufactures are increasing to a great degree, and in the large towns vast improvements are making in pavements and buildings."

Moreover, Europe's capital markets magically opened to the United States. As early as March 1791, United States securities were selling from 1 to 40 percent above par in Europe. In November 1791, European-based broker John Fry assured Hamilton that American credit overseas was secure and that European funds would stabilize securities prices. "The American Funds," Fry claimed, "had inspired no Confidence in this market 'til they had acquired a high price at home & three months ago a sale of them must have been effected here with the greatest difficulty." "The Case is now so materially alter'd," he wrote, "that one friend of mine has bought & sold near a Million of Dollars." Fry noted that Europeans at that time had more money than local investment opportunities and were looking to employ their capital in the United States. In short, Americans were able to borrow money in Europe at between 3 and 6 percent and use it to fund projects that returned 10, 15, even 20 percent per year. The strong economy made Hamilton's fame. According to one contemporary observer, "his reputation traversed the ocean and in distant climes his Name was mentioned among the great ministers of the age."

But even that rousing success was not enough for Hamilton, who possessed a truly comprehensive understanding of the entire economic process. He realized that funding and assumption, which created both national and international markets for U.S. government bonds, was only a start. The government, not to mention entrepreneurs, still did not have ample access to short-term credit, the very life-blood of commerce and manufacturing. And, Hamilton further realized, the combination of active securities markets and adequate banking facilities would prove truly awesome. The secretary therefore set out to exploit the synergy of funding and banking. The *Report on the Bank* contained one of the most fundamental elements of that synergy. Shares in the Bank were paid for mostly in government bonds, not gold and silver. Thus, bond prices would be supported as individuals bought securities to use them to purchase Bank shares. Next, the Bank would issue notes and deposits, all backed by gold and silver. Those Bank liabilities, in turn, became the nation's principal media of exchange, and could be used to purchase government bonds, other financial securities, or any asset for that matter, without the hassle of counting out payment in the potpourri of foreign coins and local banknotes that Americans had to contend with before the Bank's establishment. (Imagine trying to purchase an automobile or a refrigerator with a mix of yen, euros, and Mexican pesos.) In that fashion, the banking and funding systems worked together to enable economic growth.

Hamilton's vision for the American economy coalesced in his *Report on the Bank,* making it a masterpiece that cogently explained the importance of banks in a capitalist economy. Hamilton started by stating his "conviction"—one based on copious study of European financial theorists like Jacques Necker— that a national bank would prove "an Institution of primary importance to the prosperous administration of the Finances, and would be of the greatest utility in the operations connected with the support of the Public Credit." Next, he stressed that all the great powers of Europe possessed public banks and were indebted to them for successful trade and commerce. The implications of the comparison were clear: if young America wanted to join the ranks of the elite powers, it too would have to create a banking infrastructure. The national bank would confer many benefits. It would provide government with a ready source of loans, a safe depository for federal monies, a low-cost mechanism for transferring funds from point of collection to point of disbursement, and an inexpensive agent for meeting payments on the national debt and government salaries. After all, in 1790 technology was still quite primitive. In the absence of electronic wire transfers, how did the federal government receive a tariff duty paid in Charleston, South Carolina? How did it pay a federal judge in Boston? How did it pay interest on a U.S. government bond held by an investor in London? How did it finance the construction of warships like the fabled USS *Constitution?* The Bank provided all those services and more.

To ensure the safety of the government's deposits, the Secretary of the Treasury was empowered to inspect the state of the Bank as frequently as once a week. To ensure that the government would have access to funds when it needed loans, restrictions were placed on the Bank's ability to lend to individual states and foreigners. To make certain that the Bank made mostly safe loans, interest rates were capped at 6 percent. (Unable to charge more than 6 percent, the Bank naturally sought out the best, i.e. safest, borrowers.) The government, as the largest stockholder in the institution, would share in its profits but have no direct participation in its management. In Hamilton's view, independent managers would prevent abuse by the government and provide a necessary check against its possible perfidy, much like judicial review did for courts and legislatures. The private status of the Bank would ensure that the government could never use it as a tool of oppression. As Hamilton noted, governments were never "blessed with a constant succession of upright and wise Administrators." But the Bank, as a private institution, would have a "magnetic sense" of its "own interest . . . the prosperity of the institution" and thereby prevent the government from succumbing to "the temptations of momentary exigencies."

The model for Hamilton's plan was the greatest banking force of the day, the Bank of England. In 1790, Tench Coxe, Hamilton's assistant secretary, sent him a note with a pamphlet he wrote in 1786 that highlighted the English institution: "The Bank of England is better worth our attention, than any which has ever existed." Hamilton also drew on Adam Smith's seminal work, *An Inquiry into the Nature and Causes of the Wealth of Nations,* where financial matters, including the advantages of banks and bank money, were amply and ably discussed. Hamilton must have brimmed with excitement as he read Smith declare that "the trade of Scotland has more than quadrupled since the first erection of the two publick banks at Edinburgh." Hamilton also read Malachy Postlethwayt's *Universal Dictionary,* which suggested that commercial banks ought not to invest heavily in real estate, sound advice generally heeded until the 1980s. The secretary also relied on his knowledge of the domestic operations of the Bank of New York and the Bank of North America. Moreover, two directors of the latter institution, Philadelphia merchant William Bingham and Postmaster General Samuel Osgood, probably helped to shape the secretary's ideas.

The moment Washington finished signing the Bank bill, Hamilton's financial system was nearly complete. The national Bank, an enormous institution whose notes would circulate countrywide and whose loans would grease the wheels of commerce, agriculture, and manufacturing, was to become a reality. Investors were delighted. On July 4, 1791, fittingly enough, they eagerly snapped up "scripts" or rights to purchase shares in the new Bank. It was the most intense initial stock offering the country had yet witnessed. The offering was oversubscribed by 20 percent and sold out within hours in most locations. Subscriptions had to be scaled down pro rata. Subscribers included a broad-based group of wealthy individuals who included thirty members of Congress, Secretary of War Henry Knox, many merchants and speculators, as well as several states, the Bank of New York, the Massachusetts Bank, and Harvard University. Even Hamilton had not foreseen the tremendous demand for the Bank scripts, the price of which soared within a month from the initial $25 to over $300. Speculators, including wealthy brokers Jeremiah Wadsworth, Andrew Craigie, Joseph Barrell, and William Constable, were actively involved in buying shares in the after-market. William Duer and Robert Morris also took large positions, sometimes bullish and sometimes bearish. We will learn later that Morris loved to gamble. We will also discover that Duer made Morris seem tame, plunging his hands into every speculation imaginable and often crossing the line between speculation and fraud.

Bulls lined up on one side of the market—championed now by Duer—and bears on the other—led by Brockholst Livingston. Lawyer Robert Troup mentioned to his friend Hamilton that "the truth is that the fluctuations [in stock prices] are principally owing to the arts & contrivances of mere jobbers" and that Duer was purchasing and "is mounting fast above [Livingston]." As during the 1990s Internet craze, when individuals left good jobs to become day traders, some local businessmen got caught up in the excitement of fast and easy money. According to U.S. Senator Rufus King, the scene was one of "mechanicks deserting their shops, shopkeepers sending their goods to auction, and not a few of our merchants neglecting their regular and profitable commerce of the city" to join the trading frenzy. As always, Madison and Jefferson were incensed. Six days after the offering, Madison wrote Jefferson that the entire "business" was "shameful" because "members of the Legislature . . . were most active" in the market, "openly grasping its emoluments."

By early August, the price of Bank stock in New York produced a one-month profit in excess of 50 percent! Little wonder that shopkeepers found the temptation for quick profits too great to bear. Express carriages sped through little Jersey towns carrying "stockjobbers" in transit between the stock markets of New York and Philadelphia. Such behaviors were unprecedented in America. Many, particularly those "short," predicted that the speculative bubble was certain to burst, just like the infamous "South Sea Bubble" in 1720 had and the stock market crash of 1929 would. Hamilton soon found the wild run-up of securities prices a cause for alarm. "I thought it advisable to speak out," Hamilton told confidant Rufus King, "for a bubble connected with any operations is of all the enemies I have to fear, in my judgment the most formidable. . . . I thought it therefore expedient to risk something in contributing to dissolve the charm."

Hamilton's fears were justified. Loan curtailment would mean that money would become scarce, interest rates would rise, and securities prices would suffer. Speculators who had borrowed money to buy stock would especially feel the pinch because they would have to sell securities in order to repay their loans. The same phenomenon occurs today when calls are made on highly leveraged (indebted to the hilt) traders who buy on "margin." Using other people's money at 6 percent per year is a great game if prices move your way 10 percent in a few weeks. But if prices move contrary to expectations, speculators may end up in serious financial and legal trouble. So at the first sign of trouble, a stampede for the door ensues. If the doorkeeper, a central banker like Hamilton or Alan Greenspan, is not paying attention, more than a few end up trampled underfoot.

When the Bank of New York and other private lenders curtailed loans to the speculators on August 11, panic set in and prices of scripts soon dropped from a peak of about $325 to around $125. This type of rapid wealth destruction had not been seen before on our shores. On August 15, Hamilton, whose main concern was for the entire financial system, calmed the markets with direct open market purchases of government securities. The brokers immediately felt the relief, as one commented four days later that "stocks rather look up, and we are told the Treasury has not had much offered to him." The mere knowledge that Treasury stood ready to make purchases helped to temper the market and the mini-crisis abated. Hamilton showed that he knew how to combat crises by adding money to the system. In effect, he had opened the door, allowing speculators to exit in a somewhat orderly fashion.

By autumn, the markets had calmed and the Bank geared up to commence operations. Stockholders flocked to Philadelphia's City Hall on October 21 to choose directors in the new institution. The first board, composed of twenty-five men, was nevertheless quite distinguished, including as it did three U.S. senators and four U.S. congressmen, as well as lawyers, merchants, brokers, and even a physician. Most were members of the Federalist Party, northerners, and wealthier than average. (Representatives of Philadelphia, New York, and Boston accounted for 80 percent of the Bank board. Not surprisingly, only one board member hailed from Virginia.) Board seats were eagerly sought because directors decided who did and did not receive loans. Directors also determined salaries of all the Bank's officers and clerks and supervised the printing and supply of banknotes. The main board in Philadelphia passed judgment on loans to the government. Hamilton certainly needed to have allies on the board, as the government was soon to be the Bank's largest borrower.

The biggest question was, who would be president of the Bank? Oliver Wolcott, then working for Hamilton in the Treasury Department as comptroller, might have been the stockholders' first choice because he supported the establishment of branch offices. But Wolcott made it clear that he preferred public service. The presidency therefore devolved on Philadelphia merchant Thomas Willing, who was elected unanimously at the October 25 meeting. Willing had a strong resume and good credentials and will be featured later in "Angels Risen and Fallen." Suffice to say he was a resolute Federalist, a former judge of Pennsylvania's Supreme Court, and perhaps the wealthiest man in Philadelphia, in some part owing to a partnership with Robert Morris in the successful mercantile firm Willing & Morris. At least one board member, speaking on behalf of a "faction," argued that Willing would become Morris's puppet. The president of the Bank, he argued, "ought to be free from all suspicion of management." Willing received the nod anyway because he had served as president of the Bank of North America for about a decade and therefore was the preeminent commercial banker in the country.

The main branch opened to receive deposits on December 12, 1791 at Carpenter's Hall in Philadelphia. Soon thereafter, the Bank began making loans. Loan recipients could take their proceeds as notes, deposits, or a combination thereof. Whatever their choice, the liabilities could be turned into gold or silver coins upon demand, or tendered in payment of federal taxes. Borrowers included merchants, politicians, manufacturers, landowners, and most importantly, the government of the United States. In the spring of 1792, the Bank opened branch offices in Baltimore, Boston, Charleston, and New York, making it the first nationwide enterprise in American history.

In addition to making loans to government, Hamilton's creation performed other central banking functions. It regulated state banks by returning their notes for redemption in specie. That practice forced the state banks to hold specie reserves and effectively prevented them from over-issuing their notes. The Bank also shared macroeconomic information with the Treasury Department, and discussed with it economic conditions and policies designed to safeguard the credit system. The Treasury Department often took a paternal attitude toward the institution, particularly when the Bank stressed its independence or seemed to be overextended. Importantly, the Treasury, with the Bank's aid, acted as a lender of last resort, acting to stabilize the financial system on numerous occasions. The Treasury used various methods to achieve financial stability, including the purchase of debt securities, the manipulation of specie payments to banks, the regulation of Treasury drafts, and, when necessary, the addition of funds to ailing banks. The Treasury and the Bank, in other words, worked closely together to ensure the economy's health. As Hamilton noted a year after the Bank's inception, even "the most incorrigible theorist among its opponents would in one month's experience as head of the Department of the Treasury be compelled to acknowledge that [the Bank] is an absolutely indispensable engine in the management of the Finances."

〜 Every week several of the directors of the Bank walked downstairs to the vault to take inventory. A perusal of the vault inventory statement from March 14, 1795 provides us with a glimpse into the national bank's activities. The vaults contained banknotes, both those of the Bank and of local banks, totaling $536,000, a variety of French, Spanish, and Portuguese gold coins worth $150,000, and several chests filled with silver coins worth in sum about $13,500. The Bank's vault did not contain any U.S. coins, yet all of the sums are stated in dollars. That curious situation can be explained only by delving into the early history of the U.S. Mint.

On April 2, 1792, George Washington signed into law a bill establishing a mint, a factory for the production of coins for the federal government, under article 1, section 8 of the U.S. Constitution. (That same clause empowered Congress to "regulate the Value . . . of foreign Coin," a power that it also exercised.) The bill drew upon the earlier work on coins and mintage proffered during the Confederation period by Thomas Jefferson, Gouverneur Morris, Robert Morris, and others, and the more recent recommendations of Hamilton, whose *Report on the Establishment of a Mint* Congress had received on January 28, 1791.

The early U.S. Mint was a failure. High copper prices plagued the minting of pennies and half pennies from the start. Moreover, the 1792 law made no provision for the Mint to purchase gold and silver bullion on behalf of the public, so the institution relied entirely upon private flows of specie to provide the silver and gold for the coinage of higher denomination coins. Not until July 1794, almost two years after commencing operations, did the Mint receive a private deposit of silver, some $80,000 of French coins owned by the Bank of Maryland. The first private gold flow into the Mint occurred in February 1795, when New England merchant Moses Brown deposited $2,276 worth of gold bullion.

But private flows remained pitifully small. The Mint, which required a fairly sizeable scale of operations to run efficiently, languished, coming under repeated Congressional inquiries. Its early directors, which included famed scientist David Rittenhouse and Elias Boudinot, one of Hamilton's first benefactors, remained frustrated in their efforts to turn the Mint into an important economic force. In hindsight, the reason for their failure is readily apparent: the Mint was largely unnecessary. Bank liabilities (notes and deposits) and foreign coins admirably served as the nation's media of exchange.

Yet, Hamilton's report and the subsequent Mint Act of 1792 *were* important parts in the early credit system, for the act defined the U.S. dollar as a *unit of account*. The unit of account is a measure of value; it answers the question "what is the value of that?" just as inches answer "what is the length of that?" or grams answer "what is the weight of that?" In other words, the Mint Act defined the size of the goose's golden eggs.

Today, Americans are accustomed to conflate the unit of account with the medium of exchange because the two have been identical for decades. In other words, we measure money in the same units, the U.S. dollar, that we use to trade or exchange. If a store clerk says "the value of that item is $5," we know that, to obtain the item, we can present a $5 Federal Reserve note, write a check, or pull out a credit card. This coincidence of measuring rod and means of payment is extremely convenient. It is also a relatively new phenomenon.

In the colonial period, if a store clerk said that the price of an item was $5, the customer might tender 5 Spanish milled dollars. However, he could also hand over 37 shillings and 6 pence of Pennsylvania bills of credit, for each dollar was worth 7 shillings and 6 pence in Pennsylvania. Or, he might offer 38 chickens, each worth a shilling, and demand 6 pence in change. (There were 12 pence in a shilling, 20 shillings in a pound.) If this sounds confusing, that is because it is. Imagine the impediment to trade.

The unit of account (the measuring rod of value) and the medium of exchange are distinct things. The medium of exchange, it turns out, is relatively unimportant. What people agree to exchange, be it silver, paper, or chickens, is up to them. The key to economic growth is finding a reliable, stable method for defining or measuring value. That allows people to compare, and hence exchange, unlike things. How many chickens is a cow worth? A horse? A farm? A bond? Without a common measure, without a unit of account, answering such questions is nearly impossible.

Without a unit of account, all trade is barter. And barter, everyone knew, was extremely inefficient. "Bartering of Commodities for Commodities," one Englishman noted, "would soon be found Chargable and Inconvenient, and a hindrance to *Trade*." "Bartering one species of property for another," colonists too realized, "would be endless labour." "For some years after the settling of this colony," "A Pennsylvanian" wrote in 1768, "we had but little specie, and trade was carried on chiefly by truck or barter." "Under such inconveniences," the "man in years" correctly noted, "it was found impossible for a colony to flourish, or the inhabitants make any considerable progress in their improvements."

Accordingly, the colonies had each developed their own unit of account, their own method for measuring value. Converting from one colony's unit to another was often an arduous, mind-boggling task. Think of the trouble that would ensue if an "inch" or an "ounce" in New York were different from an "inch" or an "ounce" in Pennsylvania! Luckily for colonists, most trade was conducted between each colony and the Mother Country, so the problem was not a serious one. After independence, and especially after the passage of the Constitution, however, trade flows between the states increased significantly. The nation clearly needed a single unit of account, an identical way of measuring value. Hamilton gave it to them, in the form of the U.S. dollar. Not the physical dollars that the Mint found so difficult to produce, but rather the U.S. dollar as an abstraction, as the value represented by 371.25 grains of pure silver (416 grains of "standard silver") or 24.75 grains of pure gold (27 grains of "standard gold"). The Mint Act also defined the "standard"—but in terms too arcane to discuss here—and fixed the ratio of silver to gold at 15 to 1.

With those definitions, there emerged a distinctively American unit of account that served as the legal basis upon which all business contracts could be fairly adjudicated. A contract that called for the payment of, say, $100 could be satisfied by the payment of gold and silver as defined in the act, or by the payment of other goods and services acceptable to the creditor and valued as defined in the act. In terms of this book's larger themes, the Mint Act ensured that Americans played the game of life on a level playing field, that their inputs were commensurate to the outputs, thereby enabling a fair and consistent measurement.

But Hamilton's funding system, the Bank, and his creation of a stable unit of account would come to little if the United States did not produce anything. The Dutch had showed that there were profits to be made from acting as mere middlemen, buying from one to sell to another. But the Dutch experience had also showed the limitations of such a livelihood. Clearly, America would produce ever more prodigious surpluses of agricultural goods for market. However, demand for foodstuffs waxed and waned. Moreover, rampant competition meant that the profit margins on agricultural products would always remain thin. Significant wealth lay not in extracting the rude products of the earth but rather in working those raw materials—trees, grains, and ores—into useful goods like houses, bread, and metalware. To really get the goose to pump out its golden eggs, Americans would have to learn to add value to raw materials. In other words, they needed to invest in manufacturing.

Hamilton knew this and, in his usual style, set out to put his adopted countrymen on the correct path, whether all of them liked it or not. Before the Revolution, Hamilton made it clear that he thought America could become a major manufacturer. "Neither is there any great difficulty, in acquiring a competent knowledge of the manufacturing arts," he wrote in *Farmer Refuted,* one of the productions of his radical college days. "In a couple of years many of our own people might become proficient enough, to make the coarser kinds of stuffs and linens." During the Revolution, Hamilton continued to learn, copying much information about manufacturing into his artillery pay book. He also took copious notes on glass, asbestos, and other manufactured goods.

In the New York Ratifying Convention held in Poughkeepsie in 1788, Hamilton showed at least a general knowledge of the current development of indigenous manufactures. "Our manufactures are in their infancy," he opined, "but are they always to be so? In some of the states, they already begin to make considerable progress. In Connecticut such encouragement is given, as will soon distinguish that state." In response to his profound understanding of the importance of manufacturing, the artisans and mechanics of New York and indeed the English-speaking world generally adored him and penned him glowing letters of admiration.

As part of his comprehensive economic program, Hamilton authored a brilliant *Report on Manufacturing* where he made the case for expanding U.S. manufactures. The report was submitted to Congress on December 5, 1791, and was the fourth of his monumental state papers devoted to the development of the new nation's economy. Tench Coxe made important contributions to the manufacturing report, as we will discuss in detail in "The Judas." Importantly, Hamilton understood that aside from protective tariffs and bounties, government could do relatively little to encourage manufacturing. A national manufactory, unlike a national bank, simply did not make economic sense. Private enterprise would have to do the heavy lifting. But that did not mean that Hamilton could not again lead the way.

Hamilton, with help from Coxe, William Duer, and others, founded the Society for the Establishment of Useful Manufactures (SEUM) to demonstrate that America could create its own indigenous manufacturing base. On the banks of the mighty falls of the Passaic River in New Jersey, the SEUM attempted to build an eighteenth-century industrial park supported by the money of private equity investors. While the venture did not develop according to plan, and Duer, as he was wont to do, raided the till, Hamilton again showed that his ideas ran well ahead of those of most of his contemporaries. It would be several more decades before large-scale manufacturing would catch hold in America.

If Hamilton's financial program was as important to the development of the U.S. economy, the nation's political development, and its national sovereignty, as claimed here, why did it arouse such heated opposition? Some opposition was clearly ideological; many Republicans had a fundamentally different vision for the nation. Some opposition, however, appears to have been personal; sometimes people took a stand on an issue simply because Hamilton supported the other side. "*Fame,*" one contemporary observer noted, "begets *Envy,* and envy begets hatred."

But the root of the problem appears to have been one of perceived economic interest. Southerners wanted states rights and an agricultural economy, while northerners sought a relatively strong national government and an economy rooted in commerce and manufacturing. Indeed, Hamilton's funding system brought to the surface the recurring issue of states' rights, the rights of the colonies or states versus the rights of the imperial or federal government. Most observers thought of the question as if it were a "zero-sum" game. In other words, what one government gained the other necessarily lost. Although Congress ultimately held the purse strings, many viewed Hamilton with suspicion because he headed the powerful Treasury Department. The agrarian Republican forces feared a Treasury-dominated central government, noting that in Britain prime ministers bent on uncontested power first co-opted the Exchequer, the British treasury. Agrarian Republicans also believed that Hamilton's cronies, speculators and merchants congregated in the northern cities, favored English interests. Parts of the agrarian Republican critique contained language that suggested that the real struggle pitted merchant capitalism against agrarianism.

Other parts suggested that sectional differences, North vs. South, were the key. In the case of the Bank, sectional differences were clearly visible in the House ballot; only one northern vote was cast against the Bank while only three southern votes favored it. Representative William Branch Giles of Virginia described the sectional vote in February 1792 as indicative of a "radical difference of opinion" between North and South "upon the great governmental questions." That difference of opinion would eventually lead to the Civil War. The funding issue also contained a sectional tinge. Agrarian Republicans saw all indebtedness as pernicious. One particularly vituperative polemicist chided Hamilton for calling the public debt "a blessing" and called his reputation "bloated." His ad hominem attack also claimed that Hamilton's reports were effective only because they were so long and "fatiguing" that they "confound the judgment" and force readers into "a labyrinth of error."

The national bank merited specific antagonism because of its large size. One of James Madison's correspondents, Joseph Jones, suggested that "if the whole swarm of insects which the sunshine of the funding and banking system hath produced should be dissipated by one severe blast, I should not weep over their disaster." Detractors believed the Bank was so colossal that it was capable of many evils. They labeled the Bank a monopolistic monster that would corrupt the entire society. Why did the Bank set off opposition? In the twenty-first century, when over ten thousand banks of various sorts exist in America, it may be difficult to comprehend the hostility to it. But in the 1790s, banks, and in particular a bank with a unique national charter (charters were usually granted by states), were looked upon with profound suspicion. The anti-bank advocates were terrified that the Bank could usurp the very reins of power. After all, was the Bank not going to be guardian of the public money? And if that was the case, was that not too great a temptation for mere mortals? The entire Constitution was based on checks and balances, but was private ownership enough of a check on the Bank? Detractors also labeled the Bank as an enemy of farmers—at a time when some 90 percent of the population toiled in the fields and barns.

Southerners especially feared the institution. Many thought it would drain the economy of gold and silver. Others, who did not understand that banks had to redeem their notes and deposits for specie on demand, feared the onset of rampant inflation once its presses commenced printing. Southern delegates also opposed the Bank's two-decade lifespan. (Unlike today, all early U.S. corporate charters were of finite duration.) Commenting on the proposed length of the charter, Madison was purported to have said that "twenty years was to this country as a period of a century is to the history of other countries—there was no calculating for the events which might take place." Southerners also feared that the Bank, which was headquartered in Philadelphia, would be used as an excuse to renege on the deal struck to move the seat of government to the Potomac in 1800.

At one level, Hamilton had difficulty comprehending the agrarian critique. Unlike many of his contemporaries, Hamilton did not see the issue of state vs. federal power as a zero-sum game. He was, after all, one of the leading proponents of federalism (note the small f), the notion that the states and the national government could *share* power. The creation of the Bank of the United States, for instance, did not preclude the formation of state banks and in fact ultimately made life for state banks easier. The assumption of state debts did not preclude borrowing by state governments in the future and in fact made it easier for states to borrow again. Perhaps most importantly, the different levels of government served to check and balance each other. Again, Hamilton's thought, which did not conceive of power as a finite sum, was decades ahead of its time.

But the antagonism went much deeper than the issues. Agrarians thought Hamilton a tyrant who had designs on the reins of power. In their opinion, he had duped Washington. But ironically, while many Republicans distrusted Hamilton, they not only did not destroy the financial system but in many cases strengthened it.

≈ When Hamilton left his homeland in Nevis in 1772, never to return, agriculture was king in America. (Even ironworks, the largest manufacturing enterprises, were called "plantations" because much of their value stemmed from their forest-clearing activities.) The mainland colonies had no joint-stock banks, only a few small corporations (and their stock did not trade), and only tiny amounts of publicly traded debt. Massachusetts enjoyed the most advanced capital market, but even there government obligations were not actively traded. Governments borrowed by issuing bills of credit—fiat paper money—that often lost value. Each colony had its own unit of account and its own legal system. Colonists worked wonders with what they had. Ground rents, perpetual mortgages popular in Pennsylvania, Delaware, and Maryland, served as a form of negotiable long-term capital; foreign exchange markets provided entrepreneurs with some access to short-term loans. Overall, however, little financial intermediation existed until late in the colonial period, when a few brokers, like Hendrick Oudenaarde, began operations. In addition to chartering vessels, collecting debts, and wholesaling teas, sugars, coffee, indigo, and pepper, Oudenaarde let "money upon interest . . . upon personal Security, or Mortgages upon Houses or Lands." That was in late 1767 and early 1768, a year after Oudenaarde managed to extricate himself from debtors' prison! Suffice it to say, the scale of his money-lending operations was not large. As much recent scholarship shows, economic growth during the colonial period was torpid.

By the time *our* creator forever left his adopted land in 1804 to meet *his* Creator, the financial system was awash in intermediation. Though Hamilton fell mortally wounded on the dueling grounds at Weehawken, the financial system was thriving. Joint-stock banks were rapidly multiplying, as were other types of joint-stock companies, not all of which, thanks to Hamilton's insight, needed formal incorporation to begin operations. The credit of the U.S. was among the best in the world; U.S. bonds and stock in the Bank of the United States regularly traded in London as well as in the active securities markets of Boston, New York, Philadelphia, Baltimore, and Charleston. The nation's credit was so good that it easily borrowed to purchase Louisiana and to fight wars. The first Bank helped to keep the macroeconomy on an even keel by checking the note issue of state banks. The entire nation had a single unit of account, the U.S. dollar, that was firmly defined in terms of gold and silver. Fire and marine insurance was almost fully formed; life insurance lay just over the horizon, as did trust companies, savings banks, and building-and-loans. Great leaps in manufacturing—ultimately funded by banks and capital markets—began just a few years after Hamilton's death. Most importantly, economic growth, increases in real per capita output, was picking up steam, soon literally as well as figuratively.

Hamilton was the creator of the U.S. financial system, the engine of America's remarkable nineteenth-century economic and political transformations. Unlike the Almighty, however, Hamilton was not immortal. Nor did he work alone. In the next chapter, we learn of the contributions of one of his major helpers, Tench Coxe.

THE JUDAS

Tench Coxe (1755–1824)

To his contemporaries, Tench Coxe was "Mr. Facing Both-ways." A Tory-turned-Patriot during the Revolution, Coxe joined the Federalist Party and assisted Hamilton at Treasury. That seemed natural enough. But after the party turned to Oliver Wolcott to replace Hamilton, the embittered Coxe switched parties. Rather than hang out at the conservative edge of the Republican Party, however, he became a stalwart, one of Jefferson's most ardent supporters. Federalists labeled him a turncoat, an apostate, a traitor, a Judas Iscariot. Republicans did likewise a decade later, when Coxe tried to form a third party.

In retrospect, Coxe's transformation from Hamiltonian to Jeffersonian did not require any great personal conversion, any traumatic turn of events, any flaw of character. For all their differences, Hamilton, Jefferson, and Coxe ultimately agreed on several fundamental points. Each wanted to make America great; each thought that economic growth would be a key component of that greatness. They differed on the means to that end, with Hamilton relying more on financial development and Jefferson championing the individual farmer, but both desired a strong economy. Coxe eventually convinced both Hamilton and Jefferson that for the nation to grow really strong, Americans would have to manufacture finished goods and not just draw forth the rude products of the earth. Coxe was right, but he was not in the right, at least not to his many erstwhile friends.

William Coxe, the father of our subject, left Burlington, New Jersey, as a young man to set up as a Philadelphia merchant. In April 1750 he married Mary Francis, daughter of Tench and Elizabeth Francis. Five years and six weeks later, Mary gave birth to their third child, whom the young couple named Tench in honor of the babe's maternal grandfather. William and Mary had thirteen children together, ten of whom lived to maturity. Only Tench and Daniel W. (1769–

1852), a successful international merchant, became prominent citizens, but the Coxe family was important nevertheless due to intermarriages with leading Philadelphia clans, including the Bingham, Burd, Chew, Mifflin, Shippen, Tilghman, and Willing families.[1]

Unlike so many Financial Founders described in this book, Coxe was not an orphan. In fact, William Coxe rather doted upon his favorite child, cloistering him as much as possible from the vicissitudes of a hostile world. Coxe spent a good deal of his adolescent years socializing and reading widely in history and economics, joys punctuated but briefly by minor forays into the world of trade beginning in 1772.

As the Revolution approached, Coxe felt the need to turn his attention to politics. He found himself sympathetic to the American cause but far from a rabble-rousing radical. Nearing twenty, "Tenny," as his family still called him, also felt the need to settle down. Accordingly, he joined his father's mercantile firm, Coxe & Furman, as an informal third partner in 1776, an inauspicious time to begin a new trading business. When independence was declared, Coxe, like many in his social circle, decided to try to remain neutral but to side with the Crown if it came down to it. As British forces approached Philadelphia in late autumn, however, neutrality was not good enough. In November and December, Patriots forced Coxe and other suspected Tories out of the city. Coxe left the City of Brotherly Love on December 2, lingered for a time in New Jersey, then crossed the British lines and headed to occupied Manhattan, where he passed the next half year or so with Tory merchants like Edward Goold and Daniel Ludlow. In September 1777, Coxe returned to Philadelphia under the protection of victorious British troops.

That did little to help his political career in the long run. In the short term, however, it allowed him to profit handsomely. Save for Thomas Willing, of which more later, and some Quaker pacifists, most Philadelphia merchants had fled the approaching Redcoats, leaving the city's trade wide open to Coxe and other Tory exiles. Coxe moved into one of the city's best stores, within easy call of the City Tavern, an important mercantile hangout. He cozied up to British officers and officials, hopeful of gaining favors and contracts. Profits accrued, but strangulating trade regulations soon brought Coxe and other Tory merchants to the realization that what they needed to prosper was peace, whether or not it was linked to a British victory.

1. Tench Coxe's mother Mary was the sister of the Tench Francis who married Thomas Willing's sister Anne.

During the British occupation, Coxe formed a new partnership, of the matrimonial kind, with Catherine McCall, the orphaned daughter of Philadelphia merchant Samuel McCall. Soon after the January 1778 wedding, news arrived that the French had formally allied with the Americans. Coxe seemed unmoved and pushed ahead plans to enlarge his trading activities in Philadelphia. At first, his boldness appeared to pay off. But in May, orders arrived from England to evacuate Philadelphia. In early June, Coxe received orders to ship out all goods on hand, lest they fall into the control of the rebels. Coxe hastily emptied his store into two brigs and sent them to New York, all the while trying to collect some £9,000 due him and his partners. That a frenzied British army seized a store of his muskets and lumber did not help matters.

Meanwhile, Coxe's new bride, long a victim to tuberculosis, grew too gravely ill to undertake an ocean voyage, even the brief one to New York. When the British rear guard departed on June 18, encountering an eager Patriot patrol as it did, an apprehensive Coxe was still in Philadelphia, tending to his bride. Attainted of treason by Pennsylvania's Supreme Executive Council on May 21, Coxe was a marked man. Luckily for him, and for us, America's revolutionaries did not lust for blood as France's Robespierre later would. Radical Patriots wanted Coxe's property, not his head. They would get neither because Thomas McKean, chief justice of the Pennsylvania Supreme Court and a friend of the Coxe family, interceded on Tenny's behalf. Coxe's flirtation with Loyalism McKean chalked up to youthful indiscretion. So the "Farewell" that Coxe bid his Tory friends as American troops reentered the city turned out to be unnecessary. But the one he would soon bid his wife was permanent. She died on July 22.

Shorn of his wife, his stock of goods, and most of his friends on both sides of the conflict, Coxe spent the balance of 1778 grieving—and struggling to earn a decent profit. He was far from destitute. He had wisely put aside a goodly sum of specie, enjoyed ample deposits in his London bank, and could always draw on his father, who was safe in New Jersey. But conducting business in wartime was difficult, especially for a merchant tainted as a Tory. The British fleet, now his enemy, bottled up Delaware Bay. And asking the state to return seized property was out of the question. Like many merchants, Coxe pined for the return of peace and got on as best he could. In April 1779 he became so frustrated that he quit Philadelphia for the succor of friends in Maryland. The vacation heightened his spirits, as did frequent invitations to social functions in Philadelphia after his return that fall.

Coxe narrowly dodged conscription in the Pennsylvania line in July 1780.

He could not, however, so easily dodge the opprobrium of his Loyalist background, especially in the dark days following the exposure of Benedict Arnold's treachery that September. Coxe, after all, was distantly related to Arnold by marriage ever since the general had wed young Philadelphia beauty Peggy Shippen in April 1779. Although Coxe satisfied prominent Philadelphians that he had "no political or other connexions" to the infamous traitor, he remained fearful of mob violence. Prudence dictated that he lay low and Coxe for once was prudent. On December 20, 1780, Coxe, Furman & Coxe dissolved; Coxe waited another two years to announce the formation of his own firm based on a capital of 1,000 guineas. During those two years, Coxe continued to conduct business, mostly in the French and coasting trades, but did so cautiously and behind the scenes.

In February 1782, Coxe entered into his second domestic partnership, this time with Rebecca Coxe, his eighteen-year-old first cousin. Coxe would outlive this wife too, but not until they spent almost twenty-five happy and productive years together. Before Rebecca succumbed to tuberculosis in 1806, the partners produced ten children. Only six of them, however, managed to outlive their father.

When the peace finally came, Coxe and other American merchants hoped to reestablish colonial trading patterns. They ordered huge shipments of British manufactured goods and planned to pay for them by shipping traditional American produce—flour, horses, barrel staves, and the like—to the West Indies. The British shipments arrived but a July 2, 1783 order-in-council forbade American ships from provisioning the British West Indies. American salted fish and meats were not legally welcomed there at all, and other American articles, including lumber, horses, and grains, had to be delivered in British ships! Lax enforcement, fueled by West Indian planters' urgent demand for American produce, largely prevailed, however. By November 1783, Coxe's business was so extensive that he asked Nalbro Frazier, a Boston merchant then visiting Philadelphia, to join him as a partner. Frazier agreed; Coxe & Frazier was born.

The new firm conducted an extensive commission business, keeping 5 percent of the proceeds of all goods bought or sold by the company on the account of its numerous correspondents. It also traded extensively on its own account, using various ruses to get past British trade restrictions. Sometimes, it shipped banned goods in falsely labeled containers in legal British bottoms. The fake containers usually fooled the customs agents. At other times, Coxe & Frazier shipped legal goods in their own ships simply by paying British subjects, often business correspondents, to register them. For instance, the partners operated the brig *Betsy*, nominally owned by Moses Franks of London and Thomas Torver of Tortola, on their company's sole account.

But all the chicanery in the world could not cure a sick economy, and in 1784 and 1785 the nascent American economy was sick indeed. After suffering years of privation in the war, American consumers did just that—consumed. Mass quantities of manufactured goods poured in from Britain. But Americans had debts, debts from the colonial era held in abeyance during the war, debts from the war itself, and debts from the postwar orgy of consumption. Worse, trade restrictions and markets grown accustomed to a dearth of American produce meant relatively little income with which to pay those debts. (Coxe & Frazier, like other Philadelphia mercantile firms, ran very profitable voyages to China, but the volume of that trade was simply too small to pull America out of its economic morass.) Worst of all, perhaps, was the fact that in the years immediately after the Revolution many Americans failed to understand that the *domestic* market was to be the most important of all. Instead of encouraging interstate commerce, the early states remained jealous, imposing upon each other's merchants a jungle of regulations and taxes. Such policies hurt the economy; they hurt Coxe & Frazier.

Trade, after all, is a very good thing, both for individuals and nations. At the individual level, trade is good because it allows people to exchange for goods and services that they value. Where both parties are competent, and contract freely, trade is a win-win situation. When you buy a pack of gum for $1, you make clear that you would rather own the gum than the buck, while the shopkeeper essentially announces that she would rather own the dollar than the pack. If no fraud has occurred, for example if the gum is not past its sell-by date and the dollar is not counterfeit, both parties are better off for having traded.

At the national level trade is good because it allows for specialization, and specialization means efficiency. Imagine a person who had to make every single article of life his or herself. That person would be poor indeed, working all day to produce a few articles of but indifferent quality. (Think of Robinson Crusoe.) But that same person, engaged in making one specific thing, or providing one specific service, can churn out many high quality units. If trade is possible, all persons can specialize at what they are comparatively good at producing, and exchange it for the goods they do not produce. The total sum of goods available for everyone therefore skyrockets.

Traditionally, the American colonies had specialized in agricultural and extractive industries. They produced timber, foodstuffs, and other raw materials. By the late colonial period, they had engaged extensively in the production and exportation of intermediate or partially processed goods, turning, say, iron ore into pig iron, wheat into flour, and hides into raw leather. But much of the finishing was completed overseas, with British manufacturers transforming the pig iron into finished iron goods, British artisans turning the leather into furniture and clothing, and West Indian bakers turning the flour into bread. With its international trade partially blocked after the Revolution, America could begin to specialize domestically, with relatively infertile New England developing manufacturing capabilities, the emerging West producing foodstuffs, and the South focusing on export staples like indigo, tobacco, and cotton. (Indeed, Coxe foresaw the importance of American cotton.)

But in Confederation America, those awkward years between the end of the Revolution and the adoption of the Constitution, state trade barriers thwarted the full development of such regional specialization. It also hurt the business of Coxe & Frazier, which had tried, without success, to penetrate the southern market. Hatred of barriers to interstate commerce was one reason that Coxe supported adoption of the U.S. Constitution. Coxe was no free trader though. While he abhorred interstate tariffs, he vehemently espoused national tariffs designed to "protect" America's artisans and manufacturers from foreign competitors. Coxe's encouragement of U.S. manufacturing interests soon became his hallmark and is the reason he is included among our financial founders.

Tench Coxe could talk free trade and protectionism at the same time because he was both a merchant and an industrialist. His interest in manufacturing first appeared in 1775, when he joined the United Company of Philadelphia for Promoting American Manufacturers, one of the country's earliest joint-stock manufacturing firms. His interest in making things rather than merely in selling them increased in the 1780s when he discovered that his firm was too small to engage regularly in the lucrative China trade yet too big to arouse much sympathy from its debtors. By July 1786, correspondents owed Coxe some £4,000 on open account, yet Coxe allegedly could not collect enough to pay his baker's bill. That sum grew to £11,000, a truly enormous sum for the times, by early 1789. Those bad debts prevented Coxe from being truly rich, but nevertheless he remained one of Philadelphia's many well-to-do.

In addition to manufacturing, Coxe had one other major nonmercantile economic outlet, land speculation. He purchased properties in Delaware, rural Maryland, Baltimore, some fifty-five thousand acres in Virginia, and a big chunk of Pennsylvania's Wyoming Valley. Coxe paid for the latter with $4,000 face value worth of public securities purchased at greatly depreciated prices. He wisely held the Wyoming lands, bequeathing them to his descendants, who eventually grew wealthy off their rich coal deposits. Coxe knew that transportation improvements would increase the value of his scattered empire, so he backed public road, private turnpike, and river improvement schemes of all stripes. He also turned his attention to banking.

In January 1784 Coxe, perhaps perturbed that he had not been elected a director of the Bank of North America, tried to establish a rival institution, the so-called Bank of Pennsylvania. The January 31 stock subscription went well, so the subscribers met at City Tavern on February 5 to adopt a set of bylaws, presumably drafted by Coxe, and to select directors. Coxe was elected one of the directors and charged with taking notes at the board meetings. While Coxe went on busily making arrangements to start the new bank, the Bank of North America shrewdly offered to merge with it. Most of the Bank of Pennsylvania's subscribers thought it wiser to join an established institution than to set off on their own, so the project disintegrated. But Coxe had shown that he understood finance and possessed the administrative skills to launch a sizable new concern.

Coxe's critical stand against state paper money emissions in 1785 also held him in good stead with Hamilton. Before the Revolution, bills of credit issued by Pennsylvania's legislature or by the colony-owned loan office had been an important part of the money supply. The bills emitted in the colonial period enjoyed such good credit that merchants considered them a substitute for specie and hence would readily swap bills for coins and vice versa. Though technically a legal tender, the colonial bills maintained their value not through fiat but rather due to their acceptance by market participants. The Revolution had changed all that. Bills no longer served as a specie substitute; no one would accept them for their face value. Colonial bills of credit were eventually repudiated, and new issues made by the state and national governments were virtually worthless by 1781. Only a tiny fraction were redeemed when finally funded in the 1790s. Tender laws, rather than bolstering the value of paper money, actually caused it to depreciate because the tender provisions allowed debtors to defraud their creditors. Near the end of the debacle, debtors could obtain, say, £1,000 bills of credit for just £100 specie, then tender the bills to extinguish a debt of £1,000 specie. Not bad work if you can get it, but the damage done to creditors was enormous. Tender laws and paper money, Coxe realized, caused injustices at home but perhaps more importantly gave "the *coup de grace* to public credit" and dishonored America's "national character abroad," much to the detriment of the country's mercantile, manufacturing, and commercial agricultural interests.

The Bank of North America also did not wish to see Pennsylvania resort to a paper money emission. But "Constitutionalists," those in favor of the state's radical 1776 constitution, controlled the unicameral legislature. The state's weak executive, rather ironically styled the Supreme Executive Council, was powerless to stop the legislature from emitting £150,000 in bills of credit and then taking revenge on the Bank by revoking its charter. The Bank of course fought back. During the ensuing public debate, Coxe distinguished himself as a critic of both the Bank and the Constitutionalists. The latter were wrong, Coxe argued, for repealing the institution's act of incorporation. The former was wrong too, Coxe continued, because the Bank was a monopoly. Clearly, he smarted over the demise of his Bank of Pennsylvania. But he had a point too. If the Bank were to remain a monopoly, it needed to be more closely regulated by the state. Market forces could not effectively contain it if it was the only bank in town. Coxe therefore advocated a compromise measure whereby the Bank would be rechartered, but with a less liberal act of incorporation that would limit its corporate lifespan, place a cap on its capital, and restrict some of its activities. Coxe won the day; most of his proposals found their way into the 1787 law reincorporating the Bank of North America.

But we have only begun to narrate Coxe's contributions to the national cause. In September 1786, Coxe attended the Annapolis Convention, the precursor to the Constitutional Convention that would take place in Philadelphia the following summer. The Annapolis meeting itself was something of a bust; only twelve delegates from five states appeared. But several were real heavyweights. In addition to Coxe, also present were John Dickinson, James Madison, and, of course, Alexander Hamilton. Coxe was appointed secretary, Dickinson president. After a few days of debate, the delegates, led by Hamilton, decided it best to simply call for a larger convention with extended powers to "render the constitution of the federal Government adequate to the exigencies of the Union." The rest, as they say, is history.

Well, not quite. Not everyone was thrilled with the idea of creating a more powerful national government. Many Americans rightly wondered why they had sacrificed so much to be rid of King George if they were only to turn around and crown a new tyrant. Coxe and other merchants, however, were not about to give up their hard-won liberties merely to create a new overlord. They realized that it just might be possible to create a new form of government that would be at the same time powerful and beneficent, a government that would energetically further the interests of its citizens rather than itself. As Coxe put it, what was needed was "a system which will promote the general interests without the smallest injury to particular ones."

Coxe and other nationalists conjured up this novel, noble idea by reflecting on their own experiences as leaders—of mercantile and other business firms. They realized that nations traditionally suffered from what economists today call the principal-agent problem. The agent of the nation, which is to say the government, acted in its own interests rather than in the interests of the nation's owners, the citizenry. The same problem arose in business, when employees slacked off at work, or when commissioned agents lied about the quantity or price of goods they had sold for others. Coxe and other early businessmen were aware of such problems and solved them in modern fashion, by carefully screening and monitoring employees and other agents, and by trying to align the incentives of employees or agents with their own. The same techniques, they realized, could be used to tame governments, which were normally quite avaricious. So they built screening, monitoring, and incentive-alignment techniques into their new state constitutions and, more importantly, into the new federal compact. More popularly styled "checks and balances," the business-inspired structure of the new federal government allowed it to be relatively powerful and unthreatening at the same time.

Coxe was not an official delegate to the Constitutional Convention, but he was close at hand during the proceedings, influencing its proceedings out of doors, as the old saying goes, by talking informally with delegates. Southern delegates, for instance, he regaled with predictions of immense wealth based on the cultivation of cotton. Coxe also used his influence to keep antislavery agitators from dividing the Convention with memorials calling for an end to the peculiar institution. As we'll learn, Coxe was no friend of slavery, but he thought it a matter that could be handled later, at the state level, as in Pennsylvania. Creating a "firm and steady government" came first because without the right government, all would be slaves, to a tyrant like King George or to the anarchy experienced under the Articles of Confederation.

Coxe also played an active part in the politicking and pamphleteering that led to Pennsylvania's ratification of the Constitution. Foremost, Coxe put his pen to work, authoring some thirty major essays in support of the Constitution. None of those essays is as well remembered today as the endeavors of Hamilton, Madison, and Jay in *The Federalist*. At the time, however, Coxe's widely republished essays may have been more influential, especially given the less erudite style Coxe deliberately adopted, with the less literate. And those folks, especially if they lived in the backcountry, were the ones most in need of convincing. Pennsylvania Federalists carried the day, adroitly countering antifederalist attempts to stymie ratification. On December 12, 1787, just two months after the

Constitutional Convention adjourned, Pennsylvania became the second state to join the new union. But the Constitution would not take effect until at least nine states had ratified it, so there was still much work to be done. Coxe therefore continued to crank out the polemics, including an eight-thousand-word series under the pseudonym "A Pennsylvanian." Madison arranged for the republication or circulation of many of his essays in Virginia, then the nation's most populous state.

Aware that his Pennsylvania-oriented pieces might not appeal to southerners, Coxe wrote a new essay aimed directly at the heart of the argument of Virginia antifederalist Richard Henry Lee, whose *Letters from the Federal Farmer to the Republican* had gone through four editions. Lee's most powerful and popular argument claimed that the new union would benefit the North at the expense of the South. Coxe contended the exact opposite. His lengthy rebuttal, which won praise from Madison and Hamilton, called agriculture the "spring of our commerce, and the parent of our manufactures." While ratification hung in the balance in Virginia, Coxe turned his attention to New York, penning an essay that pointed to the economic problems that would plague the state if it opted out of the Union. Trade restrictions, depreciating paper money, and commercial chaos would likely result. But more than any essay, it was New Hampshire's ratification on June 21, 1788, the crucial ninth state, that cemented the new nation. The decision for New Yorkers and Virginians then became whether or not to join a new nation that effectively had them each surrounded. Both soon joined and that eventually drove even recalcitrant Rhode Island into the fold.

What should this powerful but benevolent new government do? For Coxe, the answer was clear: it should ensure that the United States became one big free-trade zone. That, Coxe knew, would allow the North to specialize in manufacturing, the West in foodstuffs, and the South in staples like tobacco, indigo, cotton, and sugar. How could the nation become a common market? Adoption of a common unit of account, the dollar, rooted in specie was a good starting place. Funding of the national debt and assumption of state debts was also a good step. Prohibiting local interference with interstate trade was important, as was adoption of tariffs to protect the North's "infant industries." Strict neutrality was also essential, Coxe realized. In short, Coxe and Hamilton saw eye-to-eye. It is little wonder then that Hamilton asked Coxe to serve as his Assistant Treasury Secretary. And what an able public servant he proved to be.

But first, Coxe helped to ensure that the right sorts of people would be chosen in the first federal elections. For that purpose, Coxe took over financial sponsorship of the *Federal Gazette and Philadelphia Evening Post* from Benjamin Rush, who could no longer afford the expense. Coxe and other party stalwarts saw to it that Philadelphia Federalists swept the 1788 elections at both the state and federal levels. As a nominal plum for his aid, Federalists appointed Coxe one of Pennsylvania's delegates to the Continental Congress. Though the post was hardly important at that point—the Articles of Confederation would expire in just three months, so the Continental Congress was a lame duck—opposition to Coxe's nomination was fierce. One opponent called Coxe a "PARRICIDE," another a disgrace to the "illustrious martyrs" of the Revolution. A third charged that Coxe was "hungry and voracious . . . in search of some fruit of a more *fattening* quality than the *manufacturing* fund." Worse, Coxe was "a supple, fawning, smiling PROTEUS, ready to fetch and carry as his masters bid him."

For Hamilton to make such a controversial figure his second in command demands explanation. Plain and simple, Coxe was the best man for the job despite his obvious unpopularity in some circles. Letters of recommendation from Benjamin Rush, who called Coxe "a moving common place book of knowledge," and John Jay, who called Coxe "a man of manners, talents, and information," were also important. But most of all, Hamilton chose Coxe because he realized that the former Tory knew manufacturing and manufacturers.

In July 1787, while the Constitutional Convention met in the State House in Philadelphia, Coxe had helped to create the Pennsylvania Society for the Encouragement of Manufactures and the Useful Arts. Apparently members of this organization thought some of the arts—perhaps sculpture and poetry—not "useful," but they did not dwell on the point, preferring instead to discover "the most effectual means of encouraging" manufacturing. Coxe joined a committee charged with drafting the Society's constitution, and apparently he was the lead author of the document. As its name implied, the Society was not so much a business as a charity; its twelve managers, which included Coxe, created a "manufacturing fund" used to help establish experimental factories. To help kick off the new Society, Coxe on August 12 gave a stirring speech in favor of American manufacturing in which he pointed to the nation's relative scarcity of laborers as a great strength that would induce U.S. inventors to create, patent, build, and market "machines ingeniously contrived." He hinted that anything Americans could not invent they could "borrow" from Europe, another accurate prediction that he and Hamilton would make true in the 1790s. During the speech, Coxe also correctly foretold that Europeans would eventually stream into America in large numbers, eschewing their Old World "oppressors" in favor of America's free air and increasing opulence.

But before those optimistic predictions could come to fruition, something had to be done to restore public credit. That would allow development of a domestic financial system that could attract the savings of both Americans and foreigners and fund technological progress. Enter our creator. Once his financial system was in place, Hamilton realized, he would have to set people to work, not only tilling the fields and plying the seas but *making things*. This is where Coxe stepped in, and stepped up.

For Hamilton to complete his *Report on Manufactures* in a convincing fashion, he needed data, lots of recent, high-quality data. Coxe was the right man to supply it. As a manager of the Pennsylvania Society for the Encouragement of Manufacturers, Coxe had been charged with communicating with similar societies in other states. He, therefore, had built up a nationwide network of correspondents interested in manufacturing, men like Connecticut's Jeremiah Wadsworth and New York's Walter Rutherford. Such men admired Coxe for his endeavors on behalf of American manufacturing, especially his efforts to erect cotton mills. Coxe went so far as to hire one Andrew Mitchell to attempt to steal a complete set of brass models of Richard Arkwright's laborsaving textile machinery from England. Unfortunately, the sortie ended with Mitchell exiled to Copenhagen, Coxe out a pretty penny, and British customs officials congratulating each other for their mild exhibition of competence in enforcing technology protection laws. Without British technology, a Society-financed cotton manufactory in Philadelphia's Market Street in 1788 could not compete with imports. In March 1790 the factory burned to the ground. Coxe blamed "foreign Jealousy and contrivance" for the conflagration, but it is equally plausible that Coxe set the blaze to collect the insurance on the unprofitable concern.

By 1790, Coxe also enjoyed extensive political contacts. His network, which at first consisted mostly of his old mercantile contacts, began to flourish into a faction of Coxeists during the debates over the ratification of the Constitution. It grew thicker and fuller during the first federal Congress. Without exaggeration, he was the most influential private citizen to sway that important body's deliberations. Coxe's ideas found a following throughout the Union in the late 1780s because he was a tireless and selfless advocate of the new federal compact. Congressmen naturally responded favorably to his zeal and forthrightness. Madison and of course his fellow Pennsylvanians were his most frequent correspondents, but legislators from other states also sought and received his counsel on subjects ranging from international diplomacy to internal improvements to salaries for congressmen. Perhaps his greatest success was the aid he gave to Thomas FitzSimmons regarding a draft of a patent law designed to help inventors protect their inventions from free-riding copycats, an obvious boon to all stripes of manufacturers, artisans, tinkers, and gentlemen scientists. Washington signed the important act, which FitzSimmons acknowledged bore Coxe's stamp, on April 10, 1790.

The four most controversial issues Coxe became involved with were the tariff, the slave trade, the Bill of Rights, and the permanent location of the federal capital. Everyone agreed that the federal government needed a reliable revenue stream. Almost everyone agreed that the most eligible type of tax was a tariff on imported goods. From there, consensus broke down. Consumers, or in other words people who purchased imported goods from overseas, wanted a so-called revenue tariff, basically a small tax. Manufacturers, on the other hand, wanted a higher, so-called protective tariff. The high tax would serve to keep foreign imports to a minimum, thus "protecting" the domestic manufacturers from competition. That, of course, spelled higher prices for consumers. Moreover, a protective tariff might not raise enough revenue for the national government to function and to pay its debts. Although the tax *rate* is higher with a protective tariff, fewer goods are imported (at least legally) so total revenues (the tax rate times the value of legally imported goods) may actually turn out to be lower. The higher the tariff the better for manufacturers (and smugglers) but the worse for consumers and the national treasury.

The key, as with most things, was striking a balance, or rather balances—economic and political. The economic balancing point was roughly the tax rate where federal revenue was maximized. The political balancing point might be lower than that if consumers thought that they were being forced to subsidize manufacturers. Of course, everyone had a different opinion in the matter. Two main bills soon emerged, a consumerist bill backed by Madison and a protectionist one authored by Coxe, who searched for support for his bill in the slowly industrializing North by writing a flurry of letters to legislators from the north and east of Pennsylvania. His efforts helped to solidify that section behind his high tariff recommendations. Soon, a compromise was struck and enacted. With tariffs averaging about 8 percent, northern manufacturers were partially protected yet consumers did not feel gouged. Most importantly, the compromise tariff produced enough revenue to keep Hamilton's Treasury in funds with a little aid from state banks and, a little later, the Bank of the United States.

As secretary of Pennsylvania's abolition society, Coxe was also responsible for drafting a memorial requesting Congress to pass a statute outlawing the slave trade as soon as it was Constitutional to do so. Southern legislators recoiled and the issue was, alas, buried.

Despite their differences over the proper tariff level and the slavery question,

Madison and Coxe remained mutually supportive. For instance, Coxe wrote two articles explaining and defending each of Madison's proposals regarding a federal Bill of Rights. Coxe at first had thought amending the Constitution to safeguard civil liberties ridiculous. The Constitution did not protect the right to eat, he sarcastically noted, but no one claimed that his or her right to sup hung in precarious balance. But as ratifying convention after ratifying convention urged the prompt passage of such legislation, Coxe changed his mind. His essays on the subject Madison thought important in the eventual passage of most of his recommendations.

The debate regarding the location of the capital, as we have seen, was eventually resolved with a sort of swap—Hamilton got the immediate assumption of state debts and Jefferson and Madison got a capital on the Potomac in ten years. For his part, Coxe did everything in his power, including publishing sham petitions, to further Philadelphia's bid as interim capital. In the end, Coxe would help to broker the deal that settled both issues for all time.

In May 1790, Coxe left the mercantile world behind to serve under Hamilton as the Assistant Treasury Secretary. As assistant secretary or undersecretary, rather than assistant-to-the-secretary, Coxe had his own small staff and was technically the department's second in command. Hamilton tapped Coxe for the post for several reasons. Coxe was a tall, lean, handsome man, unafraid to attend the occasional soiree or ball. He knew all the major players in Philadelphia, Baltimore, New York, and Boston, and they knew him. Though still tainted by his flirtations with Loyalism, Coxe had connections, and important ones at that. Most importantly, Coxe had proven himself in the 1780s a gifted political economist.

There was no question that Coxe would accept the offer to replace our sinner, William Duer, as Hamilton's number two after Duer's greedy machinations made his removal from office expedient. Coxe had long hoped to gain important public office, and his short stint as a Continental Congressman simply was not going to cut it for him. Neither was his self-appointment as a lobbyist on behalf of Pennsylvania's manufacturing interests. But serving Hamilton was worthy of his talents, he believed, particularly if the post soon led to yet greater prestige and emoluments. So on May 1, 1790, Hamilton made the offer and Coxe quickly accepted. For the third time in his life, Coxe rushed off to New York to improve his career. This time, he made the move in just five days by turning all his business affairs over to trusted brother Daniel W. Coxe and by leaving his wife, who was with child, at his parents' house in New Jersey. (By law, Coxe had to liquidate most of his business investments, especially his public securities and ships, to avoid any conflicts of interest.) Interestingly, Coxe moved into the same boarding house occupied by Madison.

On May 10, 1790, Coxe's appointment officially began and his long career as a professional public servant commenced. Coxe would spend almost eighteen of the next twenty years in some government bureaucracy. The closest thing to a professional economist in the new Treasury, Coxe set out to do what any good economist would do—collect as much economic data as possible for analysis. He ultimately failed in his quest to make the Treasury a great repository of commercial information like Britain's Board of Trade or Jacques Necker's Board of Research in France. But he did collect enough to publish in 1794 his only major book, *A View of the United States of America.*

His eyes firmly set on higher posts, Coxe was certain to make the social rounds, spending leisure time with everyone from John Adams to Elizabeth Hamilton to Madison, to whom he grew particularly attached. But all was not play. When Coxe arrived on the scene, the assumption question, a key component of Hamilton's financial program, was still to be decided. So too was the permanent location of the capital. Hamilton shrewdly used Coxe to help to broker the compromise that moved the capital to the Potomac and the state's debts to federal control. Eager to return to his pregnant wife, certain that he would be rewarded professionally for his exertions, and hopeful that Philadelphia as interim capital would somehow become the permanent capital before the planned move to Virginia, Coxe was elated to help.

After passage of the funding act was achieved, Hamilton put Coxe in charge of relocating the Treasury Department to Philadelphia. Coxe was delighted to locate and rent buildings—like Coxe's own former residence—suitable for the department and its staff. By autumn 1790, the Treasury and the rest of the young government had completed its move. What else his position entailed is unclear, as it appears that other major officials—like auditor Oliver Wolcott, comptroller Nicholas Eveleigh, treasurer Samuel Meredith, and register Joseph Nourse—all reported directly to Secretary Hamilton. Hamilton appears to have used Coxe as a flexible asset, part analyst, part advisor, part Tench-of-all-trades. Coxe did not mind playing that role because he thought highly of Hamilton. "He is a man of great, constant industry and immense occasional exertions" he once told Benjamin Rush, "of a very firm mind with a great deal of caution and prudence."

There was much work to be done, like negotiating contracts for supplying the army and establishing administrative procedures for transforming old Revolutionary debt instruments into the funding plan's Threes, Sixes, and Deferred bonds—bonds that paid 3 percent interest, 6 percent interest, and 6 percent beginning in 1801 (all per annum, quarterly). More importantly, two major pillars of Hamilton's revolution, the Bank of the United States and the encouragement of manufactures, still needed implementation. Coxe, of course, played important roles in both. He was also involved, though to a lesser extent, in the preparation of the crucial Mint Act and on advising Hamilton about the China trade.

Coxe, who was as we have seen only a lukewarm supporter of the Bank of North America, helped Hamilton to draft the large section of his *Bank Report* devoted to debunking the notion, held mostly of course by Bank of North America stockholders, that a new bank was unnecessary. Moreover, Hamilton's critique of the Bank of North America's governance structure followed Coxe's closely. Like Hamilton, Coxe thought banks important enough to have tried to establish one of his own, so it is probable that he and the Little Lion collaborated conceptually on other parts of the *Bank Report* as well, though clearly the wording of the final lucid product was entirely Hamilton's. Coxe also discussed, at a broad conceptual level, the grounds of the proposed national bank's constitutionality. In addition to the broad interpretation of the Constitution that Hamilton relied upon to win Washington's signature, Coxe suggested that the commerce clause of the Constitution provided grounds for the Bank's establishment. Despite the great general's approbation, the Bank was still not assured of commercial success, so Coxe pushed the institution's initial public offering (IPO) of stock to friends and family alike. Thanks in part to his efforts, Americans and foreigners clamored for shares, subscribing the $8 million available, a monstrous sum for the day, in just a few hours on the morning of July 4, 1791.

There is, however, evidence that Coxe was not entirely happy with his position. When the health of comptroller Nicholas Eveleigh gave out in April 1791, Coxe hoped to fill his vacancy, though the move technically would have entailed a demotion. Hamilton hinted that he wanted Oliver Wolcott in the slot, not Coxe. Coxe forged ahead anyway, asking Thomas Jefferson, of all people, to forward his application to Washington within *hours* of Eveleigh's death. Jefferson was more than happy to meddle in Treasury's affairs, even enclosing a blank commission in his package to the president, who was then touring the South. But Hamilton was, as usual, far ahead of the game, having already informed Washington that Wolcott was the man for the job but that a "weighty advocate" would endorse "other characters." Washington ignored Jefferson's letter and appointed Wolcott. Hamilton probably assuaged Coxe's feelings by noting that Coxe's talents were better served helping to prepare the *Report on Manufactures*.

✎ The *Report on Manufactures* was, in an era of oil lamps and quill pens, a massive undertaking. Unlike Hamilton's other famous state papers, this one re-

quired a great deal of empirical evidence on topics of which Hamilton himself
knew relatively little. To Coxe fell the task of collecting and assembling data on
American manufactures that Hamilton could craft into an effective public policy
statement. As Hamilton had surmised, Coxe found the work exciting; he
worked swiftly and with great alacrity. Coxe worked up a first draft of the report
in February 1791. Hamilton worked the draft over at least four times, adding
to it an economic justification for American manufacturing that Coxe's draft
lacked, before returning it to Coxe for his comments and corrections in September. On December 5 the report, which in many ways was as much Coxe's as
it was Hamilton's, rested in the hands of Congress, which promptly ignored it.

Coxe and Hamilton also collaborated closely in the formation of the Society
for the Establishment of Useful Manufactures (SEUM), which both men con-
ceived as a model for other American manufacturers to follow. In fact, the germ
of the idea originated with Coxe, who already by March 1791 had managed to
acquire a U.S. patent for a spinning machine—allegedly better than that of
Richard Arkwright—invented by British immigrant George Parkinson. The
machine was just the sort of laborsaving device that could make America a manufacturing giant. But a patent by itself makes nothing. To get the machines
made, manned, and spinning yarn required financial capital. Coxe had just the
idea sure to appeal to Hamilton—establish a joint stock company with a capital
composed of U.S. government securities. Then use the corporation's capital,
which was sure to generate 6 percent per year, to obtain a loan of specie from
foreign lenders. Use the specie to pay workers, construct factories, and purchase raw materials. Finally, pay the interest on the loan with the securities' interest payments. Whatever the factory earned above that would be profit.

It was a brilliant plan that would have worked perfectly were it not for one
thing—our sinner William Duer. Suffice it to say here that Hamilton supported
Coxe's plan, which was put into action soon after a charter from New Jersey had
been obtained in November 1791. Duer managed to get himself elected "governor" of the new institution but within several months had nearly destroyed it
with his outlandish securities speculations. Despite the setback, the SEUM purchased land near the falls of the Passaic River and erected some buildings. But
costs spiraled out of control because of the business incompetence of chief en-
gineer and architect Pierre L'Enfant. With its capital impaired by Duer's shenanigans and L'Enfant's opulent but dysfunctional designs, SEUM was not the
well-financed machine that Coxe or Hamilton had envisioned.

The timing was unpropitious for Hamilton, who by the end of the Panic of
1792 had made a number of political enemies. Eager to discredit Hamilton and

his achievements, critics insinuated that public monies had been invested, and subsequently lost, in the SEUM. One such attack emanated from the pen of Quaker doctor George Logan of Philadelphia, who called SEUM's charter "one of the most unjust and arbitrary laws . . . that ever disgraced the government of a free people." Logan then called the *Report on Manufactures* "flimsy" and assailed Hamilton as an aristocrat bent on undermining the liberties of Americans.

The attack on manufacturing of course incensed Coxe, who quickly crafted a telling point-by-point rebuttal that silenced Logan. Coxe's response dispelled all accusations that SEUM was a "national manufactory" in the sense of being a government entity. Since it was a private enterprise unsubsidized by taxes, Coxe implied, there was no reason for such vituperation. Sometimes businesses succeed, sometimes they fail. Sometimes they just fade away. Such was the fate of the SEUM, but not of its leading advocate, at least not yet.

In May 1792, Coxe had a close call, or so he at first imagined. Congress decided to reorganize the War and Treasury Departments, and, in so doing, it eliminated the position of Assistant Treasury Secretary. But Coxe was asked to assume a new position, Commissioner of the Revenue, created by the act. The change was largely a nominal one, save that the president, if need be, would appoint a temporary secretary instead of the appointment automatically devolving upon the assistant. Coxe continued much in the same duties as before, including aiding Hamilton in ways both large and small, but his staff was slashed in half. But now Coxe also had his own area of authority, his own demesne, the collection of the distilled liquor excise. Despite the small size of his new staff, just an office manager, three clerks, and a messenger, Coxe took up his new duties with speed, within months formulating a plan to revamp the internal revenue service that appeared so sound that Hamilton, then Washington, approved it without modification. Characteristically, Coxe did not stop there. By December he had developed an even more comprehensive plan that Hamilton and Washington also enthusiastically endorsed. Not until June 1794, however, did Congress deign to enact the majority of it.

Throughout 1793 and 1794, Coxe continued to aid Hamilton, particularly by writing tracts that defended the Treasury Department's policies and by recommending people to fill vacant offices, most of whom Hamilton agreed to. But with the *Report on Manufacturers* filed and the SEUM in tatters, relations between the two men slowly cooled. By early 1793, Hamilton found himself nodding in agreement to James McHenry's observation that Coxe "understands his business, or rather the intrigues of a court." Shortly thereafter, a cryptic warning came to Hamilton from William Heth, a customs collector in Virginia, who called Coxe a "perfidious and ungrateful friend" bent on joining Jefferson's efforts to oust Hamilton from the administration. Coxe's heart must have jumped when he heard that Hamilton had been stricken by the yellow fever in fall 1793. Hamilton was spared, but thousands of others lost their lives. Coxe avoided the contagion by staying on vacation in rural New Jersey until the frosts came.

Aside from staying clear of the dreaded plague, Coxe's biggest challenge was collecting the whiskey taxes in the western counties of his home state, the inhabitants of which disliked the federal excise taxes. Coxe gave them a little history lesson, explaining that Pennsylvania had enacted excise taxes as early as 1700 and maintained them throughout the colonial and Confederation periods. The westerners failed to appreciate Coxe's historical argument. By 1794, tax evasion had disintegrated into civil disobedience and then outright rebellion. Coxe at first advocated reconciliation and reform of the law, but by August he, like Hamilton, advocated raising an army to invade western Pennsylvania, the heart of whiskey rebel territory. A letter from Pittsburgh lawyer Hugh Henry Brackenridge threatening the invasion of Philadelphia by frontiersmen sealed their conviction.

When on September 30 Washington and Hamilton left Philadelphia to assume command of the Federal army then assembling at Carlisle, Oliver Wolcott, not Tench Coxe, was placed in temporary control of the Treasury Department. When he learned of the arrangement the next day, Coxe was at first crestfallen, then intensely aggravated. He snapped at Hamilton in one letter, and wrote brashly in several others, but then he did what every good bureaucrat does— pushed papers to cause goods to be moved, services to be provided, and payments to be made. By early November, the whiskey insurgency had been crushed. But Coxe's was just beginning.

Soon after he returned to Philadelphia in late November, Hamilton informed Washington of his intention to resign as Treasury Secretary effective January 31, 1795. Coxe soon resigned too, resigned himself to the undeniable fact that Wolcott would replace Hamilton in the top spot. He became irascible, prodding his lame duck boss time and again. Hamilton naturally pushed back. By Christmas, the two were practically at each other's throats. During the tussle of words, Coxe lost all respect for Hamilton. He even drafted a letter, one he wisely never sent, that accused Hamilton of ruthlessness and of being an enemy of free government. Coxe had crossed over to the Jeffersonian view of Hamilton. Soon, he would formally leave the Federalists for the emerging Republican Party, largely because he had to. Hamilton was weary enough of Coxe that he made certain that Washington would never bestow any additional offices or favors upon him. When Washington overlooked Coxe for the position of comptroller, the slot vacated by Wolcott, Coxe had had enough. Though he physically remained in the Treasury Department as Wolcott's subordinate, politically he ran off to Jefferson.

Anyone paying sufficient attention might have guessed that Coxe was capable of leaving the Federalist Party for the Jeffersonian Republicans. Coxe long admired Madison; he had turned to Jefferson in his ill-fated attempt to become comptroller. He had shown during the Revolution the capacity to change sides as convenience dictated. Perhaps most tellingly of all, he somewhat ironically came to loathe Britain. At first, he may have pretended to hate the land of his ancestors merely to distance himself from his own Loyalist past. Soon, however, he came to believe his own rhetoric and to favor France. By the time he finished critiquing Lord Sheffield's *Observations on American Commerce,* Coxe was a committed Anglophobe.

In 1783 Sheffield, a British aristocrat, published a lengthy polemic that purported to show that America needed Britain much more than Britain needed America. He therefore advocated treating Americans roughly in commerce. As we have seen, the British Board of Trade pretty much did so, much to the chagrin of American merchants like Coxe. But Coxe also bristled from Sheffield's accusations that American manufacturers could not possibly compete with Europeans. A prolific if somewhat prolix writer, Coxe attacked Sheffield with a sea of facts and a mountain of statistics that detailed the young nation's tremendous growth in population, wealth, and territory. He concentrated, of course, on describing the progress made by American manufactures in the few years since independence.

What were the outlines of that progress? By 1793, per capita imports had dropped because of "the constant introduction of new branches of [domestic] manufacture, and the great extension of the old branches." In that year, the value of goods manufactured in the United States was more than twice that of the country's exports and much greater than the value of its imports. Particularly after the adoption of the Constitution, manufactories had increased rapidly, producing a wide variety of articles of "comfort, utility, and necessity." Household manufacturing was particularly strong as farmers—especially farmers of grains and so-called grazing farmers who fattened livestock before sale—found it advantageous to use their down time to bring the crude materials of the earth to a usable, finished state for sale in urban marts like Philadelphia, New

York, and Boston. Coxe also thought the United States now self-sufficient in the production of crucial war material, including ships and their essential trimmings; gunpowder; cannon, muskets, and the sundry projectiles they fired; and soldiers' clothes, spirituous liquors, and "manufactured tobacco." But that was not all. Americans had also produced steam engines, flour mills, wire and nail cutters, textile card makers, and fire "engines," not to mention Franklin fireplaces, Rittenhouse stoves, and Anderson threshing machines. By the early 1790s, a list of American exports included not just the usual litany of foodstuffs but also a tremendous array of manufactured goods like boots, copper sheets, canes and walking sticks, hats, manufactured iron goods like axes and anchors, earthenware, furniture, glass, hair powder, steel, and whips.

In retrospect, Sheffield was clearly wrong and Coxe clearly right. But after the near destruction of the SEUM in early 1792, the future of American manufacturing was uncertain. One thing *was* certain—Coxe hated Sheffield and the nation he represented. Increasingly, Coxe found himself repelled by Hamilton's seemingly pro-Britain policies and attracted to Jefferson's pro-France stance. Despite the violent extremes of the French Revolution, many Americans, still thankful for French aid during the Revolution, sided with Jefferson.

So perhaps the most interesting question is not why Coxe would join the Republicans but rather why the slaveholding, agrarian Jeffersonian wing of the party would welcome into the fold an abolitionist advocate of manufacturing? Political expediency is perhaps too easy an answer, given the early success that Coxe enjoyed in the party. The Jeffersonians *embraced* Coxe. They considered his acquisition a long-term asset, not merely a temporary embarrassment to Hamiltonian Federalists. Part of the attraction was probably purely personal. Coxe liked to compliment superiors and Jefferson enjoyed such attention. For example, in 1790 one of Coxe's employees, watchmaker Robert Leslie, helped Jefferson with his *Report on Weights and Measures,* one of the Virginian's more memorable state papers. Coxe also supplied data for Jefferson's Anglophobic report on the cod and whale fisheries and helped Jefferson with his suggestion, provided to Congress just before his resignation as Secretary of State became effective at the end of 1793, to impose retaliatory commercial restrictions against the former Mother Country. (Tellingly, Coxe also helped Hamilton to prepare *the rebuttal,* which South Carolina's William Loughton Smith read before Congress in January 1794!)

Moreover, both Jefferson and Coxe thought themselves aristocrats. They could take the evening off, drink a bottle of Madeira, and discuss science, art, or history. And, over time, both came to hate the man we have labeled our financial creator, at least the three-quarters of him that was not French. Remarkably, Coxe was even closer to Madison, with whom he shared many Constitutional scruples.

Perhaps more importantly, Jefferson and Madison realized that to be truly successful, the Republican Party would have to appeal to more than just southern aristocrats and farmers. Coxe, they realized, could help the Republicans to appeal to northern artisans. As we learned "In the Beginning," Republicans did successfully attract artisanal support by 1800. Much of that success, in New York anyway, was due to the lending activities of the Manhattan Bank. Doubtless, though, some of it was due to the enlistment of pro-manufacturing men like Coxe to the party. Whatever the reasons, the Republicans adopted Coxe and he repaid the party many times over. In the meantime, Coxe maintained his position as Commissioner of the Revenue but fulfilled his duties in a perfunctory manner.

Coxe's open break with the Federalist Party occurred, fittingly enough, over the so-called Jay Treaty. In 1794, New York jurist John Jay, the lesser of the three authors of *The Federalist Papers*, headed to Britain to negotiate a commercial treaty. Jay had little to bargain with but still managed to obtain some concessions from Lord Grenville, the British foreign secretary. Jay was elated that Britain promised to relinquish western forts located within U.S. territory by June 1796, to make restitution for spoliation of American commerce, and to grant the U.S. limited trading privileges with the British West Indies. Many of his fellow countrymen, Federalists mainly, were also happy with the treaty. Many others, mostly Jeffersonians, were not. In fact, the Francophiles were upset enough to burn Jay in effigy after news of the treaty's provisions leaked to the press in May 1795. Not since the imperial crisis had Americans become so angry about commercial relations.

While the Senate debated whether or not to ratify the treaty, Coxe set his pen to work. Although he wrote under the pseudonym "Juriscola," everyone who mattered knew the identity of the author. A full three-quarters of his essay was devoted to an ardent *defense* of slavery, a strange twist indeed as Coxe had served as one of the two secretaries of the Pennsylvania Society for Promoting the Abolition of Slavery, which formed in 1787 out of two early but ineffectual abolitionist societies. Though Benjamin Franklin was nominal head of the institution, Coxe was responsible for much of its success, which included the virtual elimination of slavery in Pennsylvania by 1800. He found slavery both morally reprehensible and economically inefficient. But now, clearly, Coxe was intent on severing all ties with his former Federalist friends and forging new ones with southern slaveholders like Jefferson and Madison.

The ploy worked. The Virginians coaxed Coxe into supporting Jefferson over Adams for the presidency in 1796. Coxe understood that he had bet his future at Treasury on the outcome. If Adams prevailed, he would certainly be fired. If Jefferson won, however, Coxe could be named Treasury Secretary. But more was at stake, or at least Coxe believed. Increasingly, he came to think that Hamilton, Adams, and other Federalists had a conspiracy afoot to turn America into a monarchy. In hindsight, such fears were absolutely absurd. But in the heat of the times, the struggle between Federalists and Republicans appeared to many to be a battle between monarchy and representative government. Coxe knew he stood for the latter, represented by the French Revolution and his new friend Jefferson, and against the former, represented by the British Crown and his new enemy Hamilton.

It is important to note that Coxe continued to support banks, the funding system, and the rest of Hamilton's financial revolution. Like many, and we dare say at times most Republicans, Coxe was no enemy of finance. His problem with Hamilton was largely personal, his problems with Jay mostly commercial, his hatred of Adams almost solely political. So, like Burr in 1800, Coxe in 1796 could support Jefferson, banks, and manufacturing at the same time. And Jefferson could welcome his support though, in the end, it was only good enough to lift the Virginian to the vice presidency. Jefferson took fourteen of Pennsylvania's fifteen presidential electors, but the majority of electors from other states gave Adams the nod.

Coxe, whose support for Jefferson was conspicuously splattered across ten vehemently anti-Adams articles published in the *Gazette of the United States* and elsewhere, had gambled and lost. Federalists regularly abused him in public, and Jefferson, as vice president a mere figurehead so long as Adams drew breath, could do nothing to protect him. Coxe took his father's advice to avoid "political vexations" and pray that his administrative skills were sufficiently valued that his impolitic switch of party affiliation would be overlooked. After all, Coxe's job as head tax collector, while rather uninteresting compared to a cabinet post, was crucial to the continued functioning of the federal government. And it was by no means easy because he had to monitor distant agents, a good number of whom were borderline incompetent. Moreover, Coxe as usual had cultivated relationships with powerful people, including Secretary of State Timothy Pickering, to whom he fed reams of commercial and political information derived from his brother Daniel, who was by this time a thriving merchant. But in the end, Coxe was expendable, and expended he would be.

The attack began quietly enough, with Adams simply leaving Coxe off the invitation lists to social events. The ploy almost worked, as Coxe was so distraught that he drafted his resignation. Perhaps because he had no other career opportunities, Coxe changed his mind and did not submit the letter. But one way or another, Coxe had to go. Hamilton's replacement, Secretary of the Treasury Wolcott, began accusing Coxe of official incompetence. He scrutinized every note, every letter, and every report. By the time the New Englander was done, Coxe wished that Hamilton were still in control. Wolcott's official charge against Coxe, "deliberate misconduct in Office," was heard by the rest of the cabinet— Secretary of State Pickering, Secretary of War James McHenry, and Attorney General Charles Lee. Unsurprisingly, they sided with Wolcott. On December 23, 1797, Adams gleefully agreed to appoint a new commissioner. Most Federalists were also pleased with Coxe's dismissal, calling him a duplicitous traitor. Ever the optimist when it came to his career, Coxe beseeched Congress, and even Adams, to investigate his record and restore him to office. Charles Coxe, his father-in-law, bluntly told Coxe that his efforts had "no more chance than a Cat in Hell without claws." Charles was correct. Pennsylvania legislators put up a feeble fight on Tench's behalf, but it fell far short of success.

Coxe was now adrift and jobless, bereft of mercantile connections after years in public service, and an object of scorn in Federalist papers like *Porcupine's Gazette*. The editor of that scurrilous periodical, William Cobbett, sarcastically suggested that Coxe use his newly found free time "to write us an elegant and minute description of General Howe's triumphant entry into Philadelphia." Other papers refused to publish his rebuttals. Coxe had nothing to do but become a full time Republican Party organizer and land speculator.

≈ Coxe first got caught up in land speculation in a big way in the early 1790s. Like many other speculators, including Robert Morris, Coxe suffered dearly for his gambling. Most speculators hoped for a short-term windfall gain. Some got it, but most did not. As Coxe's descendants would learn, land was a profitable investment if held for long periods. Unfortunately Coxe learned that lesson too late, but he was able to stave off bankruptcy, however barely. One major problem was crooked land agents who, like Wall Street analysts in the late 1990s, would give the most dismal swamp high "buy" ratings. Another was gaining clear legal title to lands. A third was reselling land on credit. But the most telling blow was that demand for frontier lands simply did not, indeed could not, increase fast enough to provide the windfalls that speculators like Coxe sought. Highly leveraged, most of his assets tied up in land or nearly worthless IOUs, and increasingly unable to obtain short-term loans at bank, Coxe stared debtor's prison in the face. In the end, his father bailed him out, but at the price of cutting him out of his will.

It was more than a little ironic, then, that the first Republican patronage plum that fell to Coxe, late in 1799, was the secretaryship of the general land office of Pennsylvania. Coxe had hoped to be appointed secretary of the commonwealth, a much higher-ranking position. He had, after all, helped the new governor, Thomas McKean, defeat Federalist candidate James Ross by some five thousand votes in the 1799 gubernatorial election. Soon after his ouster from Treasury, Coxe began writing polemics for Republican newspapers. In between running errands for his younger brother Daniel, by now an important merchant, Coxe sharpened his quills and leveled them at his former party. He began by attacking Adams's foreign policy in nine lengthy articles published in the *Philadelphia Aurora,* an important new radical daily, in February 1798. Unsurprisingly, he vilified Britain while upholding France's unique brand of republic-by-guillotine. As the administration's "quasi" war with France heated up, so too did Coxe's vitriol. He certainly did not sway any Federalists to his side, but his essays undoubtedly strengthened the resolve of the party faithful.

The rhetoric grew so hot that the Federalists decided to cool tempers with legislation, the infamous Sedition Act. Benjamin Franklin Bache, slanderous editor of the *Aurora,* was one of the act's first targets. Under indictment for seditious libel and in financial trouble, Bache turned to Coxe for help. Coxe obliged by launching a fund-raising drive on Bache's behalf and by contributing a large number of essays on democracy, manufacturing, and political economy to the struggling paper. But on September 6, 1798, Bache faced a foe much stronger than the Sedition Act and was vanquished, one of thousands of victims of the yellow fever that visited Philadelphia almost every summer. Coxe again filled the breach, this time hiring a new editor, William Duane, and coming up with the financing needed to continue the paper under the ownership of Bache's widow Margaret, who promptly married Duane. Grateful to Coxe for both his job and his wife, Duane for a time became Coxe's greatest defender and the *Aurora* became the greatest outlet for Coxe's polemics.

It was through the *Aurora* that Coxe helped McKean into the governor's chair in 1799. Coxe's paper helped other Republicans to gain office too, including Albert Gallatin. Due to his role in the paper, Coxe slowly evolved into the de facto leader of the Republican Party election committee in Philadelphia county, one of the most important county-level party posts in the nation. He was so important that though he was not a candidate for office himself, Federalist pen pugilists felt compelled to remind voters that he was "Mr. Facing Bothways."

Unable to find substantive issues to debate, each party in the 1799 gubernatorial race resorted to mudslinging and character assassination. Coxe, who painted Federalist candidate James Ross as a "Whiskey Rebel," was a little better at those noble electioneering techniques than his rivals at Federalist newspapers.

Coxe was not pleased, therefore, when McKean offered the small patronage plum that the Land Office represented. But he took it anyway, perhaps because it offered a big challenge. The Land Office had grown bloated and corrupt over the years; the department needed someone with Coxe-like administrative skills to clean it up and steer it down the right path once more. The biggest problem with the job, besides the fact that it paid too little and required too much work, was that it was located in Lancaster. (Although it was little more than a rustic crossroads in the middle of nowhere, Lancaster was the state's new capital.) Coxe's children were not enamored of the move, which placed them a considerable distance from their doting grandparents. Both Tench and Rebecca missed Philadelphia's lively social life. The good news was that Coxe had little to do but work, and work he did, cleaning up the Land Office while simultaneously helping Jefferson to garner Pennsylvania's electoral votes in his successful presidential bid in 1800.

After Jefferson finally defeated Burr in the House of Representatives, a jubilant Coxe readied himself to assume his rightful place as Secretary of the Treasury. Instead, Jefferson offered that post to another Pennsylvanian, Albert Gallatin. History would not have been radically changed had Coxe been offered the spot instead. Despite his apostasy, Coxe never once questioned the importance of banks, the funding system, the Mint Act, or any other important aspect of Hamilton's financial revolution. Like Gallatin, he would have fought to extend rather than eliminate the important financial reforms of the 1790s.

Jefferson did offer Coxe his choice of two menial posts in the Treasury Department. Coxe had the good sense to turn them down but not sense enough to do so politely. In two letters almost as long as this chapter, Coxe lambasted the Virginian. Needless to say, a high federal office would not be forthcoming. He eventually begged for, and received, appointment to one of the lowly offices, revenue collector of Philadelphia. It was a job, after all, and got him out of bucolic Lancaster. And he soon moved into a slightly higher supervisory position, then into the purveyorship of the United States. Though a second-rate office, it was better than the collectorship in which he started. He continued to provide important Republicans with often unsolicited policy and political advice, but Coxe's days as a major force in the Republican Party at the national level were over. He remained, however, one of a dozen or so of the most important members of the party in Pennsylvania. He even launched his own ill-fated "Quid" or "Coxeite" ticket in 1804. After that episode, most Republicans also labeled him a Judas. He was read out of the party, but continued in the purveyorship until the eve of the Second War of Independence in 1812.

Being run out of the party did not deter Coxe from continuing to write about his hatred of Great Britain and his love of American manufactures. He was elated to learn that during his inaugural address in 1809 Madison wore a suit manufactured in America from domestic wool. To Coxe's mind, war with Britain in 1812 served a dual purpose, killing Redcoats and encouraging indigenous industry. Coxe of course wholeheartedly supported the war with his pen. But by this time he could not even garner enough support to obtain minor federal office. He took a county court job but lost that after only three years. All that Coxe had left was his reputation as a first-rate political economist.

When Coxe died in July 1824, America was a prosperous nation destined to grow ever more so. The physical basis of that prosperity was rooted in the geographical specialization of the agricultural, commercial, and manufacturing sectors. That specialization, which Coxe had trumpeted since the 1780s, was made possible by the formation of the U.S. Constitution, especially its money and commerce clauses, and by the financial revolution initiated by Hamilton, with Coxe's assistance, in the early 1790s. In general terms, the West fed the nation, the South provided it with foreign exchange, the North manufactured for it, and the East carried on its international trade and became its financial center. Because each sector could specialize in what it did comparatively best, the output of the entire nation grew. *That* is the important story underlying American history, not the tribulations of party politics. Coxe could jump from party to party because the parties were essentially the same, at least when it came to what was important, fostering financial and economic development.

That is not to say that some Republicans, like Jefferson, were not dull or jealous enough to attempt to destroy the newly formed capital markets. But the Republican Party as a whole was not so insensitive to its own self-interest. Coxe's long-time ally Albert Gallatin was the man who would save Jefferson from himself by preserving the financial system that our creator—and our Judas—so carefully created and nurtured. But Gallatin's aid may not have been required at all had not Federalist financier William Duer nearly throttled the goose in a sinful attempt to steal her for himself. To that sordid story we now turn.

THE SINNER

William Duer (*1743–1799*)

On April 19, 1792, hundreds of Manhattan's thirty thousand or so denizens surrounded the "New Gaol" chanting "we will have Mr. Duer, he has gotten our money." Some members of the mob were mere bystanders, but a good number milled about hopeful of getting their hands, or perhaps a rope, around the neck of jailed bankrupt William Duer. About a month previously Duer had, as they say, "stopped payment," essentially informing his numerous creditors that he would not be paying them back any time soon, indeed if ever. The large "riotous assemblage" deeply concerned New York's city council, which promptly called for the sheriff to restore order. As sheriffs are often wont to do, he quickly resorted to force in order to disperse the crowd. The peace and prosperity of the city teetered on the brink.

Imprisoning insolvent debtors like William Duer was commonplace in eighteenth-century America. The vast majority of such incarcerations elicited little more than comments about the debtor and his conduct. Why did Duer's insolvency and subsequent imprisonment foment such passion and violence? Clearly, this was no ordinary bankruptcy, and Duer was no ordinary debtor. Most bankrupts had a half dozen, a dozen, at the outside maybe a score of major creditors. Duer, on the other hand, had borrowed relatively heavily from everyone—and that is only a slight exaggeration—before declaring his inability to repay. According to Dr. Benjamin Rush, Duer's creditors included "merchants, tradesmen, draymen, widows, orphans, oystermen, market women, churches and even common prostitutes." The banks and major stockbrokers were also in for large sums. Duer's failure wiped out the savings of a good many, some of whom, it is claimed, wept in the streets and in their homes. Visitors to New York City reported that they "scarcely entered a house in which [they] did not find the woman in tears and the husband wringing his hands."

Contemporaries considered the ill effects of Duer's failure "beyond all description." Reverberations rippled through the economy, especially in New

York, Philadelphia, and Boston, where panicked sales sent stock and bond prices reeling some 25 percent. The young financial system was at risk, and all because of Duer's greedy aspiration to seize it for himself. In slightly more technical terms, Duer had sought to "corner" the entire U.S. securities market. He devised the most devious machination yet witnessed on America's shores to fund his financial coup attempt. His scheme fell far short of success. When John and Jane Q. Public realized that Duer was more shyster than financier, they felt betrayed and naturally sought revenge. At that point, Duer was safer in jail than he was in his own home.

Hamilton's critics believed that Duer's perfidy would finish off the entire financial system and perhaps even the creator himself. Duer, after all, had been the Assistant Treasury Secretary just two years before. But Jefferson, Madison, and their followers underestimated the resilience both of the financial markets and of Hamilton. As it would do time and again, the financial system survived the episode and, like Hamilton, actually grew stronger for the experience. Nietzsche had something right. And so too did the ancient Asian philosophers who taught there could be no thesis without an antithesis, no up with no down, no courage in a world devoid of fear. And more to the point here, there could be no saints without sinners. Duer was the quintessential poster boy for malfeasance, a sinner unequaled in the early days of the American financial system. Jefferson once called him "the King of the Alley," a reference to sordid, back alley dealings. Duer in the end was a mere pretender to the throne. But pretend he did, and so convincingly that even Hamilton fell for some of his ruses and deceptions.

Who was this sinner, this William Duer? Infamous in his time, Duer is virtually forgotten today. Before winding up in prison, he had served his country, and himself, well. In one sense, Duer possessed impeccable credentials, having served in Congress during the Revolution, on the Treasury Board after it, and as Hamilton's first right-hand man in the new federal Treasury Department. In another sense, however, Duer was nothing more than a dime-a-dozen stock manipulator, an inveterate gambler and land promoter, a shoddy government contractor, and a troubled merchant with somewhat dubious credit and more dubious business practices. No doubt Duer possessed a keen mind. But like a fox he usually turned his brilliance to sly rather than lofty ends. He became a cunning dreamer rather than a creative force. While a little self-interest was a very good thing for the financial system and the economy, Duer carried his too far. Duer was out for Duer, laws, morality, and innocents be damned. While public officials in the eighteenth century promiscuously mixed public and private affairs, Duer took the practice to new highs, or more accurately to new lows.

From whence sprang this evil? Duer came into the world on March 18, 1743 (though some claim 1747) in Devonshire, England, the son of a well-to-do attorney and a British general's daughter. Prepared at fabled Eton, young William began public life in India as an aide to the famous Lord Clive, whose soldiers drubbed the French on the subcontinent at about the same time that Clive's colleagues in North America were also defeating French armies. (A strong financial system helped the British to win the Seven Years' War, that first truly global conflict which American historians rather provincially call the French and Indian [as in Native American] War.)

Duer fell ill soon after setting foot in India, and upon returning home learned of his father's death. Duer's father had bequeathed him considerable estates in Dominica, which Duer personally surveyed in 1768 before heading north to New York as a Royal Navy mast timber contractor. Letters of introduction provided Duer with connections to two of colonial America's most influential men, William Alexander, a.k.a. "Lord Stirling,"[1] a man of wealth and privilege who resided in Basking Ridge, New Jersey, and Albany patrician Philip Schuyler. Both men would attain the rank of general during the Revolution and indirectly play key roles in Duer's life. Duer first visited Alexander; about a decade later, during the war, he would marry his daughter. Duer then headed north to Albany, where he befriended Schuyler, who would later introduce him to Hamilton. Schuyler also presented Duer, now in his mid-twenties, to the upper crust of colonial New York society. Finally, Schuyler taught his young protégé an idea that Duer would later twist to his own ends, with monstrous results. The patrician noted that although he was a public servant, he had "a right to work by night for myself." Duer extended Schuyler's notion into "a right to work morning, noon, and night for myself."

On Schuyler's advice, Duer purchased land about thirty-five miles north of Albany, in the small town of Fort Miller, and soon thereafter opened the area's first saw and grist mills. By 1775, Duer claimed to support the growing revolutionary movement, but not all found his claims convincing because he had been in the New World only about seven years, far too little time, many thought, to cast off the yoke of his English birth, breeding, and education. Schuyler and other prominent New Yorkers, including members of the influential Livingston clan and James Duane, vouched for him, positioning him as a moderate. Schuyler, major general of the New York militia, went further, offering Duer,

1. In 1759, a jury in Edinburgh, Scotland, declared William Alexander to be the nearest heir to the Earl of Stirling. Nevertheless, he was an American and a Patriot.

who had no real military experience, a commission as a colonel. Gouverneur Morris demurred, complaining that Duer was "volatile [and] unstable." Duer declined the commission, probably sensing that it would be more trouble than it was worth. Nevertheless, for the rest of his life many friends and associates called him "colonel," a sobriquet that he would much prefer to the title "King of the Alley" bestowed upon him by Jefferson.

By July 1776, Duer's commitment to American independence was sufficiently established that he was selected a member of New York State's Provincial Congress. Duer soon came to serve as an unofficial liaison between General Washington and the state government. When Manhattan succumbed to the British, Washington's army retreated across New Jersey and the state government fled to Fishkill, a hamlet on the Hudson River about fifty miles north of the island. Duer suggested that the Patriots burn New York City to the ground to limit its usefulness to the enemy, but his colleagues rejected "scorched earth" tactics.

Once safely ensconced in Fishkill, Duer, John Jay, and others formed a committee to "detect, and defeat all conspiracies against the liberties of America." Armed with subpoena powers and a troop of soldiers, Duer and his team possessed far more power than later political witch hunters like Alexander Mitchell Palmer and Joseph McCarthy would. Of course, the threat the committee faced was more palpable than the communists, real and alleged, with whom Palmer and McCarthy would later joust. Indeed, about one out of every three Americans remained loyal to the Crown and another one of three tried to remain as neutral as possible, swaying slightly to one side or the other with the winds of war. With Washington's army nowhere in sight, New York Patriots were naturally apprehensive. The committee's considerable workload was evidence enough of that. In a little over four months, the committee handled some five hundred cases, with Duer chairing about half of the indictments.

At this stage of the conflict, Duer, like many others, questioned General Washington's military prowess. Nevertheless, he agreed to continue to serve as New York's liaison to the Virginian commander-in-chief. Duer used the connection to contract with Quartermaster General Thomas Mifflin to supply the Continental Army with grain; he made a profit of $1,125 on the $45,000 deal.

In March 1777, Duer began a two-year stint as one of New York's representatives in the Continental Congress. His first task was to defend the reputation of his patron, Major General Schuyler, who had been relieved of command in favor of Major General Horatio Gates. Though many considered him but Schuyler's lackey, Duer finagled and politicked effectively, eventually winning

Schuyler's reinstatement. Indeed, the young "colonel," who was active on numerous committees and often the sole representative from New York present, impressed many, including future U.S. president John Adams and Robert Morris. Unsurprisingly, Duer and Morris served together on finance-related committees. Duer also found himself on the all-important "Board of War," the equivalent of the War Department, where he became involved in strategic military planning.

When the British occupied Philadelphia in 1777, Duer found himself on the run again, this time to York, Pennsylvania. Though many other congressmen used the retreat as an opportunity to return home, Duer, to his credit, continued to conduct the business of government. By the end of his first year, the New Yorker had served on sixty committees, most in the areas of finance, supply, or operations. Politically, Duer soon found himself largely in agreement with Washington, Schuyler, and Hamilton. For example, Washington, using Hamilton as a conduit, instructed Duer to use his influence on the Board of War to deny the approval of additional powers for newly appointed inspector general Baron Frederick von Steuben, instructions that Duer successfully carried out. Duer did not sit idly by as American soldiers starved at Valley Forge, but he found that bureaucratic red tape and political bickering limited what he could do to aid them. He soon became disenchanted, commenting that Congress reeked of "a vortex of Evil." Unsurprisingly, he was somewhat relieved not to be returned to Congress in 1779.

Freed from the burdens of office, Duer had time to pursue his two greatest loves, riches and "Lady Kitty," daughter of Lord Stirling. But Duer soon found himself implicated in a scandal. Shortly after he left Philadelphia he was attacked by an anonymous writer in the *Pennsylvania Packet,* who complained that the New Yorker meddled in Pennsylvania politics and then boldly claimed that Duer, Gouverneur Morris, and Benedict Arnold, Philadelphia's military commander, were all involved in high crimes. That charge may have arisen because a friend of Duer, William Constable, had managed to land in Philadelphia with an English ship full of scarce goods during the occupation of the city by the British. Constable remained when the British left, trading with anyone and everyone, all made possible by passes signed by Benedict Arnold, who many believed shared in the profits. Duer penned a lengthy essay in his defense, and although he made a fair acquittal of his actions, the affair clearly tarnished his reputation.

Sarah and William Alexander were unperturbed by the accusations, for they agreed that Duer could wed their daughter Catherine. Alexander, now a general, took time out from the war to give his daughter away on July 27, 1779. The ceremony was followed by a reception held in Bernards Township, New Jersey, that boasted an ox roasting. The couple would go on to have eight children, including William Alexander Duer, who would later become a New York Supreme Court justice.

But the war, marriage, and children were not the only things on Duer's mind. Drawing on the numerous friendships he forged while in Congress, Duer in 1779 launched his mercantile career in earnest. Highly leveraged and fond of living the high life, Duer found himself in constant need of credit, only part of which the nation's nascent banking system could provide. The rest of his funds he borrowed from partners, friends, and relatives and later from brokers, professional moneylenders, and anyone else willing to buy his promissory notes. When his own personal credit was exhausted, Duer cajoled prominent capitalists or politicians like Walter Livingston, Alexander Macomb, Andrew Craigie, John Pintard, William Constable, and Henry Knox to co-sign or guarantee his notes in return for information or a stake in his many ventures.

Duer's new mercantile career began inauspiciously. In 1779, Duer partnered with Silas Deane, American representative in Paris, James Wilson, the famous jurist and attorney for the Bank of North America, and a Spaniard sent to Philadelphia to acquire masts for the Spanish navy. The Spanish representative received one-fourth of the profits for securing the deal, certainly what we would call a bribe, an all-too-common occurrence. The deal turned into a fiasco and collapsed because the Spanish representative died, Deane ended up in London a suspected traitor, and the masts were of poor quality. Undeterred by the debacle, Duer forged ahead, using his father-in-law's influence to secure army provisioning contracts. That deal also disintegrated and, in a scenario that would repeat itself time and again, Duer tried to shift the blame onto his partners and away from himself.

At this early fragile stage Duer's close relationship with Robert Morris (Morris sponsored the christening of his first born, William Alexander) bolstered his as yet undistinguished mercantile career. Morris first lent Duer funds to purchase confiscated Loyalist farms in New York. Later, after becoming Superintendent of Finance, Morris helped Duer to obtain lucrative army supply contracts. Undeterred by his earlier losses on army contracts, the King of the Alley made ready to feast at the public trough. For almost a decade, Duer, sometimes alone, sometimes acting in concert, supplied the army with sundry provisions, including flour, beef, and alcohol. While some contracts he won because he offered the best products at the lowest prices, other sales fell to him because of his influence with Morris and others. Though not uncommon in the eighteenth century, such favoritism portended ill for the future.

At times, both Morris and Duer rued their relationship. Morris had to caution Duer to live up to his commitments lest his character be called into question. Ironically, on at least one occasion Morris himself had to default on scheduled payments, proffering notes instead of gold or silver coin. Strapped for cash as usual, Duer protested that he had promised his creditors specie, not paper. Both men realized, however, that the nation's moribund wartime economy was the ultimate cause of their mutual difficulties. Overall, Duer did a decent job. The soldiers were fed but sometimes the rations arrived late, or underweight, or were of inferior quality. But the situation was a far cry from the deprivations the soldiers suffered at Valley Forge or Morristown. In typical fashion, Duer blamed everyone but himself for any shortcomings.

Increasingly, Duer became more interested in profits than patriotism. In 1783, shortly after news of peace arrived, Duer and partner Daniel Parker secured a contract to supply the *British forces* in New York City. Many Patriots would not have supplied the British, the same forces that had choked off trade, treated American prisoners brutally, and rampaged over large sections of the countryside, at any price. But Duer by this time was clearly oriented towards profit. About this time, Duer and Parker embarked on other ventures, including the China trade. In typical Duer fashion, however, matters usually went awry. In this instance, Parker absconded to Europe with the firm's records and an oversized share of its profits. (Amazingly, in the late 1780s Duer would again partner with Parker, this time in transatlantic securities speculation.)

In the meantime, Duer and Lady Kitty moved to New York City, where they became fast friends with Hamilton and his wife Betsy, who was Catherine's cousin. The Duers threw lavish dinner parties at Ranelagh, their country estate in Greenwich, about two miles north of the city line. Notables including John Jay, Baron von Steuben, Robert Troup, Robert Morris, and James Madison often attended, and for good reason. Kitty and her servants served up lavish meals, many accompanied with a grand selection of wines, bottled cider, and assorted varieties of strong beer. Moreover, Duer was a major player in the city's social and business circles, a member of the chamber of commerce, a trustee of Trinity church, and an honorary member of the Society of the Cincinnati, a fraternal society of Continental Army officers.

In January 1785 the Continental Congress moved to New York City. The so-called Treasury Board, a committee of three consisting of Samuel Osgood (future first postmaster general), Walter Livingston (of the fabled Livingston clan in New York), and Arthur Lee (brother of Harry "Lighthorse" Lee and Richard Henry Lee of Virginia), replaced Morris as head of the nation's finances. When the Board noted that it needed an assistant to handle administrative details, Morris recommended our sinner. Duer accepted the post and soon thereafter Congress upgraded the position to "Secretary" and fattened his wallet to the tune of $1,850 a year, a very nice salary for the period but a sum far below his lofty aspirations.

The fox was now in the proverbial chicken coop, so it would only be a matter of time before the feathers flew. James Madison expressed concern that "the business of the treasury [board was left] to Billy Duer." Indeed, Duer's finances soon became so entangled with those of Congress that only with considerable guesswork could the two be separated. And of course Duer used his influence with the Treasury Board to help "friends," or in other words anyone willing to pay him a fee for his services. In one instance, he persuaded the Board to assign a claim against a Dutch firm to Massachusetts financier Andrew Craigie in exchange for an $8,000 "gift."

Duer spent that money on parties and bad business deals. By 1788 his financial circumstances were so dire that he felt compelled to "borrow" a warrant from the Treasury. He used that piece of paper to secure a loan from Craigie and Boston merchant and politician Christopher Gore. By the standards of any time, place, or culture, the transaction was nothing more than outright theft. But Duer's perfidy knew no bounds. His involvement in the Scioto Company would set new personal lows.

The Scioto's story is a complex, sordid one. It began in June 1786 when a group of veterans formed the Ohio Company and solicited Congress to buy one million acres of land in Ohio. Congress needed some convincing because, alas, the veterans did not have enough money to purchase such a large tract. So the company sent an agent, the Reverend Manasseh Cutler, a forty-five year old former army chaplain from Ipswich, Massachusetts, to ask Congress to turn over the land now in exchange for promises of future payments. This game, buying in bulk on credit and meeting installments from the proceeds of retail sales, was almost as old as the hills the vets wished to purchase, so Cutler met stiff resistance from Congress, which set a very high price. The veterans needed to gain approval for their plan before Congress passed pending legislation, the Northwest Land Ordinance (which would become law in 1787), that would make the land off limits, but Cutler nevertheless prepared to return to Massachusetts empty handed. But then Duer appeared on the scene. He persuaded Cutler to unpack his bags and ask Congress for five million acres instead of one million, but at a lower price per acre and with a longer payoff period. Duer believed, correctly as it turned out, that Congress was willing to sell at a lower rate in order to dispense with a larger tract.

Why was Duer being so helpful? While advising Cutler, Duer and several associates formed a second, secret company, the Scioto Company, to soak up the additional four million acres. While Scioto, a Native American word for "deer," hid in the undergrowth like a newborn fawn, Congress and the same Board of Treasury that had until recently employed Duer approved the transaction—five million acres at $0.667 cents an acre, payable in specie or certain government certificates. Meanwhile, Duer hired the famous writer and later diplomat Joel Barlow (1754–1812) to pawn off Scioto shares on unsuspecting foreign speculators. In Paris, Barlow and an associate, William Playfair, sold parcels to Frenchmen who hoped to emigrate to America to escape an increasingly unstable homeland. To further encourage sales, Barlow promised purchasers free passage to Ohio, a hut, and a year's worth of provisions in exchange for $1.20 per acre payable in installments over five years. That was more than he could honestly promise, though, because the Ohio Company, not the Scioto, held actual title to the lands.

Duer was surprised that Barlow did not simply sell the lands—as he had loosely directed him to—but instead lined up settlers. Strapped as always for cash, Duer now had to finance the French emigrants ready to quit the Old World for the New, but the reward of doubling his money and making millions he thought worth the considerable risk. Of course, if word got back to France that the initial settlers had been hoodwinked, then future sales would evaporate. Like many other Duer projects, what started as a simple deal turned into a royal mess, replete with hundreds of immigrants eager to start a new life on America's shores. Given the slow communications of the era (it took weeks and sometimes months for information to cross the Atlantic), there was little Duer could do to scotch the deal anyway. So in 1790 hundreds of French emigrants set sail for Ohio.

Duer might have been able to fulfill the promises that Barlow had made, but he also managed to get himself entangled in the newly invigorated securities market. In the 1780s, land was the major object of speculators. By the late 1780s, and certainly by 1790, real estate had given way to financial instruments as the main object of speculative lust, especially in the big port cities. For one thing, the securities market, with the numerous varieties of Revolutionary War debt daily fluctuating in value, offered many more "plays" than land sales, which were relatively straightforward buy-and-sell affairs. Moreover, the financial markets were more liquid than real estate markets. In other words, financial instruments were easier and cheaper to trade than land, allowing speculators like Duer to move more quickly into and out of positions.

Duer stretched himself thinner still when he accepted an invitation to become Hamilton's assistant at Treasury. Duer was in some ways a good choice for the post. He was, unlike his eventual replacement Tench Coxe, a firm Patriot during the Revolution and a staunch supporter of the new federal Constitution. Indeed, during the crucial New York ratification convention, he penned and anonymously published four newspaper articles that supported the Federalist cause. (Or at least attempted to support the cause. Duer made some comments that leading Federalists found impolitic.) Kitty helped to plan a reception for Washington, and Duer selected the house in which the nation's first president would reside. Moreover, Duer already lived in New York, the nation's first capital, and had extensive experience in government, including the Treasury Board, and in mercantile trade. Hamilton and Duer knew each other personally; their wives were close. Perhaps most importantly, Duer knew more about the actual functioning of the emerging securities markets than almost anyone. Had he stayed clean, Duer would have been a valuable aid to Hamilton's grand financial plan.

In other respects, Duer was a poor choice. He already had shown blatant disregard for the law, though few of his peers yet realized the full extent of his sinfulness. Perhaps Hamilton believed that Congress's attempt to prohibit any Treasury employee from dealing in public securities would keep Duer to the straight and narrow. Perhaps he believed that Duer would again place the interests of the country ahead of personal gain. Maybe he thought that their mutual friendship would keep the fox honest. In the end, however, Duer duped Hamilton as he had hundreds of others. Such is the power of the con man.

The temptations, after all, were enormous. Early knowledge of if, when, and how Congress would assume state debts, for instance, was potentially worth millions. State securities trading for just pennies, nickels, or dimes on the dollar would appreciate rapidly toward their full face value if the federal government announced that it would take over the debts on liberal terms. If assumption failed, however, the securities would at best maintain their value. Then as now, inside information was the key to making fabulous riches on the quick. And of course Duer was on the inside, at Hamilton's right hand. Once again Duer chose the road to perdition and clandestinely continued his speculative activities. Worse still, he often leaked important information, sometimes for money, sometimes merely for the fame.

In one of his larger operations, Duer partnered with William Constable and Richard Platt to purchase $170,000 worth of North and South Carolina certificates. But the partnership with Constable would not last long. Duer advised Constable to "short" (sell securities one doesn't actually own in expectation of lower prices) some state certificates. Constable complied only to learn later that the ultimate buyer turned out to be none other than the King of the Alley himself! Constable would not be tricked into selling rapidly appreciating property to Duer again. Duer next made friends with Walter Livingston, another wealthy speculator. Certain that Hamilton as usual would prevail, Duer used Congress's long debate over assumption to increase his holdings of depreciated state certificates. All told, Duer stood to gain roughly $250,000 to $375,000 if the assumption bill passed.

Even our foxy sinner could not completely hide such large dealings. The interest of members of Congress, especially Pennsylvania's William Maclay, piqued when coaches began to emanate from New York in a frenzied search for cheap state securities. Soon, all fingers pointed towards the Treasury. Many believed that Hamilton was the main culprit, but subsequent investigations all implicated only one man, or rather only one sinner.

In early April 1790, Duer resigned from the Treasury, possibly under pressure from Hamilton. Officially, Duer "left to do better." Initially, he did do well. Assumption passed Congress in August 1790 and soon after Duer cashed in on his speculations in depreciated state debts. Given his Scioto lands, army contracts, and multiple securities partnerships, Duer's business prospects looked bright. Who could have guessed that it would all crumble within two years? As usual, Duer managed to snatch defeat from the jaws of victory.

His most immediate problem was the events unfolding in Paris, where Barlow and Playfair had become financial sinners themselves, abandoning the Scioto Company in order to establish their own concern, and doing seemingly everything in their power to avoid coming to account. Duer asked Hamilton to borrow Benjamin Walker, a federal naval officer serving in the Port of New York, to go to Paris to sort out the mess. Upon his arrival, Walker discovered that Barlow was incompetent and that Playfair, who had departed with all the company's funds, was anything but. Disturbingly, he realized that two hundred French emigrants were on their way to America, steadfastly clinging to their belief that they would receive assistance, huts, and provisions. Worse yet, more French families were slated to follow.

The ill-fated immigrants landed in Alexandria, Virginia, where they put Duer's local agent to considerable expense. Scioto's guests eventually made their way to Ohio but found it a bit wilder and more dangerous than the veritable garden of Eden that Barlow and Playfair had promised. Naturally the newcomers did not find the frequent Indian raids and chronic supply problems amenable.

Duer might have survived that debacle had he not unwittingly offset his securities speculations with his major real estate position. The Scioto Company had the option of paying its installments to the Ohio Company (in turn to pay Congress) in specie or in securities. When the deal was struck in 1787, securities were trading at a steep discount. Hamilton's financial program, as we have seen, changed all that, raising securities to par. Duer made a killing buying securities cheap and reselling them at or near par. But at the same time, the price appreciation of securities raised the effective price he had to pay for the Scioto lands. Duer had neither the securities nor the cash to pay, so the Scioto Company failed and Duer lost back about $100,000.

The real victims were the French settlers. Their titles were invalid because they had contracted with the Scioto Company, not the Ohio Company, the actual owner of the land. By 1795, only eighty-five of the five hundred or so immigrants still lived on the Ohio lands upon which they had staked their hopes and dreams because to remain on the lands they had to purchase them again, this time from the Ohio Company. To compensate the French victims of the Scioto Company, a remorseful Congress in 1795 established the French Grant in what is now, ironically enough, Scioto County, Ohio.

Duer also had a role in dashing the dreams of many involved in early manufacturing in America, for he was chosen by Hamilton to be the "governor," effectively the CEO, of the Society for the Establishment of Useful Manufactures (SEUM). In September 1791 Hamilton, with Tench Coxe's influence, published an elaborate prospectus for the SEUM. The company sought not to monopolize domestic manufacturing but simply to prove that Americans could produce certain types of textiles cheaply enough to compete with foreign imports.

The SEUM prospectus, a document designed to attract investors, attacked the notion that American labor was too dear to compete with foreign. Women and children would be used to supplement the labor force, laborsaving devices would be invented, and skilled workers were sure to immigrate from Europe because of the dislocations caused by frequent wars and rebellions. Moreover, transportation costs, both from source to factory and from factory to market, would be lower, especially on the bulky, costly-to-ship products the SEUM hoped to manufacture. Thanks to Hamilton's funding program and the national bank scheduled to open its doors in December 1791, enough capital existed to implement the project on a profitable scale. Finally, a formal charter providing the company with tax shelters would be obtained. Like all of Hamilton's plans, the SEUM prospectus was brilliant in all respects but one, that it did not bar William Duer from participation. Undoubtedly, Hamilton hoped that the pretend colonel would help the company to raise much-needed cash. Unfortunately for Hamilton's reputation, SEUM stakeholders, and untold numbers of artisans, Duer raised the cash, only to walk off with part of it.

To invest in the project Duer enlisted the usual suspects, wealthy Federalists, merchants, and stockbrokers like Craigie, Constable, Troup, sundry Livingstons, and Nicholas Low, Herman LeRoy, George Scriba, and James Watson. All told, he raked in about $750,000 by offering investors a wide array of speculative tools and a good chance of healthy dividends, regardless of the fortunes of the manufacturing arm of the business. For starters, the company's stock was payable entirely in public securities, though specie was also acceptable. The directors pledged to use the securities to ensure at least a 6 percent return on capital or to secure a cheap Dutch loan. The SEUM also enjoyed extensive lottery privileges. (Lotteries are such good fundraisers that government has long since appropriated all but small church "raffles" for itself.) Its charter also allowed it to build canals, clear rivers, and charge tolls for the use of its improvements. The SEUM also planned to erect on its lands a "company town" that promised to return most of the workers' wages to the stockholders through rent and purchases of food and supplies, much like colonial iron plantations had done and coal mining companies would later do. The rents from the company's lands and buildings, most of which lay astride the powerful Paterson Falls in New Jersey, turned out to be rather substantial indeed. Perhaps most importantly, the SEUM only had to pay taxes if its profits exceeded 15 percent per annum.

The company began recruiting families to move to Paterson. On the surface, all seemed well, but behind the scenes intrigue bubbled. When he ran short of cash, Duer stole funds from the SEUM. None of this came to light until after Duer stopped payments in early 1792, of course, and by then it was too late. But Hamilton sprang into action to salvage what he could of the SEUM anyway, arranging emergency loans from the Bank of New York, working with Walker to try to recover the SEUM's money from Duer, influencing the election of a new board of directors, and serving as a liaison between the Society and various technical "mechanics," mechanical engineers akin to today's machine tool specialists. Finally, in July 1792, Hamilton wrote a draft of a "Resolution for the Society for Establishing Useful Manufactures" which attempted to revitalize the concern by recruiting a new group of mechanics to move to Paterson.

Although Paterson began to attract mechanics, and the Society recovered somewhat from Duer's depredations, public opinion turned against Hamilton and his supposed "national manufactory." Many expressed concerns about "special privileges" and the ubiquitous dominance of the Treasury secretary. Others equated the SEUM with the now much-hated Duer. Despite Hamilton's admonitions and the public's animosity, the SEUM puttered along, tried its hand at a lottery, but discontinued its manufacturing activities in 1796. The Society became dormant for a time, but its stockholders did not dissolve it. It later revived and even thrived. It played a major, though quiet, role in the development of Paterson. In the end its rents brought in more money than manufacturing on its own account ever did. It rented its buildings to various small manufacturing concerns and did especially well during the War of 1812. It also profited from its lotteries and real estate activities. Though the direct impact of the SEUM was small, its indirect effect was to give publicity to manufactures, to attract skilled laborers to America, and to encourage productive use of capital.

It is easy for Hamilton's critics, therefore, to point to the SEUM as one of his major failures. But readers must recall that Hamilton was Secretary of the Treasury during the SEUM's early years. His role in the SEUM was as large and as constant as possible given his other duties, but he was not the company's CEO, a position unfortunately given at first to Duer. Moreover, from Hamilton's standpoint, the SEUM largely served its purpose. It showed that Americans could be more than just farmers, iron producers, or mercantile middlemen. They could make textiles, an extremely profitable line of business. Moreover, the SEUM's problems resulted not from Hamilton's flawed conception but rather from Duer's sinfulness. Had Duer perished of illness in India or been taken captive by Barbary pirates on his way to inspect his West Indian properties, the SEUM probably would have thrived, and the country would have been richer for it.

〰 What ultimately destroyed Duer was his own insatiable greed. The size of his dealings simply outstripped his real wealth. Between December 1790 and February 1791, for instance, he sold $25,000 worth of securities through one broker alone. Eventually, he took some losses, got desperate to make them up, later gambled big, and, like so many big gamblers before and since, lost it all.

The beginning of the end began ironically enough on July 4, 1791, the date of the IPO of the Bank of the United States. Duer pushed the price of script (a right to purchase a share of stock) to dizzying heights, from its issue price of $25 to over $325 a month later. When Hamilton warned of irrational exuberance, script prices plummeted, but not before savvy or lucky traders like Duer had made a twelve-fold profit, in a month no less. In a scene eerily reminiscent of the Internet craze of the 1990s, the lure of such gargantuan returns encouraged mechanics, shopkeepers, and merchants to neglect "their regular and profitable commerce" to trade scripts.

True to his nickname, Duer was the most prolific trader in scripts. As a "bull," Duer looked for script prices to rise and did everything in his power to see that they did. His alter ego in this instance was "bear" investor Brockholst Livingston, who would profit if prices decreased. (Livingston sold scripts short—that his, he borrowed scripts in order to sell them at say $75 while promising to return them to the lender at some fixed point in the future. If prices decreased to say $50, he would buy the scripts at the new, lower market price, return them to the lender, and keep the difference.) Duer knew that prices could not keep increasing forever, so he looked for a break and rapidly sold out when it came. Smaller, less informed investors got stuck and suffered large losses. After prices came down in August and September, Duer started buying scripts again, hoping that the boom-and-bust cycle would continue.

He also bought in order to gain some control over the national Bank. As the owner of many scripts, Duer influenced the organizational meeting of the Bank held in Philadelphia in October 1791. Including the holdings of his close associates and agents, Duer may have controlled 1,200 of the 20,000 shares available to the public (the government owned 5,000 shares). Anticipating a price spike, Duer used his weight to convince the Bank to announce that it would establish a nationwide network of branches. The ploy worked. When the Bank made the announcement, its stock price, with help from Duer's own shill (which is to say fake) bidders, jumped and "The King" unloaded 600 shares for a profit.

Duer could engage in such schemes because the securities market was already quite liquid, with stocks and bonds changing hands quickly and cheaply. Between September 1791 and March 1792, the public appetite for securities was especially hearty. By December, new issues poured into the market, further heightening trading activity. In addition to the SEUM's $600,000 IPO, the Providence Bank sought $180,000, the Susquehanna and Schuylkill Navigation Company $400,000, and a Connecticut manufacturing company raised $200,000. In January, a large subscription for the West Boston Bridge was oversubscribed, the Massachusetts Bank doubled its capital, New Hampshire chartered its first bank, and in New York several banks, including the so-called Million Bank, were proposed. In February and March new banks in Albany, New

London, and South Carolina commenced. All told, seventeen new corporations held IPOs in those heady six months, a spate of new issues that equaled the combined activity of the previous seven years!

The new ventures all sought one thing, cash. Cash to make loans to businesses, to add value to goods, or to cheapen transportation of goods, people, and information. The golden goose was working her golden magic, matching those with savings but no profitable ideas (investors) to those with profitable ideas but no savings (entrepreneurs). Riches fairly earned were there to be made from those genuinely wealth-creating enterprises. True to form, however, Duer was interested only in riches, regardless of their manner of acquisition. On December 27, 1791, he hatched a bold plan to acquire in one fell swoop the wealth he believed that he so richly deserved. In the end, he received his just deserts.

Duer formed a secret partnership with Alexander Macomb and others, who with Duer's prodding agreed to attempt to corner the U.S. securities market, including stock of the Bank of the United States and the Bank of New York. An Irishman turned successful American speculator, Macomb, like so many others, fell for Duer's pitch. Sitting in jail a few months later, he cursed himself for believing in Duer. Indeed, Duer made Macomb look foolish, convincing him to buy while Duer secretly unloaded unwanted securities, a trick similar to that he had played on Constable years before. Alas, there is no honor among thieves.

Duer's master plan was both complicated and interesting, so a step-by-step analysis is in order. Duer realized that the new banks being formed in New York and elsewhere would weaken existing banks as stockholders in the new institutions withdrew their deposits and patronage from the older institutions. That pressure, in turn, would decrease the older banks' profits, dividends, and stock prices. Duer also hoped to control one of the new banks, the Million Bank. He failed to seize the company, ironically enough, because the speculative mania then building caused its IPO to be oversubscribed, thus preventing Duer's cabal from buying up a controlling interest.

Unable to control the Million Bank, Duer decided to kill it, and profit at the same time. If the New York legislature denied the Million Bank's charter application, naturally the market price of shares of the other bank in town at this time, the Bank of New York (BONY), would increase. Moreover, rumors abounded that the BONY might seek to join with the Bank of the United States rather than compete against it and that Hamilton would support the merger. Such a deal, Duer knew, would also cause BONY stock to soar. So Duer bought up as much BONY stock as he could. Because his finances were, as usual, stretched thin due to his engagements in the Scioto Company, the SEUM, and army contracts, he promised payment in May. He hoped, of course, that the stock price would in the meantime increase so that he could sell the shares, pay the debts he owed for their purchase, and keep the considerable balance in his pocket.

But Duer was far from done. He also moved against U.S. government securities. Hamilton's financial plan had simplified the bond market by consolidating a large variety of debt instruments into just three types of bonds, Threes that paid 3 percent interest, Sixes that paid 6 percent interest, and Deferred bonds that paid 6 percent (all per annum, quarterly) beginning in 1801. Roughly $75 million worth of the bonds existed, some of each type trading in America and the rest overseas, primarily in Western Europe.

There was method to Duer's madness. Installments on the shares of the Bank of United States were payable in four installments, the first due January 1792 and the following three over six month intervals concluding in July 1793. Of the $400 due for the par value of each share, only $100 need be paid in cash; the other $300 could be tendered in government bonds credited at their par or face value. Hamilton included the provision to encourage people to bid up the price of government bonds. By cornering U.S. securities, Duer could effectively control the prices of both government bonds and bank stock. If successful, he would effectively own the stock and the bond markets and at his leisure could sell off pieces at high prices to those who needed bonds to pay for their bank installments, foreign investors, and speculators who had sold the stock short in anticipation of lower prices.

For the plan to work, however, the confluence of events would have to be perfect. First, Duer needed to be able to borrow large sums of money so he could buy up as many securities as possible. Second, because he bought "long" and on credit, bond prices had to keep rising lest he suffer losses when the loans fell due. The more bonds fell in price, the more vulnerable he would be. Third, interference from speculators outside his circle could prove deadly. The short sellers, principally Brockholst, J. R., and Edward Livingston, tried to thwart his every move and seized any and every opportunity to hurt him. Duer was playing a dangerous game but he was not about to fold. So he borrowed and bought bonds, borrowed and bought bonds, borrowed and bought bonds. According to Macomb, Duer at this period had little trouble "raising in a few days some hundred thousand dollars."

But Duer's credit was not infinite. The professional lenders, the banks, cut him off first. Next to question his credit were his friends, who knew that he was perilously overextended. Though some still lent Duer money, it was not enough. Desperate, Duer hired Isaac Whippo, who used to make a living dredging New York harbor for oysters, to scour the streets of New York selling Duer's IOUs to anyone interested in earning 5 to 6 percent *per month*. But as purchasers of those notes should have known, high risks inhere in high returns. By late January, Whippo found it increasingly difficult to sell Duer's notes on the open market. Undaunted, in New York he sought out naïve new investors including "shopkeepers, widows, orphans, butchers, cartmen, gardeners, market women," and even "the noted Bawd Mrs. McCarty." He also dispatched agents to Boston and Philadelphia. As news of Duer's difficulties spread, the rate of interest demanded by lenders climbed sharply higher, inducing the desperate Duer to raid the SEUM's till in a futile attempt to prop up bond prices and his shaky paper empire.

In February, the Bank of the United States further injured Duer's cause. When the giant new addition to the financial system opened in December it flooded the market with its loans. Speculators cheerily borrowed the easy money, taking out loans to purchase securities. In February, the Bank realized that it had lent too much too fast. Radically reversing course, it called in over 25 percent of the loans that it had made in January, a credit restriction of over $625,000, more than enough to deflate the securities market bubble. Hamilton blessed the Bank's actions and may even have suggested that it drastically restrict its lending because he felt that rabid speculation and the multitude of new banking schemes, especially the Million Bank, threatened the stability of the financial system. He told William Seton, the Bank of New York's cashier (chief operating officer), that the new projects "pained" him because their effects were likely to be "in every way pernicious," threatening "injury to the government, and to the whole system of public credit, by disgusting all sober citizens, and giving a wild air to everything." He also worried that Manhattan was as yet unprepared for a third bank, much less a fourth or fifth one.

Equally troubling, by the end of January the securities market had reached dizzying heights due to "mad speculations." One of Hamilton's underlings at Treasury, Oliver Wolcott, thought the mania would be "cured by a few bankruptcies." Wolcott had it right. On February 10, Hamilton urged Seton to slash the Bank of New York's loans because he feared that "the superstructure of Credit is now too vast for the foundation." Within five days Philadelphia banks were also reducing loans.

Duer was now caught in a classic squeeze. The banks were calling in loans to *everybody*, essentially forcing them to sell assets, including securities, to make their repayments. Many sellers and few buyers spelled lower prices, and lower prices, as noted above, meant major pain for Duer, who found it especially difficult to unwind his position because he owned far more securities than others wished to buy under the changed credit conditions. Bears like the three Livingstons were now in control, forcing prices ever lower. The wheels came off Duer's securities carriage in early March because contracts began coming due that he did not have the cash to fulfill. On March 9, surrounded by hungry bears, he stopped payments and sought protection from his creditors. Wholesale panic in the credit markets ensued and stock prices plummeted. Business "confidence" lay in tatters because no one knew for sure who had lent to Duer. The Panic of 1792, the nation's first full-scale financial panic, was on. From peak to trough (January highs to May lows), securities prices fell on average by 25 percent. Thomas Jefferson estimated the amount of wealth destroyed in New York at $5 million, and in Philadelphia and Boston at $1 million each. His colorful description sums up the catastrophe:

> At length our paper bubble is burst. The failure of Duer, in New York, soon brought on others, and these still more, like nine pins knocking one another down, till at that place the bankruptcy is become general, every man concerned in paper being broken, and most of the tradesmen and farmers who had been laying by money, having been tempted by these speculators to lend it to them at an interest rate of from 3. to 6. pr cent a month, have lost the whole.

On top of all this, Duer suddenly found himself facing a $100,000 lawsuit brought by the federal government for his improprieties as secretary of the Treasury Board in the 1780s. In late February, Wolcott had the pleasure of informing Duer of the suit: "You will doubtless consider whether it will best promote *your interest* to deal in the words *payable* and *deliverable* or close your public transactions—it is certainly *my interest* to be no longer amused to the neglect of my duty." Duer appealed to his old friend Hamilton to help avoid the suit, but his entreaties were in vain. Hamilton would not be taken in by Duer again.

Duer became a prisoner in his own house, fearful of venturing forth. After all, he did not know who his creditors were, but they all well knew the King of the Alley. He called a general meeting of his creditors for March 24 so he could explain how he was to pay his debts. But on March 23 several creditors had him committed to jail. Macomb remained at large for several weeks but on April 18 he joined his erstwhile partner, lamenting that:

> The great fall of stocks from the prices which we gave our notes, and for contracts yet unfulfilled, is so great that, added to the daily failures of those

whose notes we hold, there is no possibility of avoiding an immense loss, which will I fear involve my ruin. . . . You can scarcely imagine the present distress in the town, and all confidence lost, no credit, failures everyday, and when we burst, it will be as bad as Law's Mississippi Scheme, comparatively taken. At present every countenance is gloomy, all confidence between individuals is lost, credit at a stand, and distress and general bankruptcy to be daily expected—for everyone gambled more or less on these cursed speculations.

Mobs numbering in the hundreds surrounded the jail calling for Duer and Macomb's heads. The unprecedented breadth of the panic—Seton called it "universal"—conjured in the minds of many the specter of a complete breakdown of the financial system, then government, then civil society itself. Cooler heads realized that such a drastic outcome was unlikely. Though distress among the poorer classes was possible, by far the bulk of the pain would fall upon the well-to-do, unlikely revolutionaries indeed. The real threat was a political backlash against Hamilton's financial system. As Massachusetts senator and merchant George Cabot put it, "public indignation" might "break thro' all restraint & demolish all the money systems of the country."

But there were more immediate problems. By late March, New York, Philadelphia, and Boston were all feeling the pinch. Massachusetts banker Stephen Higginson noted at that time that Boston's markets were "in a confused state. Stock & bills much down, no money, etc. Banks short, credit low among speculators no steady prices to anything." Similar sentiments suffused the letters of Philadelphia's financiers as well. Clearly, America's financial system was facing its most severe test to date. Hamilton and the markets, however, were up to the challenge. The Treasury secretary intervened in the markets and worked magic. Hamilton knew that liquidity would cure the goose's ills. As he had during the mini-crisis of August 1791, Hamilton injected money into the system by buying securities, the same technique used by central bankers like Alan Greenspan to this day. On three successive dates, March 19, March 25, and April 19, he told Seton to make purchases and promised further assistance should it prove necessary. "To relieve the distressed and support the funds are primary objects," he noted. The purchases lifted spirits—and prices. News that a long-sought loan from Dutch investors to the government had gone through further ameliorated the situation. Hamilton also told bankers that the time had come to increase their loans, especially to borrowers who could post government bonds as collateral.

The Bank of the United States also did a superlative job during the crisis. The main bank in Philadelphia realized the severity of the situation and acted accordingly, adding liquidity to the system by prudently extending its loans. As its cashier noted:

> In these stormy times it requires great attention and prudent cautious measures tempered at the same time with as liberal an extension of credit as the funds of the institution & other circumstances will admit of—Credit which was a short time ago pampered and overfed is now sick very sick indeed & requires tender nursing and renovating cordials to keep her from totally expiring.

With the Banks again lending and Hamilton conducting large open-market purchases, credit did slowly revive. By mid-April "bargain hunters" appeared but found few shares for sale, a sure sign that the panic had crested. By April 27 a New York newspaper reported that "prospects begin to brighten up . . . there can be no doubt of a speedy return of confidence and credit, and that business will reassume its natural course." By June, the economy was back on track and securities prices were rationally valued.

Though the economy improved, Duer's financial position did not. Duer had driven securities prices unrealistically high—the levels would not be reached again during the 1790s—and now suffered because they temporarily plummeted unrealistically low. He had taken true losses that totaled more than his net worth, so nothing could save him. But, perhaps deluded himself, he promised to repay widows and orphans first, and other creditors later. He tried to work out payment plans, but he had dug himself a hole much too deep to claw out of. After the daily mobs that gathered outside the prison began to throw stones, he pleaded with Walter Livingston to hire guards to protect him. When Pierre De-Peyster, a local merchant, managed to finagle his way in to see Duer, he promptly whipped out a brace of pistols and challenged Duer to a duel. Duer scraped up the $1,500 he owed DePeyster and avoided the confrontation. But he might have been better off had he instructed DePeyster to put a ball between his eyes. There was no way that he would be able to repay the money—estimates range from $500,000 to $3,000,000—that he owed.

Duer brought others down with him. In addition to Macomb, he bankrupted his broker, John Pintard, who eventually found himself in debtor's prison in Newark, New Jersey. Pintard would eventually recover and a decade later be instrumental in starting the New York Historical Society. Walter Livingston also declared bankruptcy and fled to his country home. Whippo too advertised to meet his creditors. Hamilton counseled Duer by mail but refused to meet his old friend in person. He realized that he had to distance himself from such a sinner. Only after Hamilton left the Treasury Department did he send small gifts to Duer, who remained in prison almost to the end of his days. Prisons in eighteenth-century America were wretched affairs. The Bridewell in New York, for instance, kept as many as ninety-three male prisoners in one "apartment" and seventy-two women in another. Comparatively speaking, then, Duer was not so bad off in debtor's prison, claiming two rooms for himself, one of which he used as an office. He even employed two clerks. Proceeds from the sale of his only major remaining asset, a tract of several million acres of land in present-day Maine, funded such relative extravagance. But even debtors' prison was a hard place, and Duer eventually fell ill. Release from prison did not restore his health. He died on May 7, 1799. Macomb fared better on earth, eventually clearing his name and debts.

By June 1792, the golden goose was alive and well and the sinner was behind bars. But the Panic of 1792 was not without repercussions for the financial system. Jefferson, Madison, William Branch Giles, and other southern Republicans had found their Boston Massacre, their Alamo, their Pearl Harbor. For over a decade, opponents of Hamilton's creation harped upon the Panic, setting it forth as a near miss, a portent of evils to come. The Bank of the United States subscription frenzy, the ensuing asset bubble, and the panic seemed to confirm their predictions that Hamilton, the funding system, and the Bank were dangerous threats to liberty. Jefferson went so far as to call it "treasonous" to recognize the Bank's right to exist.

The media did not help matters. Pamphlets and newspaper diatribes, some supporting Hamilton, others Jefferson, fanned the flames. On May 23, 1792, just as it was becoming clear that Hamilton had stymied the panic once and for all, Jefferson went on the attack, sending President Washington a letter detailing his indictment of the financial system. Jefferson first fingered the Bank of the United States, arguing that its notes would drive specie out of the country. On July 29, Washington passed Jefferson's complaints on to Hamilton, who lashed out at his opponents the following week in a letter signed "An American" in the *Gazette of the United States.* The letter openly declared that Jefferson was hostile to the new government and "more especially the provision which has been made for the public debt [and] the institution of the Bank of the United States." Yet this was only the opening salvo in a war that would last many years and almost end in Jefferson's victory. Luckily for the financial system, and hence all Americans, a little Swiss savior was at hand.

THE SAVIOR

Albert Gallatin (1761–1849)

Albert Gallatin was an exceptional Swiss-American with credentials that matched those of any Founding Father.[1] Yet when his name and face appeared on a 1¼ cent stamp in 1967, few Americans knew his story (or for that matter why a stamp needed to have a quarter cent on it).[2] Why his name has been lost to history is something of a mystery. Consider this: he served his country for *over sixty years,* held a leadership position in Congress, was a confidante of Thomas Jefferson in his successful bid for the presidency, served as the Jeffersonians' money man, holding the position of Secretary of the Treasury for over twelve years (over twice as long as Hamilton), and was, in most respects, a staunch rival of our creator. He was an inside player in both the Jefferson and Madison administrations, advised on a wide range of financial, administrative, and policy issues, and then went abroad in diplomatic service that included bringing the Second War of Independence (the War of 1812) to a successful conclusion. He died in 1849 aged eighty-eight years.

A simple story will suffice to demonstrate his prominence in the early 1800s. During their historic expedition, famed Louisiana Purchase explorers Meriwether Lewis and William Clark named the three forks of the Missouri River after leading Republicans, dubbing them the Jefferson, the Madison, and the Gallatin rivers. Several counties, two towns, a mountain range, and even a division of a university, the Gallatin School at New York University, have been named after this man. Yet two hundred years later the name, much less the story of Albert Gallatin, is virtually unknown, even to many of the students of the Gallatin School.

1. When Gallatin was born in Geneva in 1761, the city had been an independent republic for over two hundred years. The city-state joined the Swiss Confederation in the nineteenth century.

2. From July 1, 1960 to January 7, 1968, the minimum postage for a nonprofit organization to mail a letter was 1.25 cents.

Scholars of American history often gloss over Gallatin, relegating him to a passenger's seat in the Jeffersonian coach, with Jefferson, Madison, and Monroe out front managing the team. Here, however, Gallatin takes the reins as the "savior of the golden goose." As we shall see, certain Jeffersonians, including the president himself, desired to destroy Hamilton's financial system. By the time they ascended to power in 1801, the blood between Hamilton and many leading Republicans was so bad that Hamilton's support for a policy was enough to pit Republicans against it. If Gallatin had agreed with the leadership of his party, the centerpiece of the financial system, the first Bank of the United States, would have been terminated. Other corporations, the funding system, and the specie definition of the dollar may have been next. Devoid of institutional financial intermediaries and securities markets, the early United States might never have prospered economically.

We can be grateful that Gallatin stood firm. The continuation, and even extension, of Hamilton's financial revolution during the terms of three successive Virginia presidents is testimony to Gallatin's greatness. Gallatin and Hamilton personally loathed each other and disagreed on almost everything, and yet both men shared a keen understanding of finance and of the power and value of a sound economic system. Gallatin not only defended the financial system; he nurtured it, and at critical moments in U.S. history.

Born in Geneva on January 29, 1761, Albert Gallatin belonged to a family that could trace its roots back to the thirteenth century. Like many of our other Financial Founders, Gallatin was orphaned early in life, his father dying when he was four. From age five, Gallatin resided with a distant relative, Catherine Pictet, who filled the role of surrogate mother while Gallatin's biological mother struggled with business matters, until her own death when Albert was nine. Though an orphan, Gallatin was not a destitute waif. Several generations earlier, his family had wisely established a trust dedicated to helping family members in time of need. This is not to say that the lad was a spendthrift, in fact quite the opposite. Like most Genevans, Gallatin was steeped in the austerity and probity of Calvinist doctrine. So stern were the financial laws in Geneva that even *the sons* of bankrupts were disbarred from holding public office until all debts, down to the last franc, were satisfied. Despite its strait-laced reputation, Geneva, at the time an independent republic, was an intellectually stimulating place, thanks in part to the presence of renowned French refugee writer Voltaire. Several Gallatins were social friends of the *philosophe,* whom Albert as a young boy met on several occasions.

In 1779, Gallatin graduated from the academy with honors, having attained the rough equivalent of a college education today. Uninterested in the tradi-tional avenues of advancement in Geneva—a career in the public service, the law, or the church—he instead yearned to break free from the confining city. The struggle of the American colonists against the British inspired him. In 1780, with little planning, he departed westward across the Atlantic accompanied only by a friend from school, a modicum of money, a little tea, and precious little knowledge of the English language. He dared not tell his family for fear that they would attempt to interdict him. Geneva's loss would soon be America's gain.

Arriving in Boston, Gallatin and his friend attempted several small-time mer-cantile activities but found no success. In the meantime, Mlle Pictet, his surro-gate mother, tried to locate him with the aid of the United States minister to France, Benjamin Franklin. She also approached Genevans who might have contacts in Boston with the hope of locating the boy and seeing to his safe return home. All Pictet managed to do, however, was to ensure that Gallatin's roots grew strong in American soil. One of her connections helped Gallatin make arrangements to tutor students at Harvard College in French. But the lure of the American frontier, in those days just fifty to two hundred miles inland, captivated the ambitious young man. He left Cambridge, Mass., in 1783 with dreams of starting a community of Genevans who could live in peace and har-mony with the land. He first traveled south before turning west, passing through Philadelphia and Richmond along the way. Ironically, he enjoyed Richmond more than Philadelphia, although it was the latter city that would play so promi-nent a role in his future.

During Gallatin's stay in Richmond two Virginians, one who would become famous and one who already was famous, commented on his character. John Marshall, then just twenty-eight and still eighteen years from becoming one of the most famous chief justices in the history of the United States Supreme Court, asked Gallatin to become a student in his newly established law office. Gallatin realized that he had the keen analytical mind of a lawyer but not the heart, so he turned Marshall down. Patrick Henry, the revolutionary firebrand who once asked King George to give him liberty or give him death, also imme-diately took a liking to Gallatin. Henry, who was governor of Virginia at the time, sensed that the Genevan was a "most astonishing man" and correctly predicted his future as a statesman. He also tellingly noted that Gallatin was "most sen-sible and well informed," virtues that would surface time and again during his career. Reflecting years later, Gallatin claimed that his greatest asset was his "even temper," that he was not "altered by time or politics," and that he was not apt to be led astray "by passion, or to be blinded by enthusiasm or prejudice."

Though he enjoyed Richmond, the frontier beckoned. Gallatin hastened to rural Fayette County, Pennsylvania, just north of the Monongahela River, where he set up as a surveyor. There, Gallatin met General George Washington himself. In 1784 the general, who owned sizeable tracts in the region, stopped at a local land agent's office, a fourteen-foot-square log house furnished only with a large pine map table and a small cot. Accompanied by his nephew, Washington sought from local settlers and hunters information regarding the best route for opening a road across the Allegheny Mountains. A large crowd, including the twenty-three-year-old Gallatin, gathered at the small office to observe events. Maps strewn on the rough-hewn table, Washington painstakingly examined each individual's opinion regarding the best route for the road. Impatient at the duration of the discussion, Gallatin shouted out that the optimal route "was obvious" and pointed to a location on the map. All were stunned at the impropriety. Washington, a stickler for decorum, stared icily at the foreigner. Gallatin shrank at the power of the most withering stare he ever received in his life. Washington went back to the maps. After a few minutes, he put down his pen, looked at Gallatin, and pronounced "You are right, sir." Obviously impressed, Washington invited Gallatin to remain for further discussions. While we do not know precisely what was discussed, we do know that Washington invited Gallatin to stay the evening. Gallatin and the nephew slept on the floor, while the general, of course, slept in the bed. Here was one place that Washington did actually sleep, but visitors should have been more impressed to learn that Washington *and* Gallatin had slept in the cabin *on the same night* because a decade later Washington would lead an army against the whiskey rebels, and prominently among their ranks was the young Genevan financier.

With the help of a $5,000 inheritance received on his twenty-fifth birthday, Gallatin purchased a four-hundred-acre tract of land called Friendship Hill. (Interestingly, Gallatin realized the funds by selling drafts drawn on the firm of Robert Morris, our fallen angel.) Gallatin in these years sometimes trekked to Richmond, where he met Sophie Allegre. When the pair made known their desire to wed, Sophie's mother protested vehemently because Gallatin lived on the frontier, was a foreigner with weak English skills, and possessed no fortune or fame. The two wed anyway, but Sophie's mother was right about one thing, the frontier was no place for her daughter, who sadly died at Friendship Hill five months after the nuptials.

〰️ The struggle over ratification of the U.S. Constitution drew Gallatin into local Fayette County politics. In general, frontier folk opposed the document because, as they saw it, the proposed compact gave far too much power to a distant government. They had not suffered through the Revolution merely to re-place one hereditary tyrant for a nominally elected one. At best, many believed, the proposed national government would tax the relatively thinly populated frontier for the benefit of better-represented seaboard areas. In 1788, Gallatin attended a meeting called to select delegates that would propose amendments, specifically a bill of rights, to the ratified document. No one was surprised that the local politico, John Smilie, received a nomination. Gallatin himself was sur-prised to emerge as the second delegate. Rugged frontiersmen did not care that Gallatin spoke only broken English because they realized that he was an edu-cated man who could represent frontier interests in terms that city folk would understand. The four-day meeting in Harrisburg came to naught because other states had already suggested most of the same ideas that the Pennsylvanians brought forth, but Gallatin's insightful mind shone brightly.

So the next time Gallatin was not surprised by his nomination. In December 1789, frontier voters sent Smilie and Gallatin to represent their interests at the state constitutional convention. It was the first of many trips that Gallatin would make to Philadelphia over the next ten years, thanks in part to the way that he acquitted himself at the convention, where he made eloquent speeches that espoused democratic ideals and that quoted the venerable Voltaire and fabled French philosopher Jean-Jacques Rousseau. Word of his eloquent defense of democratic ideals reached his constituents in Fayette, who promptly rewarded him with election to the lower house of the new state legislature, where he served several terms. Although a member of the minority party, Gallatin took on so much committee grunt work that he came to refer to himself as the "laboring oar." Often that work was assigned to him by the Speaker of the House, Feder-alist William Bingham, a wealthy merchant and banker who recognized the Genevan immigrant's outstanding abilities. Bingham was pleased to find a rural Pennsylvanian who was pro-banks, pro-merchants, and pro-capitalist develop-ment.

Indeed, Gallatin supported the Lancaster Turnpike though it was nominally a Federalist project and at first met opposition from farmers fearful of the turn-pike's seemingly invasive nature and high tolls. The farmers quickly learned that Gallatin and the Federalists were correct; the newly constructed turnpike helped them to carry their produce to market more cheaply and easily than ever before. Soon, Pennsylvania farmers throughout the state clamored for turn-pikes. Within a few decades, the Keystone State could just as well have been called the Turnpike State. Despite all the partisan politics of the next decade, Bingham and Gallatin would remain friends.

In the legislature Gallatin also sponsored bills that sought to reform the existing penal code, to abolish slavery, and to enhance public education statewide. Gallatin's financial acumen became readily apparent when he served on the ways and means committee. His 1790–91 report especially earned him a positive reputation in the field of finance because it was a complete, accurate analysis of the state's finances.

Like any Genevan worthy of the name, Gallatin disdained debt in both private and public life. He was notoriously frugal in his personal life. According to a story current when he was Secretary of the Treasury, a stagecoach was passing Gallatin's home one night when a passenger asked the driver who resided in the abode. The driver replied "no one lives there," but the passenger retorted that he could see lights on. The driver then clarified that "no one *lives* there, but the Secretary of the Treasury *breathes* there!"

Throughout his career, Gallatin sincerely wished to see the public debt quickly extinguished, a view quite different from that of Hamilton, who believed that a properly managed public debt was a blessing. Gallatin also disagreed with Hamilton about assumption of state debts by the national government. Moreover, he believed that Hamilton had shortchanged Pennsylvania in the final settlement of Revolutionary War accounts. Such sentiments won him broad respect among proponents of the emerging Republican Party. So too did his policy prescriptions for Pennsylvania, which included retiring old state paper money, which was nothing more than debt in the form of unreliable money. Gallatin also called for an end to Pennsylvania's state income tax, an object achieved several years later.

Gallatin's fame as a financier was further enhanced in 1793 when he led an attempt to charter a third bank in Philadelphia. Both the Bank of the United States and the Bank of North America were flooded with loan applications but could not by law increase the interest rate they charged. They responded rationally, by lending to those best known to the directors, which is to say family members, friends, and business associates, most of whom were also Federalists. Republicans and frontiersmen nevertheless considered such behavior "monopolistic" and complained bitterly about it. So they were overjoyed when the Bank of Pennsylvania, with Gallatin's backing, gained a charter. Pennsylvania's economy continued to grow apace, however, so the Bank of Pennsylvania also found itself forced to lend mostly to Philadelphians, disappointing the westerners once again. Still, the episode demonstrated that Gallatin understood finance and had significant political acumen.

When in Philadelphia, Gallatin met, and later married, Hannah Nicholson, daughter of a Revolutionary War naval commander who counted as his friends New Yorker Aaron Burr and most of the Livingston and Clinton clans. Such solidly Republican connections certainly did not hurt Gallatin's political fortunes. Indeed, Pennsylvania Republicans soon tapped him to fill a long-vacant seat in the U.S. Senate. The timing could not have been worse as Gallatin was widely suspected of having authored a technical pamphlet that attacked Hamilton's funding system. As a senator, he openly called for resolutions that Secretary Hamilton furnish statements explaining the domestic and foreign debts of the government as well as a full summary of the receipts and expenditures of the federal government since 1789. His appointment and subsequent demands so annoyed Federalists in general and Hamilton in particular that they set out to oust him from his seat on the grounds that he had not met the residency requirement. Indeed, he had lived in Pennsylvania only nine of the required ten years. About three months after taking his seat, the Senate voted him out of it, fourteen yeas to twelve nays. Though he had promised to remain neutral in the matter, Pennsylvania's other senator, none other than Robert Morris, voted against Gallatin. Now as angry with Hamilton as Hamilton was with him, Gallatin returned to western Pennsylvania in early 1794, but only after selling, on credit, $4,000 worth of land to Morris. (It would have been a nice transaction for Gallatin had Morris not later gone bankrupt and defaulted on the debt.)

Gallatin returned to a Fayette County figuratively consumed by whiskey. In 1791, the national government, under prodding from Hamilton, had imposed an excise tax on distilled liquors. The tax was particularly unpopular with the backwoods farmers of the Monongahela Valley in western Pennsylvania, who, before the Mississippi Valley opened to American produce, had no economically viable means of transporting their grain to market. The frontier farmers responded rationally by processing their bulky grains into a commodity with a weight-to-value ratio that could bear the cost of overland transport to eastern marts—whiskey. The farmers were far from thrilled to learn that the new distant government that they had not supported in the first place wanted to tax their stills. In 1792 some recalcitrant settlers stopped paying the tax for a short time. New legislation and the threat of force temporarily appeased and cowed them. But the issue did not go away. Gallatin and his old political friends John Smilie and William Findlay were front and center in denouncing the tax at a gathering in Pittsburgh later that year. Gallatin expressed concern, which must have sounded very familiar to his American audience, that the excise tax would lead to more taxes "until everything we eat, drink, or wear [would be] subjected to heavy duties and the obnoxious inspection of a host of officers." Unlike the firebrands at the meeting, however, Gallatin opposed armed opposition. In the end, he lamented his decision to get involved in the Pittsburgh meeting, years later labeling his participation as "my only political sin." But a small sin it was, for his refusal to espouse violence would later save him from Hamilton's wrath.

In the meantime, tensions mounted. Westerners erected Liberty poles, symbols of freedom and rebellion that hearkened back to the imperial crisis leading to the Revolution. In July 1794, the Washington administration, led by our "Judas" Tench Coxe, again attempted to enforce the tax. The farmers openly resisted and rioting in the western counties of Pennsylvania and Virginia ensued. The rioters targeted symbols of the Federal government, including the courts, the mails, and the tax collectors. The violence turned fatal when a mob overwhelmed the grounds of a federal land inspector; several persons were killed in the ensuing melee. The small federal garrison at Pittsburgh was threatened. A "Whiskey Rebellion" appeared in full swing.

On August 7, President Washington ordered the insurgents to return to their homes. Anticipating that force would be needed to resolve the crisis, the president began raising an army of almost 13,000 troops composed of federalized militia from New Jersey, Maryland, and the eastern counties of Pennsylvania and Virginia. He also dispatched three commissioners, William Bradford, James Ross, and Jasper Yates, to visit western Pennsylvania and negotiate with the rebels, who included Gallatin. A champion of moderation, Gallatin ironically incurred the wrath of both sides: the government saw him as one of the rebels, and some rebels who were itching for a fight saw him as a liability. Indeed, Gallatin barely escaped from one of the rebel meetings with his life. Unable to sell their whiskey, many of the rebels apparently had taken to drinking it, so they did not take kindly to Gallatin's calls for reason. At the same time, Gallatin received word from a friend that staunch Federalists had placed a large bounty on his head. If that failed, assassins might be hired. Facing death on both sides, Gallatin awaited his fate.

Washington and his de facto second in command, Alexander Hamilton, viewed the rebellion as an important test for the new government. They feared that Jacobins, supporters of the recent revolution in France, were working in connection with the whiskey rebels to undermine the U.S. government. They also vividly recalled how the rebellion of Daniel Shays in western Massachusetts eight years earlier had helped to bring about calls for a new government, the government that both men had fought so hard to create and serve. In late August, Washington scolded the rebels and their supporters, arguing that "this insurrection is viewed with universal indignation and abhorrence; except by those who have never missed an opportunity by side blows, or otherwise, to aim their shafts at the general government; and even among these there is not a Spirit hardly enough, yet *openly* to justify the daring infractions of Law and order."

Reports received on August 20 that General "Mad" Anthony Wayne had roundly defeated a Native Indian force of over two thousand warriors on the Miami River in Ohio further emboldened the Washington administration because the victory, which ended a costly four-year war, was proof positive that the new national government had greatly aided frontiersmen by reducing the threat posed by the natives. As Oliver Wolcott, the second-in-command in the Treasury Department, stated: "Nothing can be more ungrateful and wicked than [the] conduct [of the rebels]. The expense of the western war chiefly on their account and of other disaffected persons, is nearly two millions per annum." The whiskey rebels remained unpersuaded. A violent end to the rebellion appeared inevitable, but Gallatin continued his efforts for peace, persuading many rebels in his county to sign the amnesty papers that were being circulated by the government.

But the signatures did not come in fast enough. In mid-September Hamilton told Rufus King, America's ambassador to England, that "nothing from the Western Country authorizes an expectation of a pacific termination of that business." Moreover, the militiamen from Virginia, New Jersey, Baltimore, and Philadelphia were all "*zealous.*" Certain that a "daring and factious spirit" was trying to destroy the Constitution, Washington on September 24 ordered the military to march west and suppress the rebellion. Hamilton made hasty preparations to join the troops, leaving instructions with his subordinate Oliver Wolcott, comptroller of the Treasury Department, to manage the fiscal affairs of the national government while he was in the field with the army. Hamilton and Henry Lee led the forces and even President Washington ventured as far as Bedford, Pennsylvania with the troops. The insurrection melted away before a single shot was fired. Again, the western farmers had behaved rationally. There was no way that two thousand or so of their number, spread over hundreds of square miles, could have defeated a federal army replete with cavalry and horse-drawn artillery and led by seasoned veterans like Washington and Hamilton. Gallatin feared that he would be punished for his participation, but the New World proved less vindictive than the Old.

Wolcott argued that William Findlay, Smilie, and Gallatin "should be hanged," after a proper trial proved their guilt of course. Though Wolcott thought the gallows a fitting end for Gallatin, he realized that Gallatin's moderate, nonviolent stance would save him from the hangman. Hamilton was not so eager to give up the quest to knock out a rival who was clearly on the ropes. He lingered in western Pennsylvania to interrogate rebels, ever hopeful that one of them would incriminate the hated Genevan immigrant and other ringleaders of the insurrection. Hamilton repeatedly pressed those in custody to name Gallatin as a conspirator, to mention any possible act of treachery on Gallatin's part, or better yet to admit that Gallatin had received French gold to finance the revolt.

But it was not to be. No one denounced Gallatin, and Washington later pardoned all of the rebels, even two convicted of treason. During the Revolutionary War, Washington occasionally resorted to public hangings to quell uprisings in the rank and file. But circumstances were changed, and Washington thought it best for the country, especially considering that the rebels had backed down without a fight, to end the matter magnanimously. It was a shrewd political move because hanging any rebels, especially prominent ones like Gallatin, probably would have created many more rebels in the future.

With the Whiskey Rebellion concluded, Gallatin was quickly returned to Congress, for which he was now officially eligible, by his constituents. There, he helped the emerging Republican Party to combat Hamilton. It was payback time. Gallatin's November 1796 pamphlet, *A Sketch of the Finances of the United States,* identified every last penny in the budget and the national debt and included the most detailed criticism of Federalist finances to date. The pamphlet also showcased Gallatin's belief that public debts were bad and should be extinguished, a notion quickly becoming one of the cornerstones of Jeffersonian political rhetoric.

When Hamilton left office in January 1795, Gallatin happily began to criticize his successor, Oliver Wolcott. Wolcott complained to Hamilton that "Gallatin . . . is evidently intending to break down [the Treasury] Department by charging it with . . . impracticable detail." Gallatin's attack on the administration extended beyond finance to every important issue of the day, including Jay's Treaty and the notorious Alien and Sedition Acts. Federalist newspapers often took aim squarely at Gallatin, a sure sign that he was one of the Republican Party's most important leaders. Indeed in 1797, when Madison missed a term in Congress, Gallatin was for all intents and purposes the party's titular leader in the House of Representatives. He also was instrumental in creating the House Ways and Means Committee, which to this day is a crucial committee charged with monitoring the Treasury Department and ensuring that Congress has a say in financial policy.

Federalists so loathed and feared Gallatin that, with extreme irony, they tried to oust him from his seat by amending the Constitution to forbid foreigners from holding high office. The measure, which was a transparent attempt to get rid of Gallatin, met defeat. The fact that all Americans born before the Revolution were technically "foreigners" aside, immigrants like Gallatin were ubiquitous in early American politics. Hamilton himself was an immigrant. Most foreigners in fact had Federalist leanings because unlike the native-born they owed allegiance to no individual state. The failure of the amendment helped gain Jefferson the presidency because Gallatin sided with the Virginian over Burr during the deadlocked election of 1800.

The intrigues surrounding the deadlock were of course intense. Complicating matters was the fact that the Constitution mandated that the lame duck House of Representatives, which had a Federalist majority, would make the decision, and not the newly elected House with its Republican majority. Many Federalists preferred Burr, a New Yorker with strong ties to the commercial and financial sectors, to the slaveholding Virginian. After thirty-six ballots, Federalists finally gave Jefferson the nod in exchange for assurances that the funding system would be left intact and that no reduction in the armed forces would be forthcoming. Now it was up to Gallatin to ensure that those assurances would be kept.

Little doubt existed, after all, that Jefferson would ask Gallatin to serve as his Treasury secretary. Gallatin understood public finance and was due a big favor for his successful efforts to thwart Burr's election in the runoff. Moreover, the only other heavyweight financier on the Republican side was the apostate Loyalist and Federalist Tench Coxe, who Jefferson believed could not be trusted with such a key post.

Gallatin had many Federalist enemies and therefore his appointment had to wait until May 1801, after the old Federalist Congress adjourned. He inherited the executive branch's largest and most important department. From Hamilton's initial staff of thirty-nine in 1789, the Treasury Department had doubled to seventy-eight by 1801. Including the customs service and internal revenue agents, Treasury employed a staggering 1,285 individuals. Gallatin needed all the help he could get because, when it came to finance, the new chief executive was behind the times. Accordingly, Jefferson turned to Gallatin for aid in just about everything that concerned money. In terms of finance, what Hamilton did for Washington, Gallatin would do for Jefferson.

Gallatin also had his own agenda to pursue. In 1801 he persuaded Congress to pass a law requiring the Secretary of the Treasury to submit an annual report to Congress. Hamilton and Wolcott had submitted reports only on an "as requested" basis, but Gallatin desired a more formal, transparent process that effectively forced Congress to monitor the nation's finance minister. Next, understandably, came repeal of the whiskey excise and other hated federal taxes, leaving tariffs on imported goods the federal government's main source of revenue. A third drain on his time occurred in the summer months, when Jefferson and Secretary of State James Madison went home to oversee work on their plantations, and Gallatin took de facto charge of the executive branch.

Gallatin at first seemed intent on eliminating the financial system. He simultaneously cut taxes, began paying down the national debt, which still stood in the neighborhood of $82 million, and ran a budget surplus. He achieved that seemingly miraculous outcome by taking a page from his Calvinist background and slashing expenditures, especially military spending. Importantly, Republicans now controlled Congress, making passage of his budgets easy. But two big fiscal storms were brewing.

First, the Barbary pirates, operating out of what is today Morocco, were incensed to learn that the U.S. had repudiated its promise to pay them $1 million of tribute annually. A war ensued that cost in the short term much more than simply paying the tribute would have. But "millions for defense and not one cent for tribute" had been the rallying cry since the XYZ bribery affair in 1798.

The second budget shock was the Louisiana Purchase in 1803, probably the greatest real estate deal in history. Great for the U.S., that is, which doubled its size for a mere $15 million, about 4 cents an acre. Overnight, the upstart nation acquired land physically larger than France, Spain, Portugal, Italy, Holland, Switzerland, and the British Isles combined. Crowning the vast territory was the magnificent port city of New Orleans, which gave western farmers a much-needed water outlet to world markets. The country could now grow westward without fear that trans-Appalachian states would secede to gain cheap access to the sea.

Napoleon sold the Louisiana Territory because he was waging war with Britain and was strapped for cash. He wrongly believed the area a wasteland and hence strongly preferred to retain instead the French colony of Saint-Domingue, which occupied the western half of the island of Hispañola (the eastern half being the Spanish colony of Santo Domingo). Saint-Domingue boasted a population of 500,000 and plantations of sugar cane, indigo, coffee, and cocoa rich enough to fill 700 ships a year. The French then promptly lost the colony when, in 1804, a successful revolution by black slaves led to the independence of the new nation of Haiti.

Jefferson was not certain, however, that the purchase was Constitutional. Recall that Jefferson interpreted the Constitution strictly, or at least publicly purported to do so. The Constitution made no specific provision for purchasing new territory, so Jefferson was inclined to believe that a Constitutional amendment might have to be passed before the nation could take title to the territory. Madison and most other cabinet members were inclined to agree. Gallatin, however, took a page from Hamilton and persuaded the president and the cabinet that the Constitution contained certain implied powers, including the inherent right to acquire territory. The movement to begin the lengthy process of amending the Constitution was dropped, and Congress quickly approved the purchase.

Hamilton cast an even larger shadow over the proceedings because the Republicans were about to start borrowing. To pay the purchase price and acquire good title, Gallatin had to pay Napoleon the full price in cash up front. As a distressed dictator desperate for cash, the little Corsican was not about to "hold the mortgage." And Gallatin had on hand only about one quarter of the cash needed to make the purchase. He therefore floated a bond issue through the Dutch banking house of Hope and Company, which promptly sold it to Baring Brothers, a British investment bank. Alexander Baring worked closely with Gallatin for five months in Washington to finalize the details. Although the two financiers formed a friendship, the price tag of the bond issue bothered Gallatin. He realized, however, that the port of New Orleans would increase federal revenues some $200,000 a year. Moreover, Gallatin and other Republicans must have savored the irony of British investors lending money to vastly increase the power of their former colonies and to replenish the coffers of Britain's arch enemy, Napoleon Bonaparte.

Financing the Louisiana Purchase alone should have been enough to seal Gallatin's fame. But he was far from done; his fingerprints were all over every important matter of his day. Not all his efforts succeeded, however. Negotiations to purchase Florida from Spain, for instance, failed. (Not until 1819 would Spain, staring down the barrel of Andrew Jackson's gun, concede.) Gallatin's attempt to tie the nation together both commercially and militarily with an ambitious program of "internal improvements," canals and turnpikes, also failed. He realized that the outlook of the typical Congressman was rather provincial, so he tried to include something for everybody. That tactic backfired, because by trying to please everyone Gallatin ended up pleasing no one. The estimated $20 million price tag over ten years was simply too large to garner enough support to pass.

When Burr gunned down Hamilton in 1804, Gallatin shed not a tear. When he received word that his long-time nemesis had been slain, he commented that "a majority of both parties seemed disposed . . . to deify Hamilton and to treat Burr as a murderer. The duel, for a duel, was certainly fair." Moreover, Burr and Gallatin remained on friendly terms, even after rumors leaked that the former vice president had tried to invade Louisiana and start his own private war with the Spanish over Vera Cruz. Though acquitted of high treason by Chief Justice Marshall, Burr fled to Europe rather than face various state charges. As he fled, Burr called Gallatin "the best head" in all of the United States. In the aftermath of his duel with Hamilton, that was probably a correct judgment.

With Hamilton gone, the Republicans won a landslide victory in the 1804 elections. Jefferson even carried Massachusetts, long a Federalist bastion. The U.S. Senate would contain only seven Federalists, the House only twenty-five. But storm clouds lay over the eastern horizon as Napoleon put the $15 million he received from British investors for Louisiana to use killing British soldiers and sailors. Initially, the neutral U.S. benefited from the war by trading with both sides. The prosperity ended, however, when the British Navy began to interdict American ships. The French and British were at each other's throats; both realized that they could weaken the other by severing its rival's trade with America. The British were also incensed that many British subjects, *former* British subjects according to the U.S. government, served on American-owned trading vessels. Undermanned British warships regularly stopped American vessels and "impressed" any of their sailors that could not prove that they were native-born Americans. The United States naturally objected to such disregard for its sovereignty but there was little it could do. Matters came to a head in the summer of 1807 when the HMS *Leopard* attempted to board the USS *Chesapeake,* in, fittingly enough, Chesapeake Bay. The *Chesapeake,* a U.S. Navy frigate, refused to allow the British to board and search for "deserters." Shots were fired, all but one by the British. When it was all over, three Americans were dead, many more wounded, and of the four U.S. sailors nabbed, only one was truly a British citizen.

Americans throughout the nation clamored for war but Jefferson demurred, favoring economic sanctions against Britain instead. Jefferson and Gallatin abhorred war, but although Gallatin thought a war would be "calamitous," he felt that the country had to prepare for armed conflict. In December 1807 Gallatin informed Jefferson that he supported only a temporary embargo and preferred "war to a permanent embargo." "Government prohibitions do always more mischief than had been calculated," he reasoned. Those words proved prescient as events unfolded exactly as Gallatin foretold.

Gallatin started tabulating the cost of a war, from strengthened coastal defenses to big increases in the size of the army and navy. A war with Britain, he estimated, would run a whopping $18 million per year. Even a short war would quickly erase the progress he had made on the national debt, which now stood at about $57 million. That figure was all that was needed to persuade Jefferson that a Nonimportation Act was a better policy choice. Jefferson of course remembered the important role that economic sanctions had played in the crises leading to the Revolution. He also knew that, thanks in part to his administration's obsession with debt reduction, the nation's armed services were unprepared for war.

What Jefferson forgot was that colonial economic sanctions had ultimately failed. Moreover, it was not clear that Britain's economy needed American trade in the 1800s anymore than it had in the 1770s. In the end, Jefferson's pacific policies did not so much stymie John Bull as cut off Columbia's nose to spite her face. His economic sanctions, the Nonimportation Act, the Embargo Act, and the Nonintercourse Act, mostly injured America's economy. Gallatin and others let the chief know that his policies were dismal failures, but Jefferson turned a deaf ear, so America continued to blockade itself.

It fell to Gallatin, and the Treasury officials who reported to him, to enforce a law that hurt the entire economy, as evidenced by everything from New England's dormant ports to Virginia's rotting tobacco crop. As Gallatin foretold, cheating commenced, as state officials, merchants, and sea captains found legal loopholes or outright broke the law. Congress closed the loopholes with passage of the Giles Enforcement Act of 1809. Instead of fighting the British, the U.S. Navy policed its own nation's sloops.

The negative impact of increased enforcement of the embargo was soon felt. One contemporary reported that Manhattan, just a few years earlier a bustling port, "looked like a town ravaged by pestilence." Such scenes sickened Gallatin, who beseeched Jefferson to moderate or eliminate the embargo and prepare for war, which Gallatin confidently and correctly predicted could be financed through government bond sales. Despite his use of bonds to finance the war, ironically, the Genevan never came around to Hamilton's view that a national debt could indeed be a national blessing.

Gallatin sensed a crisis looming. With trade at a virtual standstill, government revenues, now dependent on the tariff, plummeted. New Englanders whispered of secession. Madison came to power in 1809 but at first followed the same impoverished policy of economic sanctions that his predecessor had. Macon's Bill Number Two, which became law in 1810, was a particularly severe blunder. The law repealed the Nonintercourse Act and opened the way for renewed trade with Britain and France, but with the confusing stipulation that if one of those powers agreed to lift restrictions on American commerce, the U.S. would renew economic sanctions against the other power. Napoleon shrewdly jumped on this opportunity to receive something of value at Britain's expense. He lied to the gullible Americans, claiming that all restrictions were lifted. Madison's administration was more than happy to impose sanctions on the British. They were not so happy, however, when they learned that Napoleon's forces continued seizing American ships and cargoes.

By 1809 the inevitable occurred: a deficit commenced. As difficult as it must have been for the man who had derided the Federalists for borrowing money, Gallatin now set upon the same course of action. Many newspapers attacked Gallatin, and a resolution was brought up in Congress that questioned the Treasury secretary's capacity and integrity. It was soundly defeated because anyone not blinded by partisan rage could see that the dormant economy, and not Gallatin, was to blame. But Gallatin probably now wished that he had taken Madison's offer to switch to the post of Secretary of State. Gallatin had turned down the offer because he thought the exigencies of the times demanded that he remain at Treasury. Moreover, nasty political machinations were afoot. Those intrigues eventually led to the appointment at State of Robert Smith, whose only major claim to the job was that his brother was influential Republican Senator Samuel Smith. Madison soon grew to distrust Smith, so increasingly he turned to Gallatin to advise on diplomacy.

Gallatin still had plenty of time to devote to Treasury business, however. In fact in 1810 he submitted to Congress his own report on manufactures, not dissimilar to what Hamilton and Coxe had written almost twenty years earlier. In it Gallatin enumerated many facts and figures, and tried to put a positive policy "spin" on Republican economic sanctions by noting that the dearth of imports had stimulated good old Yankee ingenuity. He also boasted that economic freedom persisted in other parts of the economy, allowing workers to undertake the most profitable employment available, flexibility not yet enjoyed in many places in the world. The sanctions and subsequent war did indeed spur development of the manufacturing sector, but it was a high price to pay.

The following year, Gallatin and the financial system suffered a major setback. The twenty-year charter of the Bank of the United States was set to expire in 1811. The Bank's existence remained a politically divisive issue; its main supporter, the Federalist Party, was but a shadow of its former self. Because it had prestigious office buildings in Baltimore, Boston, Charleston, New Orleans,

New York, Norfolk, Philadelphia, Savannah, and Washington, and its notes enjoyed wide circulation, the Bank was by far the most visible component of Hamilton's financial revolution and indeed symbolized all of the changes that our creator had wrought. Jefferson still smarted because Hamilton had won their little duel of Constitutional logic refereed by Washington. Hamilton had lost his life in a real duel, but his Bank, which Jefferson believed was "a source of poison & corruption," lived on. Jefferson wanted it dead. In fact, during his first administration he had tried to convince Gallatin to weaken the Bank by refusing to deal with it. But Gallatin, as Hamilton predicted, had found the Bank instrumental to the Treasury's operation. The Bank moved the government's funds from one part of the nation to another with ease and speed, arranged to pay the interest payments on its bonds as they fell due, and provided it with short-term loans when disbursements temporarily exceeded revenues. Moreover, it was a safe and convenient depository for the government's surpluses.

As early as 1796 Gallatin had vindicated the Bank, arguing in his *Sketch of the Finances* that the problem was not so much the Bank itself as Federalist domination of it. Soon after becoming Treasury secretary some five years later, Gallatin wrote the Bank's president, our risen angel Thomas Willing, to make clear how important it was for both parties to support each other in the most liberal spirit. The country came first, and Gallatin understood that the Bank, though privately owned, was critical to a healthy financial sector and economy. He promised that as Treasury secretary he would do everything in his power to ensure the Bank's continued success. While the tone and nature of the letter demonstrate that Gallatin wanted to get off on the right foot with the Bank, his concern that the letter might leak to Jefferson prompted him to add the following postscript: "From the nature of this letter, especially as it relates to a monied institution, I need hardly add that it must be understood to be perfectly confidential." Confidential is an understatement! Jefferson would have been enraged had he seen this letter or heard of its contents.

Over the years, Gallatin's rapport with Willing and other Bank officers strengthened. The capital moved to Washington from Philadelphia, but the Bank's headquarters remained in the City of Brotherly Love. Gallatin desired a branch of the Bank in the new capital and requested one from Willing. Although the branch would not turn a major profit, situated as it would be in a newly formed town that served little commercial purpose, the Bank board recognized its political value and after some internal debate conceded to Gallatin's request in 1802. Somewhat ironically, establishment of the Washington branch only served to further annoy Jefferson. But Gallatin manfully continued to blunt all of the Virginian's attacks on the institution. Gallatin enjoyed a rhetorical advantage over the president because Jefferson had obtained loans at the Bank at least twice, once in November 1793, when he received an advance on his salary as Secretary of State, and once in 1809 when he needed to settle a few old debts.

Nevertheless, Jefferson and Gallatin continued to debate the Bank's merits. Jefferson once complained that foreign stockholders, who at times owned the bulk of the Bank's stock, could use the institution as a weapon against its own country. The charge was groundless because foreigners could not vote for directors and hence had no direct say over the Bank's operations. Still, Jefferson pressed on, suggesting that the government's deposits be transferred to Republican banks. Sometimes Gallatin retorted, but often he simply ignored the president. In 1807, however, Jefferson upped the ante and submitted his most virulent letter yet against the Bank, stating to Gallatin that "this institution is one of the most deadly hostility existing against the principles and forms of our constitution . . . an institution like this, penetrating by its branches every part of the Union, acting by command and phalanx may . . . upset the government. Now, while we are strong, it is the greatest duty we owe to the safety of our Constitution, to bring this powerful enemy to a perfect subordination under its authorities." As Jackson later would, Jefferson wanted the Bank destroyed and replaced by an independent Treasury, that is, a Treasury that would conduct its own banking functions, rendering it independent of the banking system.

But Jefferson was no Jackson and Gallatin was no slave. Gallatin argued against the independent treasury, noting that the Bank had done a fine job. In a letter to Jefferson, he painstakingly described the advantages of the Bank and explained that the government had the upper hand, and if need be, the Bank was "completely in our power and may be crushed." These are strong words from Gallatin, and since the Bank was clearly a creature of the government, the government could "crush" it if need be. But Gallatin wrote those words to placate the president. He would not crush so useful an institution as the Bank. Rather, he would aid it to the best of his ability.

By 1811 Gallatin was more convinced of the Bank's necessity than ever. Bank charters were serious business, as important a piece of legislation as existed. Gallatin himself noted that "of all acts of government none perhaps was more delicate, nor required greater discretion and caution to guard it against improper speculations than the granting of a *bank charter*. . . . It is an act of the highest legislative nature." Today, bank branches appear on seemingly every corner. In the early nineteenth century, however, banks were few and far between. The destruction of the nation's largest bank was therefore no trivial event. Gallatin realized that its destruction could seriously damage the financial system, so he put his own career on the line to support its recharter.

Why did Gallatin feel so strongly about the Bank and the financial system? As Treasury secretary, he felt a responsibility for the health of the economy, and he recognized that the Bank and the rest of the financial system were crucial to the economy's continued health and growth. Like his predecessors Hamilton and Wolcott, Gallatin saw himself as the federal guardian of American economic stability, the nation's unofficial central banker. The Bank of the United States was the biggest tool at his disposal for implementing his policies. As Willing correctly noted, the Bank was "the great regulating wheel of all the commercial Banks in the United States." The Bank's board minutes often demonstrate a concern for the overall health of the economy, and, much like a modern central bank, the Bank increased or restricted the money supply in response to economic developments. But ultimately the Bank was responsible to its stockholders, not to all the American people. That is where the Treasury secretary came in. The Treasury secretary was an agent of the president, and it was part of the president's job to safeguard the economic well-being of the constituents who indirectly elected him. The Treasury secretary therefore had a responsibility to the electorate, and all of the early secretaries took that responsibility very seriously.

The early secretaries used the banking system, especially the Bank of the United States, to steer the economy away from trouble. The Bank and some state banks submitted weekly balance sheets that helped the secretaries fulfill that supervisory role. The Treasury was essentially the coach and the Bank was the quarterback. The coach called the plays, but the quarterback took responsibility for execution on the field. In more technical terms, the Treasury was the principal, the policy formulator, and the Bank was the agent, the means by which policy was implemented. In modern parlance, the Treasury secretary was the central *banker* and the national bank was the central *bank*.

Central banks fulfill several key functions, all of which the Bank of the United States successfully executed. Most importantly, central banks serve as lenders of last resort. They lend when no one else will, adding liquidity (cash) to the economy when market participants are panicking. The notion is that, if the central banks make loans freely available, people will have fewer grounds to panic. They slow down, realize that everything will be all right, and stop selling at distressed prices. The textbook example of snuffing out a panic using the lender of last resort doctrine occurred in 1987 when the U.S. central bank, the Federal Reserve, *promised* to lend freely in the wake of a crash in stock market values.

The knowledge that Alan Greenspan, the central banker, stood ready to assist helped calm nerves and quell panicked selling. The potential problem with the doctrine is that if financial service companies, particularly banks, know that the central bank will bail them out, what is called a "moral hazard" is created. In other words, the banks gain an incentive to engage in risky activities. For the lender of last resort doctrine to remain an effective tool, it must be used sparingly.

The Treasury secretaries, working in conjunction with the Bank of the United States, also served as a lender of last resort. They even realized the moral hazard problem inherent in the practice. In 1801, for instance, the Bank of Columbia faced a "run" that threatened its solvency. Treasury comptroller John Steele, a stockholder in the Bank of Columbia, was nominated to find a solution. Gallatin advised Steele that he faced a dilemma: "Government cannot be [accountable] for the folly, knavery or imprudence of every small Bank." Yet, the bank's failure could have severe negative repercussions for the financial system. Gallatin therefore concluded that he would help the beleaguered bank, but only if it helped itself first. "They must help themselves," he told Steele, "in order to deserve assistance." Once satisfied that the Bank of Columbia was on the path to reform, Gallatin saved it by ordering the Bank of the United States to deposit government funds in it.

Gallatin here was merely following the footsteps of Hamilton, who ended the Panic of 1792, induced in part by our sinner William Duer, by purchasing depressed government bonds, sometimes secretly, but often very openly. The purchases had three effects: to infuse cash into the economy; to support the price of government bonds, slowing and even stopping their descent; and to let market participants know that the "smart money," the Treasury secretary, was buying, not selling. The tactic worked. Within a month, securities prices increased and no recession ensued. Gallatin used a similar tactic when he financed the impending war with Britain. He confided to John Nicholson, Pennsylvania's Comptroller General, that "we must buy money at its market price, and in order to borrow cheaper it will be necessary to keep up the price of stocks [that is, government bonds] by occasional purchases," adding that "all this is, of course, between ourselves."

Early Treasury secretaries also utilized their deposit balances to bolster weakened banks. Hamilton, for instance, supported the Bank of New York with increased deposits during the 1792 Panic. Similarly, Wolcott aided the New York branch of the Bank of the United States when a yellow fever epidemic disrupted Manhattan's economy. By ceasing to draw on his deposits with that branch,

Wolcott ensured that it had the funds necessary to continue lending to private firms whose operations were harmed by the outbreak.

Gallatin too made deposits with the Bank when he wanted to stave off an economic dislocation. In May 1804, for instance, $3 million of coins were exported in just six months. The drain left less than $100,000 of specie in the Philadelphia, New York, and Boston branches combined. Gallatin could have used the opportunity to bankrupt the Bank. He realized, however, that such an action would prove catastrophic to the economy. So instead of pressing the Bank, he manipulated government deposits to aid it. In February 1805, Gallatin again displayed concern for the banking system in central-banker fashion. In response to a liquidity crisis at several New York banks, the Bank of the United States reduced its loans and hoarded its specie reserves. Gallatin interceded, directing Willing to alter the Bank's policy and come to the aid of the faltering banks. He went so far as to use the Bank's weekly balance sheet to suggest to Willing the Bank branches best able to supply resources. Gallatin pressed the Bank to adopt a 'big picture' attitude and, if necessary, to suffer a loss on the proposed operations. The Bank concurred with Gallatin's call to "give every aid, consistent with propriety."

Mathew Carey, a Philadelphian who happened to be visiting New York during the crisis, claimed that "destruction impended on the trading world." "It was fortunately in the power of the secretary of the treasury to avert the storm," he added, clearly giving credit where it was due. So Gallatin not only saved the golden goose from antagonistic Jeffersonians, he also helped to save it from itself, or rather from its weakest and most venal elements. Like his Federalist predecessors, Gallatin understood that as Treasury secretary he was the nation's central banker and that the Bank of the United States was his major policy tool.

Although scholars usually trace the development of central banking theory to Britain in the second and third quarters of the nineteenth century, the actions of U.S. policymakers, both at the Treasury and the Bank, demonstrate that the Americans had already implemented the core ideas by 1800. That Hamilton, Wolcott, and Gallatin first developed central banking escaped notice simply because they were more interested in being central bankers than in codifying or theorizing the concepts that they developed.

〰 After Burr's self-destruction, Gallatin assumed leadership of the commercial wing of the Republican Party, which disagreed with Hamilton on political and diplomatic matters but was largely Hamiltonian where it mattered most, in financial policy. Gallatin's ability to see the Bank and the national debt for the useful tools that they were saved the financial system in its earliest, most vulnerable years under Republican rule. Even most "Old Republicans," ultra-democratic (when it came to white males) advocates of an "agrarian" economic system, came to see the value of the Bank and funding systems. But they wanted a Bank, or banks, under their control, not under the control of Federalists like Willing or David Lenox, his successor. That, in the end, is why the first Bank of the United States had to die.

In April 1808, the Bank applied for a charter renewal. Gallatin advised the Bank to wait until after the 1808 elections before approaching Congress. The timing did not matter much, however, because the national legislature was solidly Republican and would remain so. Gallatin advocated enlarging the Bank's capital from $10 million to $30 million and restricting stock sales to foreigners. He explained that the Bank would be an indispensable tool during wartime, the outbreak of which looked increasingly likely. Again, Gallatin was prescient. As we will learn in "The Saint," the federal government financed the War of 1812 only with great difficulty. But when it comes to politics, logic and prescience are not necessarily enough.

William Branch Giles, a twenty-year opponent of the institution, led the anti-Bank forces in Congress. The vice president, New Yorker George Clinton, remained bitter about losing the presidential nomination to Madison, so he too opposed the Bank. Henry Clay of Kentucky, who would later become one of America's most fabled politicians, and Samuel Smith, brother of the secretary of state, also staunchly opposed the Bank's continuance. Most Federalists backed renewal, as did Gallatin. Madison did not oppose renewal but neither did he throw his weight behind it, so the brunt of the task, and criticism, fell on Gallatin.

Bank opponents played on American xenophobia by concentrating their critique on the fact that foreigners owned a majority, at one time about 72 percent, of the Bank's shares. While it was true that foreigners therefore earned the bulk of the Bank's profits, opponents missed the point that foreign stockholders were essentially lending money to the nation's best businesses, who on average earned more than the interest they paid to the Bank. Less scrupulous politicians even raised the specter of direct foreign management of the Bank. On April 13, 1810, for instance, Representative John Love of Virginia claimed that "King George the 3rd or the Emperor Bonaparte, may send their men, the ostensible owners of the stock . . . [to take] the management of our money matters. [It is] nothing to [men who have] the resources of the continent of Europe." Such a claim was preposterous, as only citizens could vote for, or serve as, directors of the Bank. The worst the foreigners could do would be to sell their shares, which somebody else, more concerned with profits than politics, would simply buy.

The real threat of the extensive foreign ownership lay in the fact that American stockholders in the Bank held a disproportionate share of power in the institution. The owners of the 28 percent or so of the stock in domestic hands elected the directors and served on the board. Of course that was $2.8 million dollars (par value—from 5 to 25 percent higher than that in market terms, depending on the date), a sum well beyond the wealth of any American save Stephen Girard, who eventually did buy out the Bank's assets during its liquidation.

Opponents also claimed that the Bank concealed profits and conducted its operation in a mysterious fashion. Representative Robert Wright of Maryland claimed that "all the directors of the mother bank, at all times, have been Federal or worse—many of them Tories or Monarchists." Such accusations were largely political rhetoric. But the Bank, with Gallatin's knowledge, did try to hide its full size from the public to the tune of several million dollars. Gallatin was in a bind: to reveal the inflated number would surely hurt the Bank's chances for recharter, so he decided to keep it private in the hope that the charge of concealing operations and profits would blow over.

The constitutionality issue also reared its hoary head. Many Republicans still believed that the Bank was an undemocratic, highly politicized institution that simply gave too much power to the central government. Moreover, critics asserted that state banks could fulfill the Bank's major functions. Clearly, state banks were eager to obtain the government's business, which they believed was highly profitable. The selfish interest of state banks was a leading reason why many politicians, who had their own favorite local bank that might benefit if the national bank died, voted against the Bank's recharter. (History would repeat itself in 1836, as we will see in "Apocalypse No.")

To favor the Bank was political suicide. Senator William H. Crawford of Georgia, a Bank advocate, lamented that "the member who dares to give his opinion in favor of the renewal of the charter is instantly charged with being bribed by the agents of the bank, with being corrupt, with having trampled upon the rights and liberties of the people, with having sold the sovereignty of the United States to foreign capitalists, with being guilty of perjury by having violated the Constitution." Despite the political risks, Gallatin wrote avidly in defense of the Bank and found himself, not a little ironically, in the role that Hamilton once played. In his March 3, 1809 report to Congress, Gallatin "pray[ed] for a renewal of the charter," stating that the Bank had been skillfully managed and operated. But it is doubtful that Hamilton himself could have saved the institution. The critics simply had too much ammunition, including the Bank's failure to establish any branches west of the Appalachians, save at New Orleans.

Although the charter did not expire until March 4, 1811, the official renewal process commenced in the House on March 28, 1808 and in the Senate on April 20 of that year. The matter developed slowly and was referred to Secretary Gallatin for an opinion. As noted, Gallatin recommended renewal on March 3, 1809. A House committee began debating the issue on January 29, 1810. On February 19, the committee reported in favor of renewal and sent the bill to the floor of the House, where debate commenced on April 13. The bill stopped dead in its tracks, so stockholders resubmitted it on December 10. Despite an intense debate, the bill was again killed in both houses, but by the narrowest of margins. On January 24, 1811 the House defeated recharter by a 65 to 64 margin. On February 20, the Senate decided against the Bank on the casting vote of Vice President Clinton, currently an enemy of both Madison and Gallatin, and an old foe of Hamilton himself.

Writing several years later, Gallatin lamented that "in 1810 the weight of the administration was in favor of renewal, Mr. Madison having made his opinion known that he considered the question as settled by precedent, and myself an open and strenuous advocate. We had the powerful support of Mr. Crawford in the Senate, and no formidable opponent in either House but Mr. Clay, a majority of political friends in both Houses, and almost all the Federalist votes on the question . . . yet the question was lost."

The loss was a large one, for both the country and for Gallatin politically, who suffered from many scurrilous attacks by Republican newspaper editors. Gallatin was so livid at Secretary of State Robert Smith that he gave Madison an ultimatum—fire him or Smith. Madison chose the illustrious Treasury secretary over the backstabbing Smith, but that only further incensed the radicals and firebrands. Future president James Monroe replaced Smith at the State Department.

In accordance with law, the Bank of the United States closed its doors on March 3, 1811. Gallatin knew that if a financial crisis now ensued it would be difficult to stop. As usual, Gallatin read the future correctly. War with Great Britain loomed, so Gallatin hastened to raise funds to finance the impending hostilities. He went to the state banks for loans, but they did not feel it prudent to lend to the national government the sums required. Their reluctance to lend forced Gallatin to issue Treasury notes, or direct obligations against the U.S.

government similar to the bills of credit issued by American colonies and states before adoption of the Constitution.

Given the nation's unfavorable financial condition, it would have been best to avoid war with Britain. But Americans felt their sovereignty was at stake. Indeed, what we now call the War of 1812 was at the time referred to as the Second War of Independence. British impressment of U.S. sailors and incursions into American territorial waters were clear violations of the country's nationhood. British forts on American territory and a standing army in Canada were also clear threats. It is difficult to argue that the war was inevitable because the British took a conciliatory tone near the end. Indeed, had news of their more liberal policy arrived earlier war might have been averted. But it would be equally difficult to argue that the war was fought for light and transient causes. Those with close commercial or family ties to Britain, however, wondered why the United States did not go to war with France, which had been equally abusive. In short, the war was a controversial one, perhaps more controversial than even the conflict in Vietnam would prove to be.

The War of 1812 ended as a draw. Notable U.S. military victories on the Great Lakes (Oliver Hazard Perry), in the open seas (the USS *Constitution,* better known as "Old Ironsides"), and at Baltimore (inspiration for the national anthem) and New Orleans filled Americans with pride. On the other hand, because Jackson's stunning victory at New Orleans occurred after the peace treaty had been signed, it gave the United States no bargaining power at the peace table. Indeed, the impressment of sailors was not even mentioned in the document! Moreover, the war almost shattered the Union as New Englanders, with their close ties to Old Englanders, vehemently opposed the conflict and even threatened secession. The war also proved embarrassing at times, particularly the sacking of Washington on August 24 and 25, 1814, when British forces burned the Capitol, the White House, and many other buildings, including Gallatin's residence. (The British generously removed his furniture before lighting the blaze.)

Most embarrassing of all was the nation's finances. The war, which in 1813 alone cost some $20 million more than the government's revenues, forced Gallatin to reinstitute Federalist-style excise and other direct taxes, to sell Federalist-style bonds, and to beg and plead for loans from state banks now that the Bank of the United States no longer existed. Congressional unwillingness to beef up tax revenues significantly and New Englanders' reluctance to purchase war bonds further stressed the Treasury secretary. When the domestic capital markets appeared closed to the national government, Gallatin was forced to turn to private investment bankers, including David Parrish, John Jacob Astor, and our saint Stephen Girard, to sell the government's bonds. Even then, the risk pre-mium (higher yield, to compensate for increased risk of default) demanded was considerable. It was noted with a touch of irony that Geneva-born Gallatin, French-born Girard, and German-born Astor and Parish teamed up to save the finances of newborn America in her war with Great Britain.

Gallatin knew that the only way to save the nation's finances was to end the war as quickly as possible. He also grew weary of criticism from armchair financiers and of his poor relationships with other cabinet members, particu-larly Secretary of War John Armstrong. So, Gallatin asked for a leave of absence as Treasury secretary to join the peace talks about to take place in Europe. (Per-haps too he pined to see the Old World, devastated though it was by almost two decades of intense warfare.) William Jones, who in a few years would almost ruin the second Bank of the United States, sat in at Treasury during Gallatin's absence. Before heading off to St. Petersburg, Russia, the initial site of the peace conference, Gallatin left behind several important tax bills and the outline of a charter for a new Bank of the United States.

Gallatin sailed for Russia on May 9, 1813, but did not officially relinquish his post at Treasury until February 8, 1814. To this day, he holds the record for the longest tenure as Treasury secretary. He had made his share of friends and ene-mies on both sides of the political aisle, and his support of the Bank was politi-cally costly. But, like Hamilton's, his actions were immensely important to America's subsequent economic growth. Historians have often highlighted the sharp differences between Federalists and Republicans, with Hamilton's phi-losophy on one end of the spectrum and Jefferson's on the other. Although it is true that Gallatin followed Jeffersonian principles in reducing the federal debt and internal taxes, he was forced to rely on both by the end of his tenure. Per-haps more importantly, Gallatin set the important precedent that Treasury secretaries were to be guardians of the financial system and the economy first and foremost above any party affiliation. Gallatin supported, used, and ex-panded on the financial framework put in place by Hamilton: a central bank, a unit of account defined in specie, a system of corporate intermediaries (banks and insurers), and securities markets. Though Gallatin failed to win a charter for a new national bank before leaving for the peace talks, itself an important mission for the financial sector, he planted the seeds that would grow into the second Bank of the United States.

☜Gallatin continued to serve his adopted country with distinction for many more years. Foremost, Gallatin was the most influential of the three Americans who helped to negotiate the Treaty of Ghent, which ended the War of 1812, though both other negotiators, Henry Clay and John Quincy Adams, would eventually prove far more popular politically. Upon conclusion of the negotiations in 1815, Gallatin traveled the continent. He visited his native Geneva for the first time in thirty-five years, which we know from his letters was a very emotional experience. Gallatin later served as U.S. minister to France. After a seven-year stint, which also took him to London and Brussels, Gallatin and his family returned home to Friendship Hill.

Soon after his return, he was tapped to run for vice president on Treasury secretary William Crawford's 1824 presidential ticket.[3] Gallatin quickly agreed but almost as quickly dropped out after his nomination generated a hail of criticism that ran the gamut from his birthplace, to his participation in the Whiskey Rebellion, to his support for the national banks. Crawford grew too ill to win anyway, but garnered enough votes to throw the election into the House of Representatives, where John Quincy Adams carried the day by entering into what opponent Andrew Jackson's followers called a "corrupt bargain."

In 1825, Gallatin threw an uncharacteristically lavish party at Friendship Hill to celebrate the visit of Revolutionary War hero the Marquis de Lafayette, who was touring the country. Hundreds of guests were in attendance to pay respects to the famous Frenchman. The following year, Gallatin returned to London to treat with the British over boundary disputes. Two years later, the now venerable senior statesman returned home, where he involved himself in debates over the tariff. Congress rejected his calls for trade-friendly low tariffs, passing instead a highly protectionist "Tariff of Abominations" that led to the Nullification Crisis.

By 1831, Gallatin and his family had taken up residence in Manhattan. Despite his seventy years, he would not retire, spending the next eighteen years as an active participant in the financial, intellectual, and social circles of the metropolis. He even served as president of the National Bank of the City of New York. As a bank president, Gallatin became involved in the fight over the second Bank of the United States. In 1830, he penned an influential pamphlet, *Considerations on the Currency and Banking System of the United States,* which not

3. Article II, Section 1, Clause 5 of the original U.S. Constitution stated that "No Person except a natural born Citizen, or a Citizen of the United States, at the time of the Adoption of this Constitution, shall be eligible to the Office of President." So despite frequent assertions to the contrary, Gallatin, Hamilton, and others born elsewhere could have been elected to the presidency.

surprisingly supported the Second Bank. Gallatin disagreed with President Jackson's attack on the Bank, but he also disliked Nicholas Biddle's handling of the situation, especially his policy of credit contraction implemented in 1833. The Second Bank's actions hurt his own bank but more importantly took its toll on the economy at large. Gallatin witnessed the shuttering of the Second Bank, the Panic of 1837, and the financial and economic dislocations, including suspension of specie payments by the nation's banks, that buffeted the economy for the next several years. Gallatin resigned as president of the bank in 1839, succeeded by his son James. In 1865, the bank, which despite its name was a state-chartered institution, had to change its name. It chose to call itself the Gallatin Bank to honor its famous first president.

In one of his last writings, Gallatin again spelled out his views on the central bank issue in *Suggestions on the Banks and Currency of the Several United States, in Reference Principally to the Suspension of Specie Payments,* published in June 1841. Gallatin drew on his experiences with the First and Second Banks to argue in favor of a third Bank of the United States, but only if it would be properly administered, as the first Bank of the United States had been. His recommendation came to naught.

Though no longer a force in national politics, Gallatin remained active in local affairs. For instance, he helped to found New York University, although he resigned from his post before the university officially opened due to differences in opinion concerning the proposed curriculum and the school's funding. After opening its doors, the university soon adopted many parts of his proposed curriculum, and a division of the school was named in honor of its famous founder. Gallatin also spent eighteen months researching and writing a 422-page book, *A Synopsis of the Indian Tribes Within the United States East of the Rocky Mountains, and in the British and Russian Possessions in North America.* He also publicly denounced slavery, warned that admitting Texas to the Union could lead to a war with Mexico, and wrote at length about the Oregon boundary question. In December 1843, President John Henry Tyler offered to appoint Gallatin Treasury secretary. Gallatin respectfully declined, arguing that at age eighty-three it would "be an act of insanity." Actually, Gallatin lived another six years. When the inevitable occurred, he was buried in New York's Trinity Church in the same graveyard, though at the opposite side of the church, where lay his longtime nemesis, Hamilton. We could not have concocted a more fitting ending.

Thomas Willing (1731–1821) &
Robert Morris (1735–1806)

Late in the summer of 1777, Washington and his army lost a major battle to the British at Brandywine Creek southwest of Philadelphia. That defeat, which was quickly followed by another, sealed the city's fate. While the Redcoats took their time plundering Chester County and destroying rebel iron furnaces along the Schuylkill River, Philadelphia Patriots fled to the relative safety of Reading, Lancaster, York, and other inland towns. Those who stayed behind seemingly signaled that they did not fear the approaching army, and maybe even that they welcomed it. To stay in Philadelphia was almost to proclaim oneself a Loyalist, a defender of the Crown.

Philadelphia merchant Thomas Willing was one of those who stayed put. With that act, the former Pennsylvania legislator, Supreme Court justice, and Continental congressman effectively ended his political career. It was perhaps the lowest point in a life that spanned almost ninety years. Willing, who refused to take the oath of loyalty to the Crown or to attend the many social entertainments thrown by British officers during the occupation, ultimately recovered from his decision and regained the confidence of most of his fellow Patriots. In the end, he led the nation's mightiest financial institution, the first Bank of the United States, for over fifteen years and was held in such high esteem that while on his deathbed he was nominated to head the second Bank of the United States. A staunch proponent of modern financial contracts like life insurance and negotiable ground rents, Willing ended his life one of the nation's richest men and most well-known financial innovators. Having transformed himself from alleged Crown sympathizer into a leading financier, Willing is our risen angel.

The career of Willing's longtime partner followed the opposite trajectory. Robert Morris fled Philadelphia as the Redcoats approached in 1777. A few years later, as the superintendent of finance, he almost single-handedly financed the final years of the rebellion. But within a dozen years of that success he began experiencing financial difficulties that ultimately led to ignominy and his imprisonment for debt. Morris, therefore, is our fallen angel.

Truth be told, Thomas Willing stayed in Philadelphia during the occupation because General Howe had personally written to assure him of his personal safety should he stay. Howe, it turned out, wished to use Willing as a go-between, a conduit with which to start peace negotiations with Congress. Willing also hoped for the opportunity to exchange his old colonial bills of credit, which were worthless since July 4, 1776, into a more stable species of property, while simultaneously protecting his real estate and wharves from British depredations. Congress rejected the peace overtures and imprisoned the messenger that Willing sent to deliver Howe's note to Congress. "I am surprised," George Washington lamented, "Thomas Willing should suffer himself to be imposed on by such flimsy measures."

Washington was surprised because Willing sprang from one of Philadelphia's richest and most reputable Anglican families. From his birth on December 19, 1731, he wanted for nothing, including a London law degree. His father, Charles, was the son of the successful London merchant for whom Thomas was named. Charles had settled in Philadelphia in the late 1720s and soon thereafter married into the prominent Shippen clan, quickly establishing himself in the upper business and social echelons of the burgeoning colonial port.

In 1740, at the tender age of eight, "Tommy" traveled to England for a proper education. By sixteen, he was a law student in the Inner Temple, one of London's famous "Inns of Court." He returned to Philadelphia in May 1749 and immediately began to work for his father's mercantile firm, Charles Willing Company. In 1751, after running the company successfully in his father's absence, he became a partner. Only three years later, he had to assume full ownership of the company when his father, aged only forty-four, died after a short illness. Just twenty-three years old, Willing had to care for his mother and eight siblings, the youngest just a baby. Luckily, in addition to his extensive education, a £6,000 inheritance, and a sterling reputation, Willing possessed an uncanny, if conservative, nose for business. He put that nose to the grindstone, foregoing marriage until 1763, when, at the then advanced age of thirty-two, he took nineteen-year-old Anne McCall as his bride. Anne was the daughter and granddaughter of wealthy Philadelphia merchants. She bore Willing thirteen children, ten of whom survived that tenuous first year. But poor "Nancy," as Willing called her, passed away just two months after the birth of the thirteenth child. The infant died shortly thereafter. The year was 1781, the same year that Willing began his long career as a banker. Married to his post and deeply devoted to his surviving children, all of whom did well in life, he never took another wife. That hardly mattered; between his siblings and children, Willing was already related to, in business with, or close friends with almost all of Philadelphia's most important families, Quaker and Anglican.

Willing's elevated social status certainly did not hurt his many business interests. Willing headed one of the colonies' leading mercantile houses, Willing & Morris; his partner was our fallen angel Robert Morris. The company exported Pennsylvania's agricultural produce, including flour, fur, pig iron, and lumber to the West Indies and the Iberian peninsula and imported manufactured goods and indentured servants from Britain, salt, lemons, and wine from the Iberian peninsula, and slaves, rum, and molasses from the West Indies. Willing & Morris also acted as an international banker by buying and selling bills of exchange, commercial debt instruments roughly analogous to checks.

Even during the colonial era, Willing innovated in the fields of marine insurance and real estate finance. Willing & Morris often invested considerable sums in ships and cargoes, so it had to obtain insurance to hedge against possible loss. Like many colonial mercantile firms, it found obtaining marine insurance in London both expensive and cumbersome. But where most found inconvenience, Willing & Morris found business opportunity. During the French and Indian War, Willing & Morris built an armed transport ship that was so fast and powerful that underwriters slashed its premium by six percentage points. The underwriters had perhaps underestimated the ship's strength. In one engagement, she fought off four French privateers. On the return leg, however, privateers again swarmed and eventually took her. "What are our ships of war doing?" Willing wondered aloud.

Undaunted, Willing took a more sophisticated approach in 1757 by forming Philadelphia's first marine insurance company, Thomas Willing and Company. At first composed of six principals, the company underwrote through insurance broker William Bradford at the Old London Coffee House. The insurer wrote risks as high as £1,000 on the credit of the combined assets of all six principals. After several years the insurance company disbanded, but Willing & Morris continued to underwrite large marine risks on its own.

Willing also innovated in real estate finance. In the colonial era potential purchasers of real estate had few financing options. Many simply saved until they could pay for a plot with cash. Of course that was a time-consuming strategy. Others obtained mortgages, often from the seller himself. Early mortgages, however, were much different from today's affairs. Many fell due after only a year or two. Though often allowed to continue if interest was punctually paid, they were thereafter essentially callable at the will of the lender.

Willing saw that ground rents, essentially perpetual mortgages, were, especially in urban settings, much preferable instruments for both the buyer and the seller. Instead of receiving a lump sum payment, say £100, for a piece of land, the seller could instead accept the interest on £100, say £6 per year, forever. The buyer gained by obtaining the land in fee simple for a small outlay; the seller gained by obtaining a relatively secure annuity. Both parties gained from the liquidity the ground rent contract created. The buyer could sell the land, subject to the ground rent of £6 per year, at will. Likewise, the seller could sell the right to receive the ground rent when he or she saw fit. Willing took advantage of that flexibility, both buying and selling real estate on ground rent whenever possible.

In the early years, Willing made most of the company's day-to-day business decisions. As he entered deeper into public life, however, he increasingly turned control over to partner Robert Morris. Some of Willing's forays into politics were clearly tied to his business interests. His attendance at the Albany Congress in 1754 and subsequent tenure as an Indian trade commissioner clearly aided his company's endeavors to obtain furs. As a Supreme Court justice Willing gained important business information, both as he rode circuit around southeastern Pennsylvania and as he sat on the main bench, helping to decide appeals with potentially important legal ramifications. Similarly, as a Philadelphia common councilman, alderman, and mayor, Willing helped to sculpt the city's business regulations. During his two terms in Pennsylvania's colonial legislature, he did likewise for the entire province, pushing particularly for improvement of its docks, rivers, and roads.

As the imperial crisis deepened, Willing's political interests became more activist, more geared toward influencing the wider political environment in which his firm had to operate and his large family had to live. With help from Morris, Willing led the protest of Philadelphia merchants against the Stamp Act in 1765–66 by presiding over a meeting of merchants who agreed not to import any goods from Britain until the pernicious tax on newspapers and legal documents was repealed. Four years later, he presided over a meeting that imposed a non-importation agreement designed to win repeal of the Townshend Acts, a tax measure designed to wrest control of colonial governments from the colonists. This second attempt at economic coercion failed, however, and within a year the agreement was rescinded. Heartened by that victory, and deeply in debt, Britain imposed a new series of colonial taxes and regulations, none of which found much favor among Americans, many of whom were increasingly dismayed that they were not directly represented in Parliament. In 1774 Willing co-chaired a meeting that affirmed Philadelphia's support for the port of Boston, which in the wake of its infamous Tea Party had been shut down and occupied by Red-coats. From that meeting, and a follow-up one a month later also co-chaired by Willing, sprang the seeds of such important Revolutionary institutions as the Continental Congress and the Committee of Correspondence.

In some ways, Willing's prominent role in the early stages of the Revolution is surprising. He had more to lose than to gain; he had close family and business ties to the mother country. Perhaps he became involved, as some have suggested, to steer the movement away from radicalism. More important, we think, was the fact that Willing was a natural leader, with the wealth, education, and bearing to match. In fact, Willing resembled George Washington physically and in temperament. Both enjoyed granite-like facial features that signaled the solemnity of their characters. Similarly, both were scrupulously honest and deeply conservative, Willing so much so that he acquired the nickname "Old Square Toes." Washington and Willing resided next door to each other for a time and often dined together. Perhaps most importantly, both were outstanding businessmen because they knew that high returns entailed big risks. Each would occasionally take a gamble, but only with a small portion of his wealth. Through hard but smart work, each became, and more importantly remained, rich. The same could not be said for Willing's partner.

Robert Morris was born in 1735 to a Liverpool merchant turned Maryland tobacco factor. Like Hamilton, Gallatin, Girard, and Jackson, Morris was an orphan. His mother died when he was so young that he professed no recollection of her; his father died in a freak cannon accident in 1750. Morris followed in his father's mercantile footsteps. At age fifteen, about the time of his father's death, he apprenticed to Charles Willing (Thomas's father), one of midcentury Philadelphia's most important merchants. Armed with that important connection and a healthy inheritance, Morris took on the world—and eventually lost.

Morris was a precocious youth. Legend has it that while still in his teens he cornered the flour market in Philadelphia, making a bundle for Charles Willing Company in the process. Charles Willing admired Morris's bravado, but in 1754 he fell victim to yellow fever, which forced young Thomas to assume command of the firm. Thomas Willing allowed Morris to watch the markets and travel the seas while he remained in Philadelphia, using his legal training to attend to contracts and other legal matters.

Morris acquitted himself well and began to attract offers of partnership. Willing, reluctant to lose the services of his daring friend, convinced Morris to partner with him. Effective May 1, 1757, Willing & Morris (at times a.k.a. Willing, Morris & Company) commenced business. Morris was only twenty-two, but he had already made several voyages to the West Indies, including an ill-fated one that led to his capture and eventual escape from French privateers. Within a few years, with Willing busy on the political front, the firm relied on Morris to make most of the day-to-day business decisions. Willing continued to supply the firm with his capital, his reputation, strategic advice, and legal talents.

Many a night in the 1760s, Morris visited the Willings in their fine home next to the city park. Morris would bounce Ann, who later married merchant William Bingham, on his knee while he and Willing discussed business. Then promptly at 9 p.m. the partners would down a glass of Madeira. Square Toes would promptly go to bed; Morris often would hit the town. A bachelor, he enjoyed quite a reputation as a lover of wine, women, and song. Willing felt more at home running the Assembly dances, arranged for the city's social elite. Though he found them a bore, Morris met his wife, Mary White, at one of them. They married in March 1769, a month before Mary's twentieth birthday.

Within a few years, however, the imperial crisis would shatter the domestic and business tranquility of the partners. Upon hearing of the skirmishes at Lexington and Concord, Morris and Willing became committed Patriots. Both were elected to Pennsylvania's seven-member delegation to the Continental Congress in November 1775. To Morris fell responsibility for constructing a Continental navy. Manning the boats turned out to be more difficult than building them because most mariners knew that there was better prize money to be won and less danger to be faced when sailing on privateers, private ships commissioned to seize enemy ships and sell them to the highest bidder. Only a handful of the twenty-six Navy vessels that Morris constructed ever set sail.

Morris also headed a secret committee charged with importing arms and gunpowder for the Continental forces. Willing & Morris naturally handled the contract. But neither Morris nor Willing really desired war; neither voted in favor of the Declaration of Independence. When that famous document was finally signed on August 2, however, Robert Morris put his pen to the paper. Willing never had the chance to, as he was not returned to Congress as a delegate, quite possibly because of his stance on independence. He later recalled that he "thought America at that time unequal to such a conflict as must ensue." He was almost right. But by August both Morris and Willing were fully devoted to the cause of independence and the defense of Pennsylvania.

ALEXANDER HAMILTON
Portrait by John Trumbull, 1806. Andrew W. Mellon Collection.
Image © Board of Trustees, National Gallery of Art, Washington.

WILLIAM DUER, MEMBER OF THE CONTINENTAL CONGRESS
Etching by Max Rosenthal, ca. 1885. Emmet Collection, Miriam and
Ira D. Wallach Division of Art, Prints and Photographs (1253348).
The New York Public Library, Astor, Lenox and Tilden Foundations.

ALBERT GALLATIN

Etching by Henry B. Hall, 1870. Emmet Collection, Miriam and
Ira D. Wallach Division of Art, Prints and Photographs (425066).
The New York Public Library, Astor, Lenox and Tilden Foundations.

THOMAS WILLING
Print by Henry B. Hall. Emmet Collection, Miriam and Ira D. Wallach
Division of Art, Prints and Photographs (422398). The New York Public
Library, Astor, Lenox and Tilden Foundations.

ROBERT MORRIS
Reproduction of a painting by C. W. Peale. Pennsylvania Academy of
Fine Arts. Copyright by Detroit Publishing Company, 1913. Image courtesy
of Library of Congress, Prints and Photographs Division, Washington, D.C.
(LC-USZ62-3596).

STEPHEN GIRARD
Etching by Albert Rosenthal after a portrait by John Lambdin.
Copyright by the Pennsylvania Historical Publishing Assn, 1903.
Image courtesy of Library of Congress, Prints and Photographs Division,
Washington, D.C. (LC-USZ62-123051).

ANDREW JACKSON

Engraving by A. H. Ritchie after a portrait by D. M. Carter. New York :
Ritchie & Co, 1860. Image courtesy of Library of Congress, Prints and
Photographs Division, Washington, D.C. (LC-USZ62-5099).

NICHOLAS BIDDLE
Emmet Collection, Miriam and Ira D. Wallach Division of Art,
Prints and Photographs (424753). The New York Public Library,
Astor, Lenox and Tilden Foundations.

BANK OF THE UNITED STATES, IN THIRD STREET, PHILADELPHIA

Drawn, engraved & published by William Birch & Sons, 1799.
Courtesy of Independence National Historical Park.

SECOND BANK OF THE UNITED STATES
By William Henry Bartlett.
Courtesy of Independence National Historical Park.

MODERN VIEWS: FIRST AND SECOND BANKS OF THE UNITED STATES
Photographs by Thomas L. Davies. Courtesy of Independence National
Historical Park.

In December 1776, the British pushed seemingly effortlessly across New Jersey from their new stronghold in New York. A panicked Congress fled to Baltimore, leaving Morris in charge of the government and its already troubled finances. The paper money that Congress had emitted to pay its debts, the infamous Continental Dollars, rapidly lost value as the Patriot cause teetered on the brink of disaster. To fill the breach, Morris pledged his personal credit. He also personally solicited loans from the few Philadelphians of standing who remained in the city. The amazing thing was that some of the motley band of Loyalists and Quaker pacifists actually lent him money. Morris's efforts were sufficient to give the British forces pause. They tarried on the east side of the Delaware. Thanks in part to Morris's fundraising, including $50,000 in specie sent to Washington's forces at a crucial hour, the Continental Army did not disband. Its morale bolstered with gold and silver, it proved that it could face trained European soldiers and win. Coins clinking in their purses, Washington, Hamilton, and company defeated British forces, first at Trenton and soon thereafter at Princeton. The British flood had crested, at least for the time being.

Congress returned to Philadelphia in March 1777. There it stayed, lackadaisically legislating a war through cumbrous committees until the British threat appeared anew late that summer. Not eager to retrace its steps through the wilds of New Jersey, and painfully aware that the rebels had effectively obstructed the entrance to the Delaware River, the British army in New York decided to attack Philadelphia from the south. The British mounted an amphibious assault at Head of Elk, the north end of Chesapeake Bay, then headed overland to the rebel capital. With the British army between it and Baltimore, and New York still strongly garrisoned with British troops, Congress this time could flee only one way, to the hills west of Philadelphia. It did so post haste. And this time Morris went with it, leaving Willing behind to tend to company business.

As we have seen, the British marched into Philadelphia with little difficulty. After a failed counterattack, Washington and the Continental Army set up camp for the winter in Valley Forge, Pennsylvania, on the west bank of the Schuylkill River about twenty miles to the northwest. There the common soldier endured a cold, hungry, shoeless winter in order to block British sorties towards Congress, still ensconced in Pennsylvania's equivalent of the Ruhr Valley. The strategy worked; the British, fearful that a French fleet could bottle it up, evacuated Philadelphia in mid-1778.

Despite the war, Willing & Morris continued to earn large profits, a good deal of which came from sneaking shipments past the British blockade and outfitting privateers to harass the enemy's shipping. From the war's start, the French supported the rebel cause under the old dictum that "my enemy's enemy is my friend." For strategic reasons, France did not wish to enter the war directly if it could help it, so at first it supplied the Patriots surreptitiously by transshipping ammunition, armaments, European manufactured goods, and medicine by way of Saint-Domingue, Martinique, and St. Eustatia, much of it through William Bingham, a Willing & Morris agent. The company's ships, smaller, faster, more heavily armed, and less heavily laden than in peacetime, also ran the gauntlet back to the islands laden with American tobacco, flour, rice, and indigo. The risks were high but the returns higher still. "One arrival," Morris told Bingham in late 1776, "will pay for 2 or 3 or 4 losses." Square Toes took part and prayed for the best because there was no other way to trade during the war. But he could take only so much. At the end of 1777, the partnership dissolved. The breakup was amicable; in the future the pair would often team up on specific projects, both business and political ones. But dissolution of the firm in the meantime allowed Willing to continue in his usual, conservative track and freed Morris to rapidly amass profits via new, risky partnerships with the likes of Jonathan Hudson, Samuel Inglis, Peter Whitesides, Silas Deane, French entrepreneur John Holker, and a slew of other players.

The fog of war, combined with the engagement of some awful agents in France, made it difficult to discern exactly who did what and when. Many shipments left port without the usual invoices. Some were seized and lost. Others were seized but retaken by colonial privateers weeks or months later. Public and private mercantile "adventures" mixed promiscuously. The resulting confusion led many to believe that Willing & Morris, or at least Morris, waited to see what happened to ships before accounting for the cargo. In other words, ships that successfully ran the blockade he claimed were brimming with his own private property, while those taken he maintained were fully stocked on the public's account. A disagreement over ownership of the cargo of the *Farmer,* which was seized by the British soon after it left Baltimore, brought that matter to a head. Detractors charged that Morris simply helped himself to public funds. What else could explain his financial success in wartime? Morris denied any wrongdoing and demanded a full investigation. Congress complied and eventually exonerated both Morris and the firm.

The animus directed at Morris prevented many from seeing the wisdom in his policy recommendations. Instead of establishing its credit by levying and collecting taxes adequate to retire its debts as Morris and other fiscal conservatives recommended, Congress instead issued reams of paper money. As the value of its money disintegrated, Congress tried to prop it up with decrees, price fixing, interstate embargoes, and legal tender laws. Such pseudo-legal tactics served only to further injure the nation's already shaky credit. All those laws interfered with free trade. The tender laws were perhaps the most onerous because they forced people to accept pieces of paper of no intrinsic value in exchange for valuable goods and services.

Frustrated in Congress, Morris jumped to the state legislature, where he lobbied heartily against Pennsylvania's first state constitution, a radical frame of government that Morris rightly believed did not provide the checks and balances necessary to prevent predatory government. Morris believed that government was necessary to protect property and liberty, but he also knew that a government left unchecked in its ambitions was, ironically enough, *the single* biggest threat to both. As a staunch defender of market forces, he feared the radical new government would impose harmful regulations upon business interests and thereby injure the entire state. Commerce, he argued, should be "free as air to place it in the most advantageous state to mankind." Later, as the superintendent of finance, he would "ask for no embargo, no regulations. On the contrary, I wish and pray that the whole detestable tribe of restrictions may be done away, and the people be put in possession of that freedom for which they are contending." Here, clearly, was a man who understood the environment that would help the golden goose to thrive!

The state's first constitution was a very democratic document. Many, therefore, took Morris's attacks upon *it* as attacks upon *democracy*. That, combined with further accusations of war profiteering, made Morris a marked man, afraid for a time to venture forth from his home after dark. Later in the war, his controversial tenure as the superintendent of finance made him the most hated man in the country besides Benedict Arnold and King George. It also made him the most loved.

Morris and Willing had long hoped to establish a commercial bank. During the severe deflation brought about by the end of the French and Indian War and the passage of the Currency Act, which severely decreased colonists' control over their monetary policy, the pair had tried to form a private company designed to emit printed bearer notes. The scheme fell under the scrutiny of jealous business competitors and unsympathetic British officials, however, and was quickly abandoned. But the dream died hard. In 1780, Morris and Willing saw their main chance to enter the banking business and seized it. By that time, Congress was more or less broke, unable to borrow money, to collect taxes, or to emit currency. Its bills of credit were worthless, or nearly so. The several states were almost as bad off.

Farmers and manufacturers responded to the crisis by withholding their productions and their coins from the market, forcing the army to endure chronic, severe shortages. A near mutiny in May at Washington's headquarters in Morristown demonstrated just how precarious the war effort had become. Morris, Willing, James Wilson, and other leading Philadelphians ameliorated the situation by forming the Pennsylvania Bank, a private nonprofit institution capitalized with the private bonds of leading merchants. The pooled pledges of the bank's founders, which totaled some £315,000 Pennsylvania currency, immediately made the new institution more creditworthy than the bitterly divided and ineffectual national government.

But the Pennsylvania Bank could do only so much. Congress, its back against the wall, turned to Morris for a miracle. On February 20, 1781 it unanimously elected Morris Superintendent of Finance, a new position designed for him and him alone. After negotiating for more authority and the right to continue his private mercantile pursuits, Morris formally accepted the challenge. After winding up some important commonwealth business, including fighting for the repeal of Pennsylvania's onerous legal tender law, he took the oath of office on June 27. Gouverneur Morris, an unrelated friend, became his assistant, and an able, diligent, and intelligent assistant he proved to be. Morris eventually enticed Congress to add a slew of capable financiers to his team, men like Philadelphia merchants Michael Hillegas (treasurer), Joseph Nourse (register), and John Swanwick (cashier). Morris also forged important business relationships with the nation's best and brightest exchange brokers, the most important of whom was Haym Salomon.

Salomon, a Polish Jew, is an important example of the credit market's inherent fairness. Born in 1740, he emigrated to New York in the early 1770s and quickly joined the Sons of Liberty, a secret organization of colonists opposed to British rule. Fluent in eight languages, he was an important addition to the Patriot cause, especially after war broke out. His language and commercial skills allowed him to supply goods to the Hessian forces while concurrently spying on them, to help French and American prisoners of war to escape their captors, and to encourage foreign mercenaries to desert the British army by providing them with funds. After the British finally figured out what Salomon was up to, they arrested him. Legend has it that he escaped hanging by bribing a Hessian guard. Whatever the case, Salomon was clearly no longer welcome in New York, so he made haste to Philadelphia. The Redcoats retaliated by seizing his assets, which amounted to some $120,000, leaving him virtually penniless. Too re-sourceful to be ruined by that seizure, Salomon quickly rebuilt his fortune out of his new counting house on Philadelphia's Front Street.

In 1781, Salomon sold $200,000 of government bonds by endorsing them with his personal credit. Salomon's credit was better than that of the national government because he had never defaulted on a note and was well known as a man of integrity and a true Patriot. Indeed, he bought government bonds when no other broker wanted to touch such risky assets. Scores of diary entries attest to the fact that Morris often relied on Salomon's talents in the financially dark days of 1781, 1782, and 1783. Soon, with Morris's blessing, Salomon advertised himself as "Broker to the Office of Finance." Shrewdly, he bought French bills of exchange, keeping the market for those assets stable. The local French minister noticed this deft move, so soon Salomon was asked to assist Morris in co-ordinating loans with the French and the Spanish. The linguistically gifted Pole also acted as paymaster general for the French forces in America.

When Morris was at his wit's end, he called for Salomon. Morris's diary entry of August 28, 1782, for instance, notes that Morris urged Salomon "to leave no stone unturned to find out money and the means by which I could obtain it." If he could not find the funds elsewhere, Salomon often advanced them himself, at low interest. Thomas Jefferson, Thomas Mifflin, James Wilson, Baron von Steuben, and General Arthur St. Clair all received either low or interest-free loans. Young delegate and future president James Madison also borrowed from Salomon, informing Edmund Randolph that when he was hard pressed for money, he relied on the "kindness of our little friend in Front Street" who assisted him with loans but "obstinately rejects all recompense." Perhaps Salomon's greatest feat was quickly raising $20,000 to help fund Washington's secret march from New York to Yorktown to trap Cornwallis.

Riddled with tuberculosis since his imprisonment by the British, Salomon lived only long enough to see American independence. He died in 1785 holding over $353,000 in depreciated Continental currency, the market value of which was $44,372. Though he of course did not sign the Declaration of Independence, Salomon did pledge his life and property to the cause and, as was his habit, paid both in full when due.

Earlier generations of Americans revered Salomon. Wacker Drive in Chicago is home to a Revolutionary War memorial with life-size statues of Washington flanked by none other than Morris and Salomon. In 1941, President Franklin Roosevelt extolled the "genius" and "unselfish devotion" of those two financiers, noting that their efforts were of crucial importance to the war effort. In

1975, the United States Postal Service issued a commemorative stamp in Salomon's honor. The reverse side of the stamp correctly noted that Salomon was "responsible for raising most of the money needed to finance the American Revolution and later to save the new nation from collapse."

Though he relied heavily on his trustworthy broker to beat the streets for money, Morris alone understood the grand plan that would save the rebellion. Even a vibrant economy, Morris understood, could get by with only a small amount of hard cash provided people and businesses were willing to extend credit. Tender laws, which forced creditors to accept depreciated paper money at full face value, had by all accounts "extinguished all credit." Why give up a team of horses, or a barn full of grain, for a piece of paper of doubtful value? Why lend someone real money—gold or silver coins—only to be repaid with paper? (Today, tender laws again support the value of our money. The difference is that the United States is now the world's most powerful nation and economy, so worldwide demand for dollars, rather than the law, gives our currency its value.)

Once both the tender laws and the depreciating currency were eliminated, confidence and hence private and public credit could be restored. Confidence in the future of the country would become a self-fulfilling prophecy because if people believed the rebellion would succeed they would not press for immediate payment in coin, the financial pressure on the national government would be relieved, and Congress would indeed win the war. But how could Morris start this virtuous circle? Morris's personal credit, the collection of in-kind taxes, the establishment of a bank, and a loan from the French proved key.

The French had little love for Americans or their ways. But by stirring up trouble for France's leading rival, Great Britain, the rebellious colonies had done the French a great service, for which they grudgingly paid in specie. The sum paid was a pittance in the scheme of things, but it proved adequate to Morris's needs.

Before the French funds could be realized, however, Morris found it necessary to order supplies for the army, still encamped at Morristown, New Jersey. No one in their right mind would advance anything of value to Congress, but they would to Morris. So Morris used his personal credit to ensure that the army got fed. Their bellies full, American soldiers did not pillage the farms of upstate New York, New Jersey, or Pennsylvania. Those farmers therefore remained Patriots, all thanks to the mystique of Morris's signature.

In-kind taxes, the collection of taxes in farm produce, also helped in the short run. Though grossly inefficient in many ways, payment in wheat or cows was of course superior to no tax revenue at all. Morris turned over some of the taxes directly to the army, which at least got fed. The rest he exchanged at home or abroad for hard currency, foreign exchange, munitions, clothing, or other necessities. The breadth and magnitude of this commerce was stunning. His reputation enhanced further by his adroit handling of such an extensive trading empire, Morris found that he could issue his personal promissory notes to a large sum. Such notes, ultimately met with French coin, helped to fund Washington's successful foray against the British at Yorktown.

Though the victory at Yorktown ultimately ended the war, it took two more years for the British to come to terms. In the meantime, the army's readiness had to be maintained. In-kind taxes and Morris's personal credit, however, could extend only so far. What was needed was a way to pool the credit of many powerful merchants like Morris. The Pennsylvania Bank had proved the basic soundness of the idea. Something more was needed, however. Morris somehow had to multiply the little specie he had available. He had to stretch his cash as far as possible, in effect to increase the supply of money at his disposal. The vehicle for so doing was the nation's first true commercial bank.

Just three days after accepting the office of superintendent of finance in June 1781, Morris submitted to Congress a plan to establish a bank. The plan called for a joint stock corporation with a capital stock of $400,000 divided into 1,000 shares, each of $400 par value. The corporation, styled the Bank of North America, would be headed by twelve directors and would enjoy the explicit legal right to issue bearer notes. The notes were not to be a legal tender, but they would be redeemable at the bank in specie on demand, an arrangement far superior to a tender provision.

With rare unanimity and vigor, Congress quickly approved the plan, though it stopped short of formally incorporating the institution. Newspaper editors throughout the nation provided free publicity for its initial public offering. But subscriptions to the Bank's capital stock came in slowly. After years of war and economic dislocation, few could bring themselves to invest $400 in a novel unproven institution. Momentum picked up when Morris negotiated a debt-for-equity swap with the subscribers to the Pennsylvania Bank. But that swap did nothing to bring hard coin into the Bank's vaults. Things really got rolling when Morris used the specie proceeds of a French loan to purchase shares in the Bank on the government's account. To avoid British cruisers, the ship carrying the specie put in at Boston. Anxiety ran high as an ox-driven wagon train carrying the coins traveled overland to Philadelphia, carefully skirting British-controlled downstate New York. The precious cargo, which had been under the protection of Tench Francis, Willing's partner and Morris's brother-in-law, arrived safely in early November 1781. As the institution now clearly had a fighting chance to survive, preparations for its grand opening proceeded apace. (Fittingly, Francis would soon be appointed the bank's cashier.) The full capital stock had not yet been filled, so Congress was reluctant to authorize it to open. But expediency won out; on the final day of 1781, Congress officially chartered the bank, granting it corporate legal rights and perpetual existence. Because many doubted Congress had the right under the Articles of Confederation to incorporate a bank, the institution later received several state charters as well, including one from its state of domicile, Pennsylvania.

The Bank of North America began operations on January 7, 1782, and immediately began to lend considerable sums to Morris on the national government's account, $400,000 by mid-year in fact. For over a year, the Bank lent the national government large amounts, both on long-term loan and by discounting its accounts receivable. Morris paid off some of the loans with cash, bills of exchange, or the Bank's own stock, but usually he met notes coming due with discounts on new notes. The exact figure is shrouded in the mists of history, but the Bank probably advanced the government in the vicinity of $1 million all told. In April 1783, the government repaid all its outstanding loans by turning over its remaining stock in the company. Because the dividend rate on its stock exceeded the 6 percent it paid for its loans, the net cost of the government's borrowing from the Bank amounted to just shy of $30,000. Paying only around 3 percent interest was quite a trick for a government with such a shoddy credit history.

It should be noted too that the Bank also indirectly aided the government by helping to revive the nation's economy. A stronger economy, after all, meant larger tax receipts. But prosperity was still several years down the road. In the meantime, Morris struggled to collect the nation's taxes and to retrench its expenditures.

Soon after the bank opened, Morris dropped the inefficient in-kind tax system. Requisitions for specific provisions often went unheeded or were only fulfilled with inferior produce. Moreover, transportation costs were high and many goods spoiled in transit or simply arrived too late. Morris pressed the several states to collect their taxes and pay specie over to Congress, but try as he may he could not draw blood from those stones. Since Morris, unlike state authorities, had no legal authority to force taxpayers, or even tax collectors, to pay up or face the sheriff, he could do little but exhort. Predictably, state officials dragged their feet. Each state, Morris soon came to realize, feared that it had contributed more than its fair share to the Revolution and that it would not receive proper credit for its exertions. Moreover, it proved politically impossible for Morris to induce the states to agree on a fair basis for adjusting their accounts. Uncertain where they stood, most states adopted the politically astute position of ignoring Congressional requisitions. Morris implored states to pay, so that the country could "become independent, really and truly independent, independent of our enemies, of our friends, of all but the Omnipotent." Rhetoric and moral suasion, however, proved insufficient. The situation became so bad that Morris misinformed the states about the extent of French assistance in order to alarm them into action. But even that desperate ploy failed.

The solution to the problem was clear: the national government needed a direct income independent of the states. Morris therefore urged Congress to enact the so-called impost, a national 5 percent ad valorem tariff (tax) on imports. But this revealed an inherent weakness of the Articles of Confederation. Eventually every state but one, tiny Rhode Island, agreed to the impost. But the Articles proclaimed that unanimity was necessary for a revenue measure to pass, so Rhode Island's intransigence spelled the end of the crucial revenue measure. Britain's increasingly tight blockade of American ports would have rendered the impost of little immediate practical aid anyway.

Faced with anemic tax receipts, Morris tried to reduce government expenditures without cutting into its effectiveness. The Confederation government, Morris found, was riddled with duplication of effort and other inefficiencies. He slashed the government's civil expenditures, which were relatively minor, by cutting personnel. Military expenditures were a much more intractable problem because they had to be maintained. The military procurement apparatus then in place, basically the old commissary-style system, where officers procured the supplies, was extremely wasteful. Morris therefore replaced it with a new contract system whereby private firms contracted to supply the army with rations over a fixed period for a prearranged price. Morris took sealed bids from competing contractors to ensure the best deal. Problems arose, mostly due to the use of subcontractors by some of the larger contractors, to the assignment of some of the contracts to unscrupulous types like William Duer, and to the so-called "winner's curse." (The lowest bidder often bids too low, so today bids often go to the *second* lowest bidder.) But overall the system "gave more satisfaction." In other words, it was much more cost-efficient than the old commissary system.

Despite his efforts to make the national government more efficient, Morris could not force an increase in tax receipts to the level needed to fund the war. Of the $8 million requested in 1782, the states paid over a paltry $422,000, much of it in produce accounted for at inflated prices. Eventually, not even the Bank of

North America could continue to provide the national government with loans. At that desperate juncture, only foreign loans and personal credit kept the American war effort looking healthy enough to persuade the British that further fighting would be futile. Because the size and timing of the foreign loans were difficult to predict, Morris often sold bills of exchange without knowing if the bills would be honored once they arrived in Europe. In 1782, the British stepped up its blockade of the American coast, strangling trade. According to Morris, the British managed to stop fully 95 percent of American shipping. With trade levels so low, demand for bills of exchange plummeted, leaving Morris in the odd position of controlling more assets overseas than at home. Of course knowledge of those assets, safely in the hands of American agents in France and Holland, helped to bolster confidence in Morris and the national government. So more than once Morris's personal printed promissory notes, bearer instruments called "Long Bobs" or "Short Bobs" depending on their term to maturity, and similar notes issued by John Swanwick, Salomon, Hillegas, and others filled the void and kept the Continental Army in the field.

It was a close shave nonetheless. By early 1783, Morris was fed up with Congress's general impotence and the impending failure of a second tariff bill, this time at the hands of New York. So on January 24, 1783, Morris tendered his resignation to Congress, effective at the end of May. Events would conspire, however, to keep him in office almost another two years. In March, the infamous Newburgh Conspiracy, some vague rumblings among army officers camped in upstate New York, induced Congress to ask Morris to remain in office. Morris agreed, and it was a good thing he did. The government still owed many soldiers years of back pay. By June 1783, eighty Continental soldiers of the Pennsylvania line felt they had waited quite long enough to be paid for their sacrifices. They decamped from Lancaster and descended upon Philadelphia, where they proceeded to frighten Congress. The mutinous men demanded their pay and threatened to seize Congress and break into the Bank of North America. Fearful that the militia might join the mutiny rather than suppress it, Congress and the governments of Pennsylvania and Philadelphia cowered. In fact, as soon as the coast was clear Congress fled to Princeton. When word of this fiasco reached Europe, the last shred of the nation's credit vanished.

The renewed crisis induced Morris to stay at his post. When the British officially capitulated on September 3, 1783, Morris was still in office, attempting to close up his many accounts. To help to quell the army's discontent, Morris had emitted more than $1 million of his own notes with six months to maturity. Luckily, peace brought a resumption of trade, which in turn eased tax collection. Some $820,000 trickled in, allowing Morris, with help from yet another

French loan, to honor his notes as they fell due and were presented for payment. He finally left office on November 1, 1784, whereupon he published a full statement of his accounts. "The Master," he told the public, "should know what the servant has done."

When Morris became superintendent of finance in 1781, he inherited an economy in the throes of hyperinflation. To turn the economy around, he had to drastically reduce the money supply. His policies caused a lot of pain, especially in the hinterland, but not as much pain as all Americans would have suffered had he allowed prices to continue to spiral upward. The cost of his success was the political fallout that his retrenchment policy caused. To this day, left-leaning historians vilify him. But through luck, pluck, and a good dose of administrative and financial genius, he had preserved the nation's independence by finding the funds necessary to keep the war effort afloat and nurtured the golden goose while it was still a feeble hatchling. His office actually showed a small surplus when he finally left it. But unlike Hamilton, Morris was unable to enact the tax revenues necessary to fund the national debt. He had, however, saved the Revolution and established an institution new to America's shores, the commercial bank, which would play a major role in the new nation's future economic success.

Thomas Willing's biggest claim to fame is that he was the nation's first commercial banker. Robert Morris, the brainchild behind the Bank of North America, could not physically or politically serve as both the superintendent of finance and president of the Bank. So naturally he turned to his old conservative friend to head up the new institution. Because Morris, Willing, and their friends initially held almost half the bank's stock, assuring Willing a directorship was simple. Getting those directors to elect Willing their president was also relatively easy.

Under Willing's conservative stewardship, the Bank of North America aided the national government, the Pennsylvania state government, and private businesses with timely loans. At first, it lent heavily to the national government, but soon it learned to spread its largesse to a diverse set of borrowers in Philadelphia and across the country. The troubled economy and the novelty of the enterprise conspired to make the institution's early months relatively rocky ones. By July 1782, however, the Bank was thriving and paying high dividends to prove it. After news of peace arrived in March 1783, its subscription book finally filled. Soon thereafter, its stock rose above par. By November 1783 its shares traded in European capital markets. But its prosperity brought with it jealousy and misunderstanding. Those envious of the Bank teamed up with those ignorant of its principles in an effort to smash the institution. In the short run, the effort met success; the Pennsylvania legislature repealed the Bank's charter in 1785. But in the long run, the Bank won. It continued to operate despite the loss of its charter, and in 1787 the legislature awarded it a new though somewhat less advantageous act of incorporation.

The Bank of North America deserved its recharter because it was an indisputable aid to the economy. For starters, it shared important practical administrative information with the founders of new banks, including the Bank of New York and the Bank of Massachusetts. The Bank was a scrupulously honest corporation; it contained many internal "checks and balances" that effectively prevented peculation. Moreover, its notes and checks were extremely costly to counterfeit. Those facts, combined with the Bank's supply of specie, gave the community great confidence in the quality of the new institution.

After a slow start, the Bank's liabilities, its notes and deposits, served as media of exchange without the aid of a legal tender law. The Bank's notes were far better than Continentals or state bills of credit because they were redeemable for a fixed amount of specie on the demand of the holder. Everyone knew that the Bank did not have $1 of gold or silver in its vaults for every dollar of its notes or deposits outstanding. But soon most people grasped that only a fraction of the bank's liability holders wanted specie. Most were content to hold notes and deposits. So, "fractional reserves" were not only adequate, the practice of holding only a portion of liabilities in gold or silver coins actually added to the supply of ready money. The Bank could put, say, $1 million of banknotes and deposits into circulation backed by only $200,000 or $300,000 in specie. People could hold the Bank's liabilities in confidence because they knew that the Bank was well run and solvent. They knew, if only from the vociferous complaints of rejected applicants, that the Bank screened loan applications carefully. They also knew that the Bank lent for short periods, at first only thirty days. That policy made it easy for the Bank to quickly increase its specie reserves if necessary by simply not renewing loans as they fell due. Some people complained about that practice, but most market participants understood that the complaints proved that the Bank was carefully run.

The Bank's contribution to the economy went way beyond just supplying it with reliable money. Indeed its main function was intermediation, the linkage of savers to entrepreneurs. Despite much lore to the contrary, early Americans were not any more inventive than other peoples. They were, however, more likely to obtain the financing necessary to make their inventions and business innovations a reality. The Bank supplied one such type of financing, the short-term business loan or "discount." With the aid of such loans, American entrepreneurs helped to increase the efficiency (units of output for a given amount of input) of their firms and ultimately the entire economy.

Consider, for instance, the story of Philadelphia tinmaker Thomas Passmore, one of the many master artisans or nascent manufacturers to receive loans from the Bank. Passmore realized that he could produce more wares more cheaply per unit by increasing the scale of his operations and by dividing the production process into more but simpler operations. So instead of employing one skilled journeyman artisan who made tinware from start to finish, he employed six relatively unskilled mechanics, each of whom completed only one or two operations. Soon, however, Passmore's tinware flooded the Philadelphia market. He had to find new markets or revert to the older less efficient ways.

With help from the Bank, Passmore was able to continue to churn out his tinware. He did so by selling his products to shopkeepers in the South and the interior towns of the North on credit. In exchange for the tinware, the shopkeepers gave Passmore their promissory notes, their promise to pay in the future. Passmore then discounted their notes at the Bank, providing him with the cash necessary to pay his tin suppliers, his employees, and his landlord. Demand for his products, not working capital constraints, now determined the volume of Passmore's business. And demand there was aplenty. Multiply this story by the Bank's several thousand early borrowers, and its contribution to the economy becomes clearer. But we must multiply its effects yet more because its customers did not sit on hordes of borrowed money. Rather, they used it to pay for goods, including the productions of farmers. As early as August 1784, farmers selling in the Philadelphia market received not credit or depreciating bills of credit but specie and banknotes. Writing for the *Pennsylvania Gazette* on August 4, 1784, "S.G." forcefully stated the case for the Bank:

> Is not the bank the nest-egg of public and private credit? Has it not extended the trade of our state? Does it not furnish prompt payment to the miller and farmer? Has it not allured merchants to settle among us, with immense capitals, from every part of the world? Has it not compelled the great houses in our sister states to open houses in our city, for the convenience of transacting business? Has it not given our city a pre-eminence above all the cities in the United States? Above all—Did not the bank raise, feed, cloath, and in part pay that army (when every other resource for money failed) which compelled Great-Britain to withdraw her troops, and finally to acknowledge our independence?

The Bank of North America's success did not go unnoticed. Hamilton used the bank as a model for his Bank of the United States, which as we have seen was one of the pillars of the highly successful financial reforms he initiated in the early 1790s. Willing's successful stewardship of the Bank of North America also did not go unnoticed. Indeed, the Bank of North America lent money to the new federal government before the formation of the national bank, so Hamilton was well aware of Willing's banking prowess. Who would be the president of the newly formed Bank of the United States? Though some New Englanders, including Fisher Ames, wished to see one of their own, Oliver Wolcott of Connecticut, elected to the presidency, Wolcott preferred his role as comptroller of the currency in Hamilton's Treasury Department. The Bank's directors then offered the presidency to Willing. Ames hoped to persuade Hamilton that Willing would be nothing more than Robert Morris's puppet. Ames was wrong. Willing proved to be an outstanding choice, a true leader not swayed by personal or political intrigues.

In fact, part of the genius of the Bank of North America and the Bank of the United States was that, as stockholder-owned institutions, they were relatively independent of political control. That allowed them to steward the economy in the interests of business, which is to say the American people, and not in the interests of politicians seeking office. As president of the Bank of the United States, Willing worked closely with Alexander Hamilton, Oliver Wolcott, and Albert Gallatin, America's three most important early Treasury secretaries. With the help of Willing and his Bank, the new national government demonstrated its vigor by implementing an efficient tax system, by vastly improving its credit rating overseas, and by putting down agrarian rebels who sought to damage both. Willing headed up and coordinated the country's first nationwide business, as the Bank's nine offices stretched from Boston in the North, to Savannah in the South, and across the gulf coast to New Orleans. Under his tutelage, the Bank lent millions of dollars to the government at critical times, and lent millions more to wealth-creating entrepreneurs. All the important financial transactions of the era, from the transfer of the government's payment for the Louisiana Purchase to the funding of warships like the fabled USS *Constitution,* required Willing's input. The nation and its financial system were blessed to have found a steady and even-keeled bank president. Aided by the national bank and the emerging strength of the central government, the U.S. economy boomed in the two decades following the passage of the Constitution.

Willing remained president of the Bank of the United States until 1807, when illness and seventy-six years of life forced him to retire. But he was not yet done contributing to the financial system. After leaving the Bank, he gave American life insurance a big boost. Willing understood the need for life insurance when at a tender age he had to shoulder the responsibility of settling his father's estate and caring for his many siblings. Had Charles owned a life insurance policy, Willing realized, his tasks would have been much simplified.

As he aged, Willing also clearly saw the need for life insurance's alter ego, the life annuity. Life insurance hedged against the risk of dying too young; life annuities protected against the risk of dying too old, after the ability to generate income had declined. For himself and his family, Willing used ground rents to approximate the properties of life annuities. But he realized that ground rents were not optimal for that purpose. Thus Willing was a major supporter of the nation's first true joint-stock life insurance company, The Pennsylvania Company for Insurance on Lives and Granting of Annuities. When the new company had difficulty selling its shares to the public, Willing interceded with an important pamphlet called *An Address to the Citizens of Pennsylvania Upon the Subject of a Life Insurance Company.* In that pamphlet, Willing patiently explained the many uses to which life insurance and life annuities could be put. With Willing's backing, the Pennsylvania Company filled its subscription and played a leading role in the early development of American life insurance.

That was no minor contribution because life insurance and life annuities would soon come to have a profound effect on the American economy. In addition to becoming the largest financial intermediaries in terms of assets, life companies also played an important role in bringing U.S. birth rates down to modern levels. In the colonial and early national periods, couples had numerous children, often more than ten. They did so partly to compensate for high infant mortality, but mostly they wanted to provide an income in old age and, perversely, a form of life insurance whereby older children would take care of younger children if a parent died, much as Willing had been forced to do. Life insurance companies allowed couples to hedge against the risks of life, both dying too young, or in other words while still productive, and living too long, or in other words past the productive years, using financial instruments instead of children. That allowed couples to have fewer children and hence to invest more in the education and training of each of them.

In the end, therefore, Willing contributed at least as much, and arguably much more, to the nation's financial development as did his erstwhile partner. In the end, Old Square Toes also fared much better in business. Morris sank into bankruptcy and died, while Willing lived on and on, growing ever so slightly richer by the day.

When separated during the Revolution, Willing in a letter professed to "love" Morris. Their relationship was entirely Platonic, of course; such expressions were common among men, and women, in the eighteenth-century Atlantic world. But clearly Willing missed Morris's dashing brilliance; perhaps Morris missed Old Square Toes' steadying hand. Whatever the reasons, in 1783 Willing, Morris, and John Swanwick joined in partnership. The new company was much like the colonial company: it imported manufactured goods and tropical products, exported Pennsylvania's produce, underwrote maritime risks, and dealt in exchange and real estate. The firm dissolved in 1794 when Morris sold his interest to Swanwick to raise cash. Willing had long acted as a brake to Morris's wild enthusiasm and optimism. With their business relationship severed, Morris was free to take greater risks in the hope of larger returns.

Willing tended to mine new markets deeply and methodically while Morris liked to play hit-and-run, corner-the-market, or high-leveraged games. The China trade is a prime example of their divergent approaches. In late 1783, Morris, Willing, Bingham, and other U.S. merchants dispatched a ship to China. Despite the fact the Chinese desired nothing of America but its silver, the ship, aptly named the *Empress of China,* earned a healthy profit of 25 percent. Willing remained extensively engaged in the China trade, slowly but surely increasing his presence in the Far East. By the 1790s, he was able to sell his bills of exchange in the Orient, effectively paying for its riches with his promise to pay at a time when other American merchants had to pay hard cash up front. Willing later made successful inroads into the South American trade. Morris, on the other hand, soon turned his back on trade altogether because he found it insufficiently remunerative for his tastes!

Similarly, while Willing limited himself to a few partners, the activities of whom he monitored closely, Morris busily spread his capital thin, forming additional partnerships, including one with Tench Tilghman in Baltimore and another with William Constable in New York. The latter company spent a good deal of time, and more importantly £80,000 sterling of Morris's money, in an unsuccessful attempt to monopolize the French tobacco market. After the debacle, Constable lost all faith in Morris's business capacity, writing Gouverneur Morris: "I have a very bad opinion of Robert Morris's Talents." Constable might also have questioned Morris's appetite for extravagance.

Old Square Toes lived well, but not opulently. Morris, on the other hand, was prone to ostentation. At "The Hills," his country estate, for instance, he maintained an expensive hothouse that produced a trickle of tropical fruit of indifferent quality. Hiring the extravagant French architect Major L'Enfant to build a mansion for him in the city was another major blunder. Vastly over budget, past deadline, and "violently ugly," the mansion soon came to be known among Philadelphians as "Morris's Folly." Morris spent a colossal sum for the day, reportedly $1 million, on the property though it was never completed.

In another show of extravagance and folly, Morris was not content sending his sons Robert and Thomas to provincial schools like the University of Pennsylvania or Princeton College. So off to Europe to study they went, with the eighteenth-century equivalent of father's gold credit card in hand. Upon hearing reports that young Bobby did not wash himself or his clothes because his father was rich, Morris reproached him. "I am ambitious not of giving you a large fortune," Morris told his wayward namesake, "but of teaching you how to make one for yourself." Morris was true to his first promise. He died a bankrupt.

Land speculation would be Morris's undoing. While Willing conservatively sold small urban lots to Philadelphia artisans on ground rent, Morris purchased huge, distant tracts of unimproved land on the frontiers. Willing's approach was slow but sure, Morris's spectacular but speculative. In the 1780s, Morris formed a number of partnerships with land speculators. With those partners he owned large swaths of frontier land stretching from New York to Georgia. One strategy, apparently, was to resell the tracts piecemeal to actual settlers. Another strategy was to sell the tracts in big chunks to other speculators. Another was to mortgage the land to Dutch bankers so that only a small portion of the plots had to be resold each year to make the interest payments. The loan could not be obtained, however, and sales were so slow that the speculations tied up big chunks of Morris's capital for extended periods. Willing, meanwhile, collected his ground rents in specie with regularity, year in and year out. Like the fabled tortoise, Willing plodded along, amassing his fortune. Morris was the hare, so in love with his own brilliance and speed that he lost sight of the finish line. As in the fable, the tortoise won this race.

The massive scale of Morris's real estate speculations was truly impressive. At the height of his empire, he owned, with sundry partners, over six million acres of land in Pennsylvania, Virginia, the Carolinas, Kentucky, and Georgia, and several million acres in New York state alone. He also controlled the North American Land Company, a joint-stock association capitalized at $3 million. Morris did not buy foolishly. The tracts he purchased, especially those in Washington, D.C., would eventually become very valuable indeed. But he was far too optimistic about the rate at which land values would increase. Only his speculation in New York's Genesee country turned a rapid profit.

In 1790, Morris purchased two million acres of western New York from

Oliver Phelps and Nathaniel Gorham for £30,000 *Massachusetts currency* (or about $75,000).He immediately dispatched William Temple Franklin, Benjamin Franklin's grandson, to Europe and informed Gouverneur Morris, then conveniently in London, of the deal. Franklin, presumably with the aid of Gouverneur, quickly sold the massive tract to Pulteney Associates, a group of British investors, for £75,000 *sterling* (or about $375,000). The quick and easy $300,000 or so that Morris netted on the deal, however, only whet his appetite for grander, more highly leveraged schemes, all of which failed miserably.

With a Constable at his side and a Bingham at his back, Morris might have been able to weather the storm that his repeated losses created. But his new business associates were made of the baser metals. Thomas Willing they were not. James Greenleaf was a particularly vexing and costly partner who seemingly enjoyed buying high and selling low on a grand scale. Eventually, Morris and fellow land speculator John Nicholson bought out Greenleaf's share in the North American Land Company and other joint ventures. But that only pulled Morris deeper into the quagmire.

Fully mortgaged, Morris, like many troubled traders before and since, became increasingly desperate. He could not find ready buyers for the properties he owned. Instead of retrenching and taking his losses, he used whatever spare cash or credit he could conjure up to buy yet more lands. That strategy, however, was still a losing one, especially when he bought lands with dubious titles. And when it was learned that he mortgaged the same land to two or three different lenders, the capital markets closed to him. When the money market also went against him, his game was over.

Morris may have relied too much on the Bank of North America to keep his numerous schemes afloat with liquidity loans. After all, Morris had created the Bank and saved it from its political enemies in the mid-1780s. His friends directed the institution. All that aside, Morris may have owned more assets than any other person in America. So he certainly deserved to borrow. But by the mid-1790s it became clear that Morris had liabilities that matched, or perhaps even exceeded, his tremendous pile of assets. That, of course, spelled trouble. On April 16, 1795, the Bank threatened suit unless he coughed up some cash. Morris arranged for a loan in Holland, but his hopes were dashed when the French invaded the Low Countries.

Ironically cut off from the bank he helped to create, Morris had to enter the money market, where loans could be had if the borrower agreed to pay high enough interest. For the first time in his life, he had to pay usurious rates of interest in order to raise cash. Promissory notes signed by the same hand that once carried the nation to victory over John Bull now sold for 15 cents on the dollar. Once news that he was willing to borrow at extravagant rates reached the ears of his creditors, Morris was finished. Nothing could stymie the ensuing run.

Despite his business troubles, Morris continued to serve in public office, including the Pennsylvania Assembly, the Constitutional Convention, and the U.S. Senate. Legend has it that he was offered the position of Secretary of the Treasury but refused it, noting that it was Hamilton's turn. Undoubtedly our creator and Morris collaborated often on financial and fiscal questions. But on at least one occasion, Hamilton got the better of him because Morris and Pennsylvania's other senator, the vituperative William Maclay, split over the location of the national capital. Morris wanted it along the Delaware in Trenton, where he owned land. Maclay wanted it along the Susquehanna in Harrisburg, where he owned land. Their split created the opportunity for Hamilton to broker the compromise that moved the capital to the Potomac after a temporary stay in Philadelphia and that allowed the federal government to assume the Revolutionary War debts of the states.

Morris was on the slippery slope toward bankruptcy, and nothing, not even the fame of public office, could stop the slide. His lands in Georgia and North Carolina evaporated because he failed to pay the taxes due on them. They sold at public auctions for a song. Nobody would purchase his large, ugly, unfinished mansion. Friends would lend to him no more. He took refuge from his creditors at the Hills, which he soon took to call "Castle Defiance," munching on little green bananas and awaiting the inevitable. In those days, a man's house was truly his castle. As long as Morris remained on his property, he could not be arrested for his debts. Agents of his creditors camped just outside, looking for their main chance to imprison one of the nation's greatest patriots. Morris remained locked away, a prisoner in his own home, unable to stop the slow sale of his empire at auction. He gave in to pressure on February 15, 1798 and made the trek to the debtors' prison at Walnut and Prune (now Locust).

Morris at last realized that he had tried to feed the golden goose too much, too fast, and a fare that it did not desire. He told his son Thomas to keep his dealings "within bounds." "You will grow rich fast enough," he noted, "and enjoy yourself much more." But it was too late for Morris himself. His unfinished marble palace sold at auction for a mere $46,000, the cost of the lot alone several years earlier. Although released from prison on August 26, 1801, under the terms of the first federal bankruptcy law, Morris never again obtained a lucrative position or made a favorable trade. His vast fortune reduced to a few household items and a broken gold watch that had belonged to his father, Morris and his wife Mary lived off a $1,600 annuity. His heart ceased beating on May 8, 1806, but Robert Morris had died long before.

Willing, by contrast, lived for another fourteen years after his retirement from the presidency of the Bank of the United States, finally dying in 1821. He certainly died a very wealthy man; in all likelihood, he also died happy. His surviving children had all done well in life. Willing had the pleasure of declining the request of Louis Philippe, a pretender to the French throne, to marry his daughter Abigail. "If you have no claim to the throne of France, you are no match for my daughter," Willing told the duke, "and if you ever become King," he quipped, "she will be no match for you." Some years later, Abigail married Pennsylvania plutocrat Richard Peters. Anne Willing had done best of all. After marrying William Bingham, she became the social center of the Federalist court, her beauty, elegance, and elevated status forever captured in Daniel Huntington's famous painting, "Lady Washington's Reception." Despite the painting's title, Mrs. Bingham stands in the visual center of the painting, light from above washing over her, while Robert Morris's face barely emerges from the crowd in the background. Tragically, Mrs. Bingham died in Bermuda on May 11, 1801, but her daughter Anne, whose beauty was compared to that of Helen of Troy, lived on as Lady Ashburton, the wife of the great London financier Alexander Baring.

The moral behind our risen and fallen angels is that early America's goose distributed its gold eggs as equitably as the prevailing social and political systems allowed. When left unsullied by prejudicial laws and attitudes, the goose doled out its rewards with remarkable precision. Those who fed the goose the right foods at the right time received just the right number of eggs in exchange. Those whose guesses about what the golden goose would eat at a given time turned out to be wrong, however, lost their investment and suffered the consequences. In both cases, it mattered not whether one sprang from a wealthy, prestigious family or from poor immigrants, whether one financed independence or remained a lukewarm Patriot, whether one was educated at Princeton or apprenticed to a lowly pettifogger, or whether one was a sociable butterfly or a recluse. All that mattered was what one contributed to the economy. The returns could range from millions of dollars to utter destitution and ignominious death. That same basic parable underlies the next chapter.

THE SAINT

Stephen Girard (1750–1831)

Stephen Girard, an early philanthropist unfamiliar to most present day Americans, actually risked his life in the service of others. Arguably America's richest man in the early nineteenth century, Girard usually made his money through acumen and wise business decisions. He also influenced the financial system in powerful, positive ways. However, even his business reputation was at times disparaged. Yet in 1793, at the height of the worst plague to hit America's shores, he risked his life to save his fellow Philadelphians. Thirty odd years later, Girard in death again helped to save lives by bequeathing his vast fortune to Philadelphia's impoverished orphans. For those reasons, he plays the figurative role of saint in our story.

Girard was born to Pierre and Anne Girard in Bordeaux, France on May 20, 1750. He was christened Etienne after his godfather, Etienne Souisse, one of his father's friends. (Girard used the Anglicized version of his name after taking up residence in America.) At age twelve, Girard mourned the death of his mother but did not draw closer to his workaholic merchant of a father, with whom he maintained an intense love-hate relationship. Though but a lad, Girard took over the day-to-day management of his seven living siblings, a responsibility that pushed him closer to a life of solitude and hard work. Very early in life Girard displayed personality traits, including a quick temper and long bouts of solitude, that plagued him until his death. Technically an orphan after his mother's death, Girard also suffered a major physical handicap, the loss of his right eye. The teasing of other boys induced him to eschew social contact in favor of labor. Still a mere boy, he learned by rote a sentence that guided the rest of his life: "My love of work is the greatest pleasure that I have upon this globe." Ironically, strict adherence to that maxim led to further social ostracism, as in many people's eyes he became little more than a miser. In business he could be quick-tempered and quick to blame, surviving largely thanks to his intense work ethic, self-confidence, and uncanny ability to time markets. But no scrooge or grinch was he. In life as in death, no one gave more.

To this day, almost 175 years after entering his grave, Girard still touches lives. Since its establishment, Girard College, his longest lasting legacy, has provided Philadelphia's most deserving orphans with free tuition, room, and board. The charitable trust that Girard established to fund that institution was the largest bequeathed by an American in the first half of the nineteenth century. Tragedy lay at the heart of the donation. Girard's wife, the lowbred but pretty Mary Lum, found it difficult to conceive. Worse, she slowly grew insane. She spent the last quarter century of her life in the Pennsylvania Hospital after repeatedly attacking Girard with invective and, more dangerously, sundry pieces of household furniture. She gave birth only once, after she had been committed. The child, who was named for her mother, died before the difficult question of her patrimony was resolved. Despite the circumstances, Girard found it impossible to obtain a divorce. Mercifully, Mary died in 1815. Bereft of legitimate heirs, Girard gave all but $140,000 of his vast personal fortune of $7 million, a truly princely sum at the time, to the college. Donating money to charity after one's death was not at all unusual for the period. The scale of the donation, however, was unprecedented and has rarely been equaled, even in nominal terms, to this day.

Estranged from his numerous siblings and half-siblings after a fight over his father's estate, Girard gave to those he thought most worthy, "poor white male orphans" bereft of hearth and home. The orphans were indeed worthy of assistance. In the first half of the nineteenth century, lower life expectancies, only tiny amounts of life insurance in force, and a dearth of public funding meant that orphans were both numerous and often impoverished. Girard's siblings, in contrast, were little better than a cadre of gold diggers. When their father Pierre died in 1788, they ransacked his offices in search of hidden coins. Finding only 30,000 livres, which they found too small a sum for their tastes, they made off with a hundred barrels of wine too! Girard eventually netted a grand total of $92.36 from his father's estate. Some of his siblings, and even strangers who happened to be named Girard, later had the audacity to ask him for handouts. Moreover, Girard thought it wrong to bequeath more than $5,000 to any one person. That sum, he believed, was enough to launch the meritorious on a career but insufficient to allow him or her to slip into a life of idleness and profligacy. No wonder then that Girard sought a broad charitable outlet for his immense wealth.

Girard College's trust fund has grown enormously and is estimated today to be worth approximately $375 million. The beneficiaries now include all orphans regardless of sex, creed, or color. Indeed, though reared a Roman Catholic, Girard decreed that the school be nonsectarian. Each individual, he believed, should be free to choose a religion upon his or her maturity. Girard's last will and testament held religion to be inseparable from human character but ultimately a decision best left to individual conscience. Religious leaders eager to take control of the trust objected to this provision, but Girard's will prevailed.

Over almost two centuries, many thousands have benefited from attending the boarding institution. Curators of the school's library and museum, usually Girard College graduates, look upon Girard and the school with reverence. They speak of their benefactor in glowing terms, as a father figure they never knew, and on occasion their eyes swell with tears as they recount stories about this special man. They boast not of his impressive riches, but of the orphan, shunned by society for his handicap and his obsession for work, who literally risked his all to save the lives of others.

Unlike many philanthropists, Girard did not wait until he died to start helping others. His finest hour occurred during Philadelphia's great yellow fever epidemic in 1793. That episode, largely forgotten in American history, was one of the greatest disasters to befall any American city. The gravity of the epidemic increases when one realizes that Philadelphia was at the time the nation's temporary capital. Yellow fever, so named because the victim's skin turns a yellowish hue, is fatal to as many as half of those who contract it. If the afflicted does not successfully resist the disease, he dies a tortuous week-long death filled with bouts of high fever, chills, black vomit, and diarrhea. Were this not awful enough, the alleged cure for the malady, the one pushed by Philadelphia's leading physician, the famed Dr. Benjamin Rush, involved bloodletting and mercury purges. Rush, like Girard, bravely stayed in town and tried his utmost to aid the sick. Unfortunately, Rush's harsh treatment plan caused untold deaths.

In 1793, the population of Philadelphia and its suburbs was approximately 45,000. Diseased mosquitoes slipped into the city during the summer, on the same ships that brought two thousand French-speaking West Indian refugees to the capital. Absorbing the refugees, who fled slave rebellions and yellow fever epidemics at home, was no easy task. Girard and other leading members of the city's elite organized the "Societe Francaise de Bienfaisance de Philadelphie" to provide relief and housing for the new arrivals. Unfortunately, the mosquitoes also found Philadelphia a hospitable habitat. A dry summer left the city and its environs covered with stagnant pools—ideal breeding grounds for the fecund little flying vampires. Philadelphians did not stand a chance. Before the epidemic ended with the November frosts, some four to five thousand Philadelphians, about 10 percent of the city's population, lay yellowed and dead in pools of vomit and excrement. In a typical day just prior to the plague, an average of three Philadelphians died. On October 11, at the peak of the plague, 119 persons met their excruciatingly painful end.

Yet the numbers do not tell the whole story. When the existence of an epidemic was announced in mid-August, the city fell into complete panic. The "Fever" did not discriminate: rich and poor, young and old, doctors and dockworkers were all coming down with the disease. And because no one knew what caused the dreadful malady, scapegoats were numerous and largely defenseless. Some blamed the refugees. Others cited the city's teeming refuse piles. Still others blamed Girard because his ships frequented the West Indies and because stevedores unloading his ships were the first to succumb.

According to Secretary of State Thomas Jefferson, by September 1 everyone who could afford to had fled the city for the outlying suburbs. As many as twenty thousand citizens left the city limits. Those who stayed faced as somber a time as the city had ever seen. In early September, in response to the mounting crisis, city leaders established a temporary hospital in Bush Hill, an unoccupied mansion on the city's northern boundary about one mile from the center of town. One year before it had been occupied by John Adams, the vice president, and his wife Abigail, but when the fever struck, its owner, William Hamilton (no relation to Alexander), did not reside in Philadelphia and had not found a suitable replacement for the Adamses. The exigencies of the emergency dictated that the city take his property. The state later gave him $2,000 for it, a sum he thought well shy of its pre-plague value.

Sadly for those infected, few volunteers assisted at Bush Hill because most people suspected that the disease was contagious. Indeed, many of the afflicted died alone after urging their loved ones to flee and save themselves. Faced with such melancholy prospects, masters sent their servants to Bush Hill at first sight of the slightest symptom.

No one great or small was immune to this plague. None other than Alexander Hamilton caught the fever on September 5. Soon thereafter, his beloved wife Betsy also became ill. Dr. Edward Stevens saw to their recovery, which became instant front-page news. Stevens's treatment was much milder than the aggressive bloodletting and purging that Dr. Rush espoused. Soon, controversy over the proper course of treatment divided Philadelphia's doctors and leading citizens. After they recovered, the Hamiltons and their servants attempted to take sanctuary in Manhattan. The fear there was so great, however, that they were denied admission. In an effort to avoid the ravages of the fever, the city had placed itself under strict quarantine. Undaunted, they retreated to Betsy's father's house outside Albany, where they received a less than cordial welcome. They were placed under guard with their servants while their clothes, baggage, and carriages were burned. Not until five reputable physicians swore that the Hamiltons were in good health did the phobia subside.

Philadelphia suffered another blow to its morale on September 10 when President George Washington left for Mt. Vernon. While it was Washington's custom to depart in the early fall for a vacation until Congress met again, many Philadelphians interpreted his departure as an ominous sign. Secretary of War Henry Knox was now nominally in charge of the executive branch, but he too decided to vacate. Like Hamilton, Knox ventured to Manhattan only to be rebuffed. Knox eventually found refuge in Elizabethtown, New Jersey.

Meanwhile, back in the capital, its leaders hundreds of miles away, the national government ground to a halt. Mail delivery ceased; four of the city's five daily papers closed. In the Treasury Department alone six clerks contracted the disease. Oliver Wolcott tried to manage affairs during Hamilton's absence, attempting to reassemble the staff near the Schuylkill River waterfalls. Most of his clerks, however, were either dead or had fled. The one exception was Joshua Dawson of the Register's Office. Dawson, who oversaw import tonnage and duties on spirits, worked out of his Arch Street home rather than the offices of the Treasury Department. He lost his young daughter to the plague but avoided infection himself. Thomas Willing, the president of the Bank of the United States, also took ill but eventually recovered.

Stephen Girard could have, indeed should have, simply left town. But instead, he chose to risk his life to save others. Though awkward physically, Girard was no coward. During the Revolution, he rebuffed an army officer who tried to take liberties with his Mary by challenging him to a duel. So Girard was not about to allow a little black bile to frighten him. He rolled up his sleeves and plunged into the fight, the fight against the disease itself, the fight against physicians with quack cures, the fight for the honor of the French refugees who many blamed for the scourge, and the fight for his business and reputation. Unlike some fifty merchants who ran away and reneged on their financial obligations, Girard defended his credit, his honor, his people, his city.

Girard knew that the afflicted desperately needed his help. When the call went out for volunteers, only thirty-seven stepped forward. Clearly, the hospital at Bush Hill was no place for the faint of heart; the stench of death, vomit, and excrement filled the nostrils, overpowering even the strongest. After inspecting conditions at Bush Hill, Girard realized that such a small number of volunteers would prove insufficient unless they were efficiently organized. Therefore, at the September 16 meeting of the emergency plague committee, Girard and fellow Philadelphian Peter Helm offered to supervise the volunteers. Girard's actions, which many viewed as a death sentence, took observers aback.

But Girard was not suicidal. He had experienced a brief bout of fever in August but brushed it off, proudly announcing that "Frenchmen do not die as easily as Americans." Like Hamilton, Girard, who was conversant with the principles of medicine due to his youthful experience as a sailor, shunned Dr. Rush's harsh treatments in favor of the milder approach of Dr. Stevens. Moreover, Girard did not believe that the disease was contagious, attributing the far-reaching nature of the epidemic instead to the widespread distribution of the city's filth.

Girard and Helm quickly went to work at Bush Hill, dividing the tasks between matters related to the inside of the hospital, Girard's domain, and to those on the outside, Helm's realm. It was a daunting task made all the more difficult by the fact that Girard had to convince the emergency committee that his preferred choice of medical chief, a French doctor who had seen yellow fever before in the West Indies, should lead the staff, not an American team influenced by Rush. Girard prevailed, so mercifully no bloodletting or mercury purges took place at Bush Hill.

For sixty straight days Girard managed the makeshift hospital and cared for the ever-growing number of sick. When overcrowding became a problem, temporary shelters sprang up around the mansion house. A contemporary observer noted that Girard had to perform "many disgusting offices of kindness for [the patients], which nothing could render tolerable, but the exalted motives that impelled him to this heroic conduct." In the words of one historian, "for the dying, Girard acted as confessor and chaplain, comforter and attorney."

The public recognized that Girard and Helm personally saved many from death. So the city readily adopted Girard's recommendation that Bush Hill become a permanent hospital. And it was a good thing that it did, because in the future both Girard and Bush Hill would provide succor to many more victims of the city's intermittent yellow fever epidemics. For those risky, unselfish actions, we dub Girard our saint.

＊ Girard, like Alexander Hamilton, came to America on the eve of the Revolutionary War. Salt water had run in the veins of the Girard family for generations, so it is little surprise that young Stephen inherited a love of the sea. A poor athlete and scholar due to his bad eye, both hard labor and the learned professions were closed to him. But he could bark out orders to sailors and business correspondents, so a life in the mercantile way beckoned. No doubt he both relished and blanched at the thought of following in the footsteps of the father he both loved and hated.

In 1764, at the age of fourteen, Girard made his first voyage to the West Indies. Unhappy at home, where his babysitting duties weighed heavily on him as his father alternated between stints of work and philandering (first with Girard's aunt and later with his stepmother, who Girard abhorred), Girard returned to the islands multiple times over the next ten years. In 1774, he purchased some wares from Bordeaux traders and landed in Saint-Domingue (later, Haiti) ready to resell them to local French planters. Unfortunately the goods were out-of-fashion merchandise, so one of his earliest attempts at trade came to nothing. Forced to sell the goods at a loss, Girard owed debts in Bordeaux that he did not have the resources or credit to discharge. Fearful that he would be sent to debtors' prison if he returned to France, Girard set out for America. The episode taught Girard several life-long business lessons that induced him to switch his focus from dry goods to foodstuffs. He also concentrated on the trade between the West Indies and the mainland British colonies because he believed that shorter travel times would make for greater flexibility in business decisions.

For several years, Girard sailed the New Orleans-New York route for Thomas Randall, a well-to-do merchant. By shipping goods for sale to the Indians, including firearms, on the New Orleans leg on his own account, Girard was able to amass enough money to purchase a ship of his own. In 1776, he sailed his ship to Philadelphia, where rebels promptly confiscated it for the use of the Patriot cause. Keenly aware that prices would soon skyrocket, Girard purchased a stock of goods and foodstuffs and set up as a shopkeeper. On October 27, 1778, with the war raging, he took the oath of allegiance to the Commonwealth of Pennsylvania, an act that forced him to renounce his French citizenship. His allegiance to his adopted country would never be called into question. Indeed, Girard was more "American" than many Americans were. Unlike the typical Frenchman, whom Girard considered lazy and shiftless, the stereotypical American bustled from dawn to dusk looking to increase his wealth. Though of course not all Americans were like that, enough of them were to make Girard feel right at home, thousands of miles away from home.

In Philadelphia's active, relatively free atmosphere, Girard excelled as a merchant. He parlayed his gains from the successful shopkeeping stint into privateering, a form of lawful pirating and private military parrying rolled into one. After the war, he chartered ships laden with goods from the continent and the

West Indies. While there are no indications that he was involved in the slave trade, he did personally own several slaves for use in his house in Philadelphia, not an uncommon practice at the time. One of those slaves had been his brother John's mistress. Girard also held a silent partnership interest in a coffee plantation on Saint-Domingue, managed by John, which of course utilized slave labor. (Although the Catholic Church, other Christian denominations, and half of America at that time countenanced slavery, Girard's complicity in this institution is the one asterisk to our dubbing him for sainthood.)

Girard's command of English was not strong, so he conducted much of his business in French. As his stature and profits grew in the 1780s, he posted clerks at the entrances to his counting house and required written applications from those who called to see him. Other Philadelphia merchants grew jealous of this Francophile and his receptionists, but none doubted his ability to judge the market for everything from linens to foodstuffs. As he was not a social creature and spoke broken English, he did not sit in the coffeehouses schmoozing with other merchants. This, and his almost maniacal insistence on following all private contracts to the letter, reinforced his reputation as a cruel outsider. After his wife Mary was moved into an insane asylum, his social interaction declined further. Yet he did have female companionship, taking on several mistresses over the years. First to share his bed was beautiful Quakeress Sally Bickham. For all intents and purposes she played the role of Girard's wife after Mary's madness became unbearable. Sally garnered a side benefit in that Girard set up her brother Martin in business despite the fact that she eventually left the millionaire to marry a younger, more joyous man. Girard promptly replaced her with an even younger girl, laundress Polly Kenton. Nevertheless, our saint continued to treat Martin as the son he never had, setting him up in trade on generous terms. Only when Bickham proved himself more avaricious than sensible by engaging in wild slaving expeditions did Girard withdraw his support.

Tellingly, Girard's employees, apprentices, and indentured servants spoke highly of his kindness, as did his godmother, whom he supported financially until her death in 1824. Untold numbers of destitute Frenchmen passing through Philadelphia also found Girard willing to give up a few minutes of his time and a few dollars of his treasure. The many young boys who served valuable apprenticeships in his counting house also praised him. A successful stint with Girard was the eighteenth-century equivalent of an MBA degree from a top tier program like those at Harvard, Wharton, or Stern.

For all his private kindness, Girard was naturally distrustful. This trait held him in good stead in the dog-eat-dog world of eighteenth century commerce.

Due to the tremendous distances and time lags involved, agents found it all too easy to bilk their principals. By trusting no one very far, Girard avoided the fraudulent schemes that other merchants usually fell prey to. He also had a good nose for bargains, picking up wares on the cheap at sheriff's sales and auctions. On one occasion, for instance, he purchased an enormous 364-ton ship for only £900. It needed some repairs, but less than £100 later, it was ready to start paying for itself. In another shrewd move, Girard leased out much more space than he needed, subdivided it, and subleased it at higher rates per square foot. So good was he at this game that he rarely was out of pocket for any rent at all because his subtenants paid him enough to cover his own rent.

Our saint was not perfect, but generally he learned from his mistakes. For instance, during the Revolution he fell in with Joseph Baldesqui, the treasurer of Count Casimir Pulaski's Polish Cavalry Legion, a small force that came to America to help further the cause of liberty. In September 1788 Baldesqui and Girard formed a partnership and commenced sundry mercantile operations. Unfortunately for the future students of Girard College, Baldesqui was inept. To make a series of long stories short, the man liked to buy high and sell low. Girard soon learned to avoid him.

Girard later partnered with his brother John, for Baldesqui's follies made him forever wary of forming mercantile partnerships with nonrelatives. His stormy partnership with John, who also had a penchant for losing money, soon made him wary of entering into any partnerships at all. With typical luck, Girard found himself free of his brother and his plantation on Saint-Domingue just as that French colony became convulsed in the opening phases of a revolution that led in 1804 to the founding of the nation of Haiti. Girard's take from the enterprise was $30,000—a nice profit for the day—although he lamented that the sum was far below what he thought he would have made on his own.

Now twice burned, for the rest of his career Girard preferred employees to partners. Here, matters were generally more satisfactory. In fact, he long enjoyed the services of at least four exemplary employees, Creole John Henry Roberjot, from Saint-Domingue, in his countinghouse, cashier George Simpson in his bank, and captains Ezra Bowen and Myles McLeveen at the helms of his ships. In each case, Girard found just the right mix of fixed salary and bonus incentive to keep the men productive, sober, loyal, and obedient. From his lesser employees he also demanded unflinching loyalty but in return paid good wages and board. In fact, Girard's sailors were among the healthiest and happiest in the world. That allowed Girard to keep his ships at sea a larger percentage of the time than other merchants found possible.

Partnership troubles aside, during the 1780s and early 1790s Girard amassed a fortune with his shipping interests, market knowledge, and a little regulatory rule bending. He traded around the globe, including the profitable, perfectly legal (in America), and, at the time, moral opium trade in the Orient. (Indeed, opium was one of the few medicines that eased his wife's pain in the worst throes of her mental illness.) In addition to the West Indies, his ships regularly visited Europe's major ports as well as Calcutta, Batavia, and Canton, the big three of the China trade. It was not unusual for his ships to leave Philadelphia laden with $75,000 worth of produce and to return a year and a half later bearing goods that would sell for $150,000 or more. Indeed on one trip the *Voltaire* turned $68,000 into $248,000, a phenomenal rate of return.

The uncanny ability to buy just the right product, at just the right time, held him in good stead. He purchased sugar, for example, *from specific hills* that he knew to yield only the sweetest canes. And as a connoisseur of coffee and tobacco he was unequaled. He reminded his purchasing agents, for example, never to sample tobacco on unusually warm or cold days because temperature affected its flavor; he knew just the right hue of coffee that would attract buyers like moths to the flame.

Girard generally specialized in the highest quality foodstuffs. He could afford to pay a little bit more to obtain the best products because he cut costs elsewhere. His notorious miserly instincts, for instance, led him to entrust young apprenticed Americans with his cargoes in foreign ports. Though young and inexperienced, his agents passed through his rigorous apprenticeship program, so he knew that they had the right stuff, that they would follow orders when voyages went as planned, but could act intelligently should plans go awry. By paying less and getting more, Girard improved his profit margins. The seasoned merchants who lost the high consignment fees that they would have charged Girard were of course less than amused. They lost no opportunity to slander the poor rich man. But the bottom line for Girard was written in dollars and cents, not popularity. Girard's many customers would have been quite happy with his use of apprentice boys had they known that it was responsible for the relatively high-quality, low-cost food on their plates.

Girard also proved adept at skirting trade barriers, particularly those of Pennsylvania, France, and Saint-Domingue. When convenient, his ships changed names, owners, captains, crews, and/or manifests. Consumers profited from his legalistic manipulations because they received a wider variety of goods at lower prices than they would have otherwise. Of course, Girard profited from the adventures as well, as did his captains, mates, and sailors. And on occasion customs officials benefited too, when they found a gold guinea or two trans-

ferred to their possession during a handshake. Girard also manipulated shipping records to ensure himself the lowest insurance premium possible.

Girard also found lending a profitable endeavor. Usury laws prevented banks
from charging more than 6 percent interest. Real market rates were often considerably above that. So everyone who needed ready cash first tried to get a bank
loan. If turned away from the banks, loan applicants sought out the likes of
"note shavers," men like Girard who purchased promissory notes (IOUs) for
less than their face value. There is nothing inherently wrong with buying a
promissory note at a discount—U.S. Treasury savings bonds sell at a discount,
for instance—but shavers bought at a steeper discount than allowed by law. As
large public institutions, banks could not get away with such flagrant violations
of the law. But individuals like Girard who were involved in a variety of commercial activities found the usury laws easily evaded. The simplest technique
was simply not to write down how much the shaver paid for the note. Better yet,
get the borrower (the seller of the note) to sign a receipt that stipulated a legal
selling price. Borrowers were more than happy to oblige because, after all, they
were not being forced to borrow. They valued the smaller amount of ready cash
now more than the larger amount of cash they would have to pay in the future.
Like drug laws, usury strictures were difficult to enforce. Once again, Girard
found that the interests of free trade and his purse were closely aligned.

Of course, not everyone believed in free trade. To such people, Girard was
an unprincipled loan shark worthy of public derision. One particularly damning cartoon lampooned him as "Stephen Graspall." Girard persevered because
money lending was part and parcel of being a merchant. So too was conducting
foreign exchange operations. And because he was involved in global markets his
entire adult life, Girard developed considerable expertise in that important
field. He soon understood foreign exchange as fully as he did sugar, coffee, and
flour, buying and selling bills of exchange, the international checks of the day,
as market conditions warranted.

For all of those reasons and more, money began to pour into his coffers. By
1788, he was too important, and too involved in multiple ventures, to sail with
his own ships. He began his final sea venture in late 1787, landing in Marseilles
because he still owed debts in his native Bordeaux. He never again personally
visited his homeland, or any foreign nation for that matter, but continued trading internationally from his desk in Philadelphia.

≈ Unsurprisingly, Girard sided with the Republican admirers of the French
Revolution and against the Anglophile Federalists. Though roundly defeated
when he first ran for elective office, he exercised his Constitutional right to make

his sentiments known, going so far as to call a town meeting near Independence Hall on July 22, 1795. Tensions were running high because John Jay had returned from London with a treaty bearing on some outstanding issues between Britain and America, including the removal of British troops from forts in the American west and the establishment of commissions to resolve disputes over shipping seized during the Revolution and over the border with Canada. There was no mention in the treaty, however, of the most vexing issue to Americans, British impressment of American sailors on the high seas.

Girard claimed that his meeting, which in thinly veiled language called for war against Britain, attracted six thousand loyal Americans. Federalists retorted that it brought forth only "two shiploads of Irish and fifty French immigrants." Despite Girard's efforts, the federal government chose peace with England and a possible naval war with France. Girard of course denounced Jay's Treaty, which signaled a rapprochement between America and the mother country, nodding approvingly when mobs burned an effigy of John Jay and a copy of the treaty in front of the British minister's house. He later donated enough of his money, time, and reputation to the Republican cause to gain election on the Jeffersonian ticket to Philadelphia's Select Council. Girard worked hard in office, helping to make his adopted city a cleaner, healthier, more efficient place. His political support ended at the city line, however, as demonstrated by his repeated failure to convince the state legislature to grant him a divorce.

Despite the war and his political dalliances, in the latter half of the 1790s Girard's business grew ever larger. One ship grew into several, then a half dozen. Named for Enlightenment philosophers like *Rousseau, Voltaire, Helvetius,* and *Montesquieu,* Girard's ships plied a complicated trade that brought North American produce to Europe, European finished goods to the Orient, and Asian fineries to North America. With each trip, the world's welfare increased because producers the world round found larger markets for their wares and consumers had access to a wider variety of goods, often at lower prices. And with each successful trip, Girard found his personal wealth increased.

The latter half of the 1790s and first years of the new century also witnessed an increase in Girard's financial activities. Occasional exchange dealings or note shavings in the hundreds of dollars grew into regular dealings worth thousands of dollars per transaction. The level of Girard's investment in public securities, mostly bank stocks and government bonds, also dramatically increased. His operations in this period, however, did not develop in new directions. In the early nineteenth century, four key international and political developments would conspire to change that: the Napoleonic Wars; the Embargo and Nonintercourse Acts; the shuttering of the Bank of the United States in 1811; and the War of 1812.

As they had so often during the prior centuries, in early 1803 the French and the British went to war. This time, Napoleon Bonaparte's visions of grandeur were at the root of the conflict. Initially, this war proved a bonanza for American merchants. As a neutral third party, they traded, and quite profitably at that, with both sides. As the war in Europe intensified, Girard, always with a nose to profits, realized that the prosperity could not last forever. With his ships, cargoes, and money spread throughout the major European trading centers, including Amsterdam, London, St. Petersburg, Hamburg, Copenhagen, and other ports, Girard grew nervous. Late in 1807, shortly after the British warship HMS *Leopard* mauled the USS *Chesapeake*, he decided to repatriate his overseas assets. He believed that America would now find it difficult to remain out of the fray.

President Jefferson hesitated. The *Leopard's* attack was an act of war, and everyone knew that the president's party preferred taking the side of the French against the British, but Jefferson realized that thanks to his administration's failure to maintain the U.S. armed forces, the nation was ill equipped to fight anyone. Jefferson opted for economic sanctions. Had Hamilton not died at Weehawken, he surely would have died the day that Jefferson and his Congress passed the Embargo Act rather than defend the nation's honor.

That invidious act, and the various trade restrictions that followed it, were the products of wishful thinking on the part of the Republicans. Jefferson and his friends convinced themselves that Britain needed America more than America needed Britain. In fact, as major trading partners they needed each other equally. Moreover, since Britain was locked in a desperate struggle against Napoleonic authoritarianism, it did not look kindly on the actions of its former colonies. Worst of all, the embargo damaged the American economy because it crushed all those involved in international trade, which meant that farmers and artisans suffered right along with the merchants. Only subsistence farmers, rare individuals found mostly in historians' dreams, were left untouched.

Girard did not wait for the depression to hit. As soon as he learned of the embargo, he ordered Baring Brothers, his London banker since the insolvency of George Barclay's bank a few years earlier, to invest his funds in portable liquid assets, especially the equities of American corporations and U.S. federal bonds. After Hamilton funded the national debt, American securities traded in European capital markets, especially those of London and Amsterdam. By repatriating his assets in the form of securities instead of merchandise, Girard avoided both the embargo and the risks of wartime seizure. Girard also realized that the embargo would wreak havoc on the value of the dollar, so he speculated on changes in the dollar-sterling exchange rate as well. In so doing, he proved that he could predict the financial world as ably as he spotted mercantile price trends.

On March 1, 1809, Jefferson repealed the Embargo Act, substituting in its stead the Nonintercourse Act. Girard still had a significant part of his fortune overseas and wished it returned, so again he moved quickly to repatriate his funds. He sensed that rumors of war would depreciate U.S. bonds, so this round he ordered his European agents to purchase on his account as many shares in the Bank of the United States as possible. Luckily for Girard, at that time foreigners, primarily in England and Holland, owned some 75 percent of the Bank of the United States. But here a political risk loomed because the charter of Hamilton's central bank would expire in 1811 and recharter was uncertain. Clearly, were the charter not renewed the Bank's stock would sell off sharply. So buying Bank shares was fraught with risk, but so too was doing nothing.

Politically, Girard sided more with the Francophile Republicans than with the Francophobe Federalists. In fact, legend has it that Girard personally supplied the gunpowder for the cannon salutes that greeted news that the House had chosen Jefferson over Burr in the 1801 runoff. But Girard could not agree with President Jefferson's financial or fiscal views. Moreover, Girard believed that the Bank of the United States should be rechartered because it was indispensable to the nation's commerce. He rejected the Jeffersonian claim that the Bank was a Federalist plot to usurp the liberties of the people, or the equally ridiculous charge that foreigners, who were lawfully barred from voting for directors, controlled it.

Girard hired agents to convince the Washington political circle (the capital had moved there from Philadelphia as scheduled in 1801) to renew the Bank's charter. Despite the best efforts of Girard and others, the Bank died at the hands of Vice President George Clinton, the former Republican governor of New York. On February 20, 1811, the bill for recharter tied in the U.S. Senate 17 for, 17 against, when Clinton asserted his Constitutional right to break the tie and did so in the negative. Many, including Girard, thought there still time to make another attempt. Lobbyists scurried about the capital in a frantic attempt to sway votes. Interestingly, at the same time, Girard started buying as many shares of the stock as he could, ordering Baring Brothers to clean out the London market. Girard eventually bought close to 1,000 of the 25,000 shares outstanding. As nonvoting foreigners held about 75 percent of the shares and could not vote in bank elections for directors, Girard's 1,000 shares gave him a whopping 14 percent voting stake in the institution.

Girard's gamble was not as big as it appeared to be. First, he needed to buy some type of financial instrument in order to repatriate his assets safely and Bank stock was both ample and lucrative. Second, if the Bank were rechartered, the stock price would soar. Third, even if the Bank had to be liquidated, he would have a major say in how it would be done. Fourth, he received advice from head cashier George Simpson that the Bank would prove profitable even in liquidation.

In the end, Girard and the lobbyists could not save the Bank or the American economy. The Bank's closing in March 1811 interfered with commerce nationwide. Girard himself was immediately inconvenienced when he needed to transact business in Charleston and could no longer settle the matter by transferring money between the Philadelphia and Charleston branches of the Bank. Instead, his options were to ship actual gold and silver, certainly a risky and costly proposition, or a U.S. Treasury draft, a negotiable bill backed by the Treasury Department. To his surprise, the Treasury drafts were not accepted at par value. In modern parlance, Charlestonians had imposed a risk premium on short-term government paper, which was unheard of during the Bank's existence. The truth was that citizens believed that without the Bank the federal government would no longer be able to pay its bills punctually. Girard was not about to suffer on account of the government's lack of credit, so instead of Treasury drafts he began to send to the Bank of Charleston drafts on himself. The bank readily accepted them at par value, essentially saying that Girard was more creditworthy than the U.S. government shorn of its central bank!

Clearly, sensible businessmen like Girard were appalled that the U.S. lacked a central bank, particularly when the country teetered on the verge of a war with Great Britain. The Bank and its branches (Baltimore, Boston, Charleston, New Orleans, New York, Norfolk, Savannah, and Washington) had prevented inflation by ensuring that state banks did not issue too many banknotes. It had also lent money to the federal government when it was short of funds and made all its payments for it. Now, state banks and the government were left to shift for themselves. If the nation had stayed at peace, the economy may have slowly adjusted to the new circumstances. But with each passing day, the international crisis deepened.

In response to the critical situation, Girard hatched a simple but brilliant plan to purchase all of the assets of the Bank of the United States, including its magnificent Philadelphia headquarters. Girard knew the Bank's board would accept his plan because they were very eager to liquidate the Bank's assets. Not only did Girard purchase many of the Bank's invested assets, he also purchased its buildings and, in a final stroke of genius, signed on many of its key former employees. On May 12, 1812, the bank opened under the style "The Bank of Stephen Girard." Thanks to the retention of George Simpson, the cashier or chief operating officer in modern parlance, and some former directors, the transition was almost seamless. In its basement vaults, the new bank kept watch over $3,000,000 of the First Bank's remaining stash of cash, destined to be distributed to stockholders during the liquidation process. The Girard Bank itself opened with $1,200,000 of Girard's personal capital. He soon increased that sum by $100,000. The Girard Bank's assets during its first year of operations averaged $2.5 million, placing Girard's private bank in the same size category as the largest state-chartered banks.

Girard had scored yet another financial coup. But the victory brought hardship because the enemies of the defunct Bank now became Girard's enemies. Passersby believed that Girard was in consort with the U.S. government, and therefore his bank had a special air about it even though it did not even enjoy the explicit sanction of the Pennsylvania legislature. The Philadelphia banks that did have charters were quite pleased about the destruction of the old Bank because it meant less competition and perhaps higher profits. But then Girard's Bank appeared and threatened to dash their hopes. So Philadelphia's four incorporated banks conspired against Girard and his institution by refusing to accept his banknotes for deposit. In other words, the bank tellers at the four other banks rejected Girard's banknotes when presented for deposit. Girard countered by attacking some of the financial practices of the state banks and by currying favor with the small businessmen that the state banks often refused to lend to, for artisans and other small businesses found it difficult to obtain bank loans at times.

Girard did not lend recklessly, however. He did not lend on long-term obligations like mortgages and required at least two endorsers on each note he discounted. As a result, the banknotes of the Bank of Stephen Girard usually circulated without a risk premium. (All banknotes, which were essentially sight promissory notes, traded at an increasing discount the further they migrated from the bank of issue.) In the Philadelphia region, Girard's notes were literally as good as gold. Girard kept a relatively small reserve of specie on hand to redeem his notes. A lower specie reserve ratio meant more profits because more of the bank's assets could be invested in interest-bearing loans and securities. For most banks, it would also have meant more risk that the bank might run out of specie and suffer embarrassment or even bankruptcy. But Girard realized that his personal credit and strong relationship with Baring Brothers—he was now Baring's American agent—allowed him to take on this added risk without unduly jeopardizing the safety of his bank. If unexpected cash calls came in, Girard could quickly sell a large volume of inland drafts or bills of exchange to raise the necessary cash.

Moreover, Girard closely matched the duration of his assets with that of his liabilities. In other words, loans that could be used to meet cash calls came due each day. Importantly, most of those loans were punctually paid because the bank's borrowers knew Girard's banking creed: "The principle of banking is not to furnish capital but simply to facilitate commercial operations by discounting bills or notes which result from real transactions for which value has been received." In short, Girard's name became associated with low-risk loans, sound credit, and stable finance. In today's parlance his bank was an AAA credit risk; there was nothing to be gained by testing it.

Girard took physical possession of the First Bank building and hired many of its former employees, including head cashier George Simpson. But Girard's bank was in no way the Bank's replacement. For starters, Girard's bank had no branches, no charter, state or federal, and a much smaller capitalization. Furthermore, it was not the government's depository, was under no obligation to lend to any government, and had no responsibility to other banks or the national economy. In short, the U.S. no longer had a central bank. Could the golden goose survive this new test, a banking and credit system with no central regulating body?

The question whether the goose would survive with one of its major organs missing would soon be answered in the negative. The financial system was not yet large or mature enough to go it alone, especially in the face of wartime conditions. Jefferson's trade restrictions had greatly weakened the economy; the nation was unprepared for war when it finally came in early 1812. The nation desperately needed cash to build an army, a navy, and coastal defenses. But the federal government had precious little specie and its credit standing, strong just a few years before, was now so feeble that investors, fearful of default, avoided government bonds. Moreover, sectional antagonisms threatened to tear the Union asunder. Most New Englanders protested against the war and traded with the enemy via Canada. As the war progressed and victory seemed increasingly unlikely, the nation's financial crisis mounted.

Secretary of the Treasury Albert Gallatin was in a pinch for funds. He therefore turned to the Bank of Stephen Girard for a loan of some $500,000. With the application came two sweeteners, the promise of Treasury deposits, and Gallatin's word that he would attempt to influence the Pennsylvania legislature to view the expansion plans of Girard's bank more favorably. Thus far, the state banks had used their influence in the state capital to block Girard's proposals. By agreeing to the loan, Girard could kill two birds with one stone—attract lucrative Treasury deposits and get the legislature to back down. But Girard wanted yet more. He asked Gallatin to place his private bank on the same level as all other banks. That meant that Gallatin would have to cancel some preexisting special agreements with two of the other Philadelphia banks. Gallatin balked at this last concession and for the time being the deal fell apart. But Gallatin's desperation grew deeper by the day. On February 20, 1813, the secretary floated a whopping $16 million bond issue. The bonds matured in twelve years and offered a 6 percent coupon that with special enticements effectively yielded investors 7 percent. The $16 million was a gigantic sum, the single largest bond issue in the nation's history up to that time. The Treasury was sanguine because news from the war front was good. The U.S. had recently scored some naval victories, credible reports of Napoleon's defeat in Russia were streaming in, and peace talks with the British appeared to be going well. But the bond issue flopped; investors subscribed for only about 25 percent of the sum offered, or $4 million.

Treasury Secretary Gallatin was in a bind, out of money and out of time, so he was willing to make a deal. European financier David Parish promised to underwrite about $2 million. Added to the $4 million already subscribed, about $10 million remained to be sold. Now Gallatin turned to Girard to assist in underwriting the bonds, and our saint worked his magic. He again pressed Gallatin to treat his bank on equal terms. If Gallatin agreed, then Girard would join a syndicate with Parish and wealthy New Yorker John Jacob Astor that promised to sell an amazing $10 million in bonds. Gallatin knew that the golden goose was gaunt with hunger. It needed this infusion. So he agreed to Girard's terms, which of course also included a generous sales commission.

Girard and the rest of the syndicate upheld their end of the bargain, underwriting the phenomenal sum of money. Girard kept just a little over $1,200,000 in bonds for himself and retailed off the rest at a tidy profit. The syndicate demonstrated that specialized private sector firms were better at selling government bonds than the government itself. Everyone, except New Englanders and the British, won. American investment banking was born, the government received the funds it needed to carry on the war, and investors received a fair yield.

Perhaps most importantly of all, the episode exposed the chaotic nature of the U.S. wartime financial system. Most Americans, and even some anti-bank politicians, saw the need for a new central bank.

Unfortunately for Girard, the state banks still dogged him every chance they got; his opponents were determined and had many legislators in their pocket. But as all saints do, Girard persevered. He had risked his life to save victims of the yellow fever; now, he risked his business to save victims of his own political party. In the process, he resuscitated the financial system and brought to America a whole new type of financial endeavor, investment banking. Indeed, the parallels between what Girard accomplished in 1813–14 and what investment banker J. P. Morgan did to stave off panic in 1907 are striking. Both were among the richest men in the country and both used their personal credit, their professional reputation, and their financial acumen to head off disaster at a time when the nation suffered from the lack of a central banking authority.

It was a good thing that Girard intervened when he did or the financial system may have died soon after the British set fire to Washington in August 1814. Indeed, the resulting panic forced banks outside of New England to suspend specie payments. (New England's illicit trade with the enemy kept its bank coffers full.) Specie suspension was the first step downward on the slippery slope to economic ruin. What the nation needed was a new central bank, so that is precisely what Girard and other financial capitalists, like Astor and Parish, pushed for.

Treasury Secretary Gallatin and a few select others sailed off to Europe to negotiate for peace on behalf of the U.S. government, and he eventually resigned his post as Treasury secretary. His replacement at the Treasury was none other than Philadelphian James Alexander Dallas, one of Girard's few friends. Dallas, Girard, and others urged Congress to incorporate a new Bank of the United States. In the meantime, Girard, in exchange for Treasury deposits, began to make a market (buy and sell to brokers) in Treasury notes. In short, Girard and his private bank began to serve some of the functions of the old central bank, prompting one biographer to label him the "Rothschild of America."

But Girard knew that his resources were insufficient to go it alone. Though far richer than Robert Morris had ever been, Girard's wealth was not as large a percentage of the economy as Morris's had been. Girard therefore could not by himself shoulder all of the Republic's finances the way that Morris, with Haym Salomon's help, had done during the Revolution. But that did not mean that Girard was powerless. He drafted a plan for a new central bank and presented it to Congress. By the time it emerged from committee and went to the floor for a vote, the bill was greatly changed. Committeemen had made multiple alterations, many of which Girard detested. The revised bill did not restore the specie standard and was little more than an attempted revenue grab. Girard was therefore pleased when Madison vetoed his mutilated brainchild.

The War of 1812 ended, as all wars eventually do. But the financial system was on a shaky foundation. So Girard and Dallas again pressed for the incorporation of a new central bank. With the aid of future Vice President John C. Calhoun, the "yeas" carried the day. On April 10, 1816, Madison signed into law a national charter for the second Bank of the United States. Like the first Bank of the United States, the government would have 20 percent ownership in the institution, but this time the capital would be $35 million instead of $10 million. Hamilton's creation had been renewed, three and a half times larger! And here is the irony of our story. Republicans, from Girard to Gallatin, and Madison to Calhoun, created a *second* Bank of the United States. Republicans, we daresay most Republicans, loved banks so long as they were under their control. In this case, Republicans created far and away the largest bank in the country.

Minus the government's stake, private ownership of the Second Bank amounted to $28 million. Unlike the mad scramble for shares of the First Bank, the IPO of the Second Bank stumbled, falling $3 million short of the mark. State banks as competitors of course were ecstatic, hopeful that the new Bank would be unable to commence operations. But again a syndicate headed by Girard stepped in to underwrite the deal. A mix of patriotism, astute business sense, and the profit motive had again saved the day. Girard profited handsomely. Jealous and unthinking types complained, but most Americans agreed that he who fattens the goose deserves his share of its golden produce.

Girard was not entirely happy with the new bank. Instead of following his recommendation to issue national notes redeemable at any branch, the Bank's board decided that each branch would issue its own notes. Girard also thought it unsafe and unfair for the Bank to extend preferential loan treatment to stockholders, many of whom borrowed from the bank to pay the installments due on their shares of stock! Girard also feuded with William Jones, the Bank's too-oft-intoxicated president. Accordingly, Girard resigned his directorship and in 1818–19 sold a large number of his shares. Soon after, the Bank helped to precipitate a financial panic that led to a sharp economic recession. Again, Girard had showed uncanny market timing.

But Girard was more than just a trader. He was also a financial innovator. That fact became most clear in 1823, when he bailed out the Schuylkill Navigation Company, which had run out of both cash and credit. Girard saved the company by inducing it to sell to him some $230,000 of convertible mortgage bonds. It was the perfect hedge. If the company failed, Girard would own the Schuylkill River and its improvements. If the company plodded along, he would earn interest on the bonds. If the company thrived, he would convert the bonds to stock and make yet another large profit. Although convertibles had been used previously in England, and even once before in Pennsylvania, no one had yet invested in the relatively new asset class on such a large scale. Clearly, Girard was on the cutting edge of financial development. As it turned out, the Schuylkill Navigation Company survived and continued servicing its debt to Girard and eventually to his estate.

Girard made many other spectacular deals in his lifetime, and at least one that paid off handsomely after he was gone. While serving as receiver for the First Bank's assets, Girard noticed that the Bank had come into ownership of huge tracts of Pennsylvania lands that John Nicholson and Robert Morris had pledged as collateral on some promissory notes that they never paid. Those fifty-odd square miles attracted little interest, but Girard inquired and found that coal had been discovered under them. When the lands went to auction, he purchased them and then proceeded to buy off squatters' claims. It turned out to be the best deal he ever made because the lands were rich in anthracite. Many an orphan benefited from the stream of cash that those coal lands generated.

Our saint also excelled in agriculture. During the turmoil of the embargoes and war with Britain, he decided to enter the booming "truck" business that furnished Philadelphia with fresh fruit, vegetables, and fattened beef and pork. Eschewing common garden varieties, Girard told his plantation managers to cultivate such exotics as artichokes, muscat grapes, French cauliflower, apricots, and Anjou pears. Girard could not return to France, but he was rich enough to buy part of France and grow it in the Delaware Valley! After a series of managers stumbled, mostly because they were unable to discipline the Irish farm hands, Girard personally superintended each afternoon, rain or shine. No stranger to hard work, he even did some of the manual labor himself. A pen in his hand all morning, a hoe or shovel all afternoon, this workaholic ran his plantation for profit, but he did allow himself the indulgence of beautiful flower gardens. The Horticultural Society of Pennsylvania praised his efforts, calling his pear orchard "second to none in the country," and urged others to imitate some of his methods. Unlike his mercantile practices and financial dealings, which he kept strictly secret, Girard, like many "scientific" gentlemen farmers in the era, freely shared his agricultural discoveries with the world.

The physical exertion and pleasurable time spent tending his gardens may have prolonged Girard's life. Considered an "old man" from his late twenties onward, Girard nevertheless proved quite robust, surviving into his eighties. He finally succumbed to influenza in 1831 on the day after Christmas. During his final decades he had witnessed the golden goose grow from gosling to magnificent bird. When it fell victim to the Republicans and the British, he nurtured it as he had so many victims of the yellow fever. Before he died, he saw it again grow and help the economy to prosper. By the time he died, the Philadelphia region already possessed an important, modernizing industrial economy. Girard himself developed as much as the region's economy. He began his career in the style of a traditional, if eminently successful, merchant. He ended it as a new breed of merchant, a purveyor of capital and credit. He foreshadowed the great investment banks of the late nineteenth century and helped to introduce Americans to the wonders of hybrid securities like convertible mortgage bonds.

But Girard would not want to be remembered only for his financial acumen. During the yellow fever epidemic he risked his life to nurse those abandoned by their friends, families, and masters. We close, therefore, with a resolution that the Philadelphia City Council adopted after hearing of our saint's death:

> The goodness of his heart was not manifested by ostentatious subscription or loud profession; but when pestilence stalked abroad, he risked his life to preserve from its ravages the most humble of his fellow-citizens, and wherever sorrow, unaccompanied by immorality, appeared at his door, it was thrown wide open.

Not all early financiers, however, were so good of heart. Some, like William Duer, were true scoundrels. Although the golden goose doesn't care *who* is delivering its dinner, it does care about what's in the bucket: it is very picky about the *quality* of the food it eats. The Duers of this world, who try to profit by delivering its grain late, or not at all, or adulterated with sticks, pebbles, and chaff, may gain a temporary advantage. But what they fail to understand is that they do not own the goose, or hold it captive. The goose is penned in no-one's yard. It is free to roam, and to choose what, and where, and from whom it will eat. Girard, and others like him, know that the way to get an abundance of golden eggs is to provide the goose with top-quality grain.

By the time of Girard's death, Americans were demonstrably better off, in material terms anyway, than they had been when Hamilton fell at Weehawken over twenty-five years earlier, and they were leaps and bounds ahead of the position they held when Haym Salomon succumbed to tuberculosis in 1785. But the gains were not shared equally. Some, like Willing and Girard, thrived while others, including Duer and Morris, lost their all. Most landed somewhere in between. The result was that as the financial system waxed strong, and as the size, population, and economic output of the nation grew, so too did the economic and social distance between the wealthiest of the wealthy and the poorest of the poor.

Americans were quite content to live in a system that created such large discrepancies of wealth as long as they were convinced that the outcomes were truly based on merit. A meritocratic system, they believed, was far superior to European or Asian systems where the luck of parentage, plunder, or political patronage determined one's fate. But how could the typical American be certain that he was playing a fair game on a level field? With each passing year, the nation grew larger and more complex and so it became easier to imagine conspiracies of bankers and politicians rigging the game in their favor. If enough people came to believe that distant cabals kept them from their fair share of the golden eggs, it would be tempting to seek restitution by disregarding property rights, perhaps through taxation, perhaps by force, but either way, all would be lost. By the 1830s, many Americans needed a signal that the wealth acquisition game was indeed being fairly played. An Old Hero gave them just what they sought.

Andrew Jackson (1767–1845) &
Nicholas Biddle (1786–1844)

In the early 1830s the centerpiece of the financial system, the second Bank of the United States, came under vicious attack from President Andrew Jackson. Created by Republicans in 1816, the Second Bank, like its predecessor, enjoyed a unique charter from the federal government that lasted for twenty years. But Jackson vanquished all he faced. Nicholas Biddle, president of the Second Bank, blundered into Jackson's path and both he and his institution suffered the consequences.

Skirmishes in the metaphorical "Bank War" commenced soon after Jackson's inauguration in 1829. The war turned hot in 1832 when Biddle asked Congress for an extension of his Bank's charter, which was due to expire in 1836. Though forewarned by his lieutenants to postpone the fight, Biddle's arrogance got the better of him. All seemed well at first. The Bank's forces figuratively stormed Capitol Hill, took it, and induced Congress to pass a recharter bill. But to control Washington, the Bank's soldiers would also have to seize the White House. Biddle should have known that Jackson was not accustomed to having his positions overrun, particularly when he held the high ground. And the Constitution put him atop a veritable mountain by providing him with a potent but as yet rarely utilized weapon, the executive veto.

In summer 1832, Jackson used that weapon to crush the bill extending the Second Bank's charter. But the war was not yet won because the Bank still had plenty of opportunity to gain legislative sanction before its original charter expired four years hence. So Jackson turned the so-called "Bank question" into a plank in his reelection campaign that fall, arguing that a vote for him was a vote against the Bank, and that a vote for his opponent, Henry Clay, was a vote for the Bank. Jackson told his running mate, Martin Van Buren, that "the Bank is trying to kill me, but I will kill it." Jackson meant it, and he was right. Moreover, during the struggle, firebrand advocates of "hard money" who wanted to do away with all banknotes, and perhaps even all banks, gained leverage in the Jackson camp. The survival of the financial system again hung in the balance. Would the U.S. financial system face apocalyptic political pressures?

Before answering those questions, we must delve into the backgrounds of the Bank War's two leading generals. The more fascinating, of course, was Jackson. Many students of history are familiar with the basics—his portrait adorns the $20 Federal Reserve notes to honor his stunning victory in the Battle of New Orleans, his many victories in the Seminole War, and his two terms as president. He exuded physical and emotional strength as his nicknames "Old Hickory" and "Old Hero" attest.

The usual story is that Jackson abhorred banks, bankers, and banknotes and embarked on a personal vendetta to extinguish them. All that is true, but in the final analysis Jackson squelched the Bank because he believed that it was unconstitutional. He clearly stated that "congress has no constitutional power to grant a charter" despite the fact that in 1819, in the case *McCulloch v. Maryland*, the U.S. Supreme Court upheld the Bank's constitutionality. Not everyone, and certainly not Jackson, yet recognized the Court as the supreme and final arbiter of constitutional law. Jackson believed that each part of the federal government had the right and the duty to uphold its own view of the Constitution. In other words, the executive branch did not have to bend to the dictates of judges. That way, Jackson reasoned, a few men with lifetime tenure could not possibly tyrannize the nation. In reaction to one unpopular Supreme Court decision, which protected the Cherokees from forcible removal from North Carolina, Jackson in effect said Chief Justice John Marshall had made his decision, now let him try to enforce it. Little wonder, then, that political opponents dubbed Jackson "King Andrew."

The cause of the Bank's demise turns out to be crucial to our story. Had the public perceived that Jackson's tiff with the Bank was purely personal, the golden goose would have suffered much more than it actually did. Think of it— a president destroying an important component of the financial system out of personal animus. Such an action would not have boded well for the future of the republic or its rapidly maturing economy. After all, it was an article of faith in early America that there could be no proper and steady incitement to industry where political whims, rather than hard work and market forces, ruled. A president defending a version of the Constitution that limited the size of the federal government, kept taxes low, and minimized business graft, on the other hand, was a positive signal indeed.

The notion that Jackson had Constitutional scruples is a bitter pill for some to swallow because they, like many of Jackson's contemporaries, see Old Hickory as a brutal, uneducated frontiersman. While Jackson certainly was not as polished as a John Quincy Adams, as crafty as a Martin Van Buren, or as stunning an orator as a John Calhoun, he did possess a keen strategic mind. Moreover, it turns out that among his strong Constitutional sensibilities was a belief that the Federal government could not rightfully charter corporations outside of Washington, D.C. But Jackson's Constitutional thinking has largely been lost to posterity because the other aspects of his life are more engaging. In fact, his biographers usually cannot lay down their pens until they have cranked out several long volumes detailing every facet of this intriguing man's life. We cannot help but to touch on a few of the highlights.

Jackson dueled repeatedly, took bullets, and somehow, perhaps by the grace of God, survived. His first victim was Charles Dickinson, a fellow hothead. Though a bit of a dandy, Dickinson had the reputation for being the best shot in all of Tennessee. He therefore thought little of publicly calling Jackson a "coward," an "equivocator," and a "worthless scoundrel" after Jackson belittled Dickinson's father-in-law during a dispute over a horse race wager. Dickinson aimed to injure Jackson's reputation and creditworthiness while using his own reputation as a crack shot to induce Jackson to suffer the calumny without retaliating. But Jackson quickly issued a formal challenge to duel. The pair met just over the border in Kentucky, loaded their pistols, and took marks just eight yards apart. Were it not well documented, what happened next would surely be dismissed as apocryphal.

Jackson's second, General Thomas Overton, gave the signal to fire. Dickinson fired first. His ball found Jackson's chest. Thanks to divine providence, or the baggy clothing Jackson wore, the bullet missed his foe's heart. Dickinson, dazed with disbelief, strayed from his mark. Overton returned him to it while Jackson, teeth clenched, took deliberate aim. His ball passed clear through Dickinson, who bled to death on the field. Jackson staggered away with Dickinson's ball embedded near his heart, where it remained until his death nearly forty years later.

In the meantime, Jackson had a lot of fight left in him. In September 1813, he and a small band of compatriots scuffled with Thomas Hart Benton and his brother Jesse because Jackson had been the second in a ludicrous duel where Jesse took a bullet in his posterior. Harsh words and oaths were exchanged. Jackson tried to horsewhip Thomas, but did not get in any good licks before Jesse hit him in the arm and shoulder with a blast from a pistol. Every physician in Nashville save one recommended amputating Jackson's arm, which was thoroughly shattered. Just before he slipped into unconsciousness due to blood loss, Jackson blurted "I'll keep my arm." No doctor dared draw his saw after that comment.

Jackson was bedridden for three weeks but kept his arm, which remained laden with shrapnel until the pieces were removed by a surgeon, without anesthesia or even an hour's respite from his duties as president, some twenty years later. The Bentons, fearful of the wrath of Jackson and his "puppies," fled to Missouri, where they continued to make trouble. In 1823, while both were serving in the U.S. Senate, Jackson and Benton made peace, and by the outbreak of the Bank War the president could count on his former foe as an ally. Jesse and his bruised bottom, however, never forgave Old Hickory.

Shortly before the costly scuffle with the Bentons, the massacre of 250 whites at Fort Mims signaled the opening of the Creek War. Westerners were outraged and frightened at the utter brutality of the slayings. The Indians killed the children and women in a particularly vicious fashion. Mobilization against the Indian threat was rapid. Jackson realized that he had to recuperate quickly so he could take personal command of his troops. On October 7, still pale and weak, his arm in a sling, Jackson joined his army at Fayetteville. Three days later, he marched his forces into Creek country and directed the cutting of a road and erection of forts as he went. On November 3, 1813, less than two months after almost losing an arm, Jackson ordered the destruction of an Indian village in retaliation for the Fort Mims massacre. Jackson's cavalry, which included famous frontiersman Davy Crockett, killed all 186 Indian men in the attack. The Tennesseans did not slaughter the Indian women and children, and in fact Jackson raised one young Indian boy orphaned in the attack as his own. But Jackson was not getting soft. During his military career he killed many more Indians, and as president he ordered the forced relocation of fifteen thousand Cherokees. The horrific scene that followed has been described as a "Trail of Tears."

Still, Jackson's military exploits showed unbelievable daring and courage. To prevent a mass desertion, for example, Jackson once ordered two cannon trained on the mutinous troops, then ordered their matches lit, all the while standing in the line of fire, hell's fury burning in his eyes. Sufficiently cowed, the troops returned to their posts without incident. His other military exploits, including the stunning victory at New Orleans, are well known.

Undoubtedly, Jackson enjoyed a good dose of luck or divine protection. He got luckiest in 1835 when both pistols of would-be assassin Richard Lawrence misfired. Perhaps Lawrence was too deranged to properly load his weapons.

But more than luck is needed to account for Jackson's business, military, and political careers. He must have been brighter than his detractors assumed.

A difficult question is where Jackson would rank among presidents on an intellectual scale. He certainly lacked the educational credentials of Wilson, the Roosevelts, the Adamses, Kennedy, or Clinton. But educational attainment is only one measure of intelligence. Old Hickory knew what he believed in and was confident in those beliefs. The problem was that, unlike, say, Madison, Adams, or Jefferson, Jackson did not present his ideas in a philosophical or systematic way. Moreover, he found spelling a challenge. In more than one instance, he spelled the same word four different ways, on the same page no less.

But all is not lost. Jackson faced several major Constitutional issues during his presidency. From his handling of each crisis, Jackson's profound Constitutional insights can be reconstructed. By far the most serious challenge to confront Jackson was the Nullification Crisis. Nullifiers were individuals who believed that each state government had the right, within its borders, to nullify, annul, or declare unconstitutional any federal law or mandate. This extreme version of states' rights doctrine was judicial review with a vengeance. Jackson, an advocate of a less extreme view of states' rights doctrine, could not countenance nullification. In December 1832, soon after South Carolinians, upset over the imposition of higher federal tariffs (import taxes), espoused nullification and hinted at secession, Jackson issued his so-called Nullification Proclamation. That cogent expression of Jacksonian Constitutional thought denied that states could disobey federal law and labeled any attempt at secession treasonous. Indeed Jackson once remarked that he would "die in the last Ditch" before he would "see the Union disunited." Given Jackson's past, and his immense popularity, such a threat could not be taken lightly. Most politicians, even those with nationalist beliefs, were so horrified at the thought of the Old Hero vanquishing South Carolina that they beseeched him to compromise. After the usual political shenanigans, a deal was eventually struck. The tariff was lowered, but not as much as the Nullifiers initially demanded. Most ominously, the compromise said nothing about the constitutionality of the nullification doctrine. The issue was allowed to fester and grow into the cancer that would later metastasize into civil war.

In all the excitement surrounding the Nullification Crisis, Jackson's vision of a moderate state rights' interpretation of the Constitution was lost. While Jackson thought nullification, as he put it in the Nullification Proclamation, "incompatible with the existence of the Union," he did not believe that the national government could do whatever it desired. Imposition of a tariff was clearly in its bailiwick. Sponsoring internal improvements, the construction of physical in-frastructure, was a grayer area. Jackson, like virtually all Americans, enthusias-tically supported the building of roads, canals, harbors, and other avenues of commerce and amity. The question, as always, was who should pay for it.

Jackson staunchly opposed use of federal monies to support merely local or regional improvement projects. He saw such projects as dangerous precedents that might allow the national government to one day redistribute large sums of wealth from one region to another or to balloon in size until it became an un-stoppable force of tyranny. So, he consistently vetoed internal improvement bills that were not clearly national in scope. Moreover, he thought it wrong to in-stitute a partnership between the government and private companies. That did not bode well for the Second Bank, which began its life 20 percent the property of the federal government.

By the 1830s, thanks to the continued growth and development of the Hamil-tonian system of finance, private enterprise no longer needed government aid to complete profitable projects. That was especially true after the repayment of the national debt. For reasonable ventures, long-term capital could be had from the equity and bond markets of Europe and America, and short-term financing was available from banks and commercial paper markets. A call for government aid meant that a project was not economically feasible, that to survive it had to feed from the public trough. Such projects, Jackson understood, benefited the few at the expense of the many.

Jackson's Constitutional scruples therefore led him to prefer allowing each state to make its own appropriations. Extinguishing the national debt thus be-came the solution to the internal improvement question. One of his first acts in office was to instruct Treasury Secretary Samuel Ingham to draw up a plan for extinguishing the debt. Jackson followed through on the plan and succeeded in paying off the debt in full, a feat that no sizable nation had ever before pulled off. With the national debt gone, the federal government began to run surpluses. Jackson distributed the surpluses to the several states for use as each saw fit. The effect was to further increase the credit of the U.S. government, state and mu-nicipal governments, and even private U.S. corporations.

Somewhat ironically, however, Jackson's administration appropriated more money for internal improvements than any previous administration had. The expenditures were for projects national in character, like lighthouses and ports, or to make repairs to Federal projects created during earlier administrations. Ports were national because trade followed river systems, not state boundaries. All the western states, for example, relied on New Orleans for access to world markets. And after completion of the Grand Canal, that great artificial river between Lake Erie and the Hudson River, the entire Great Lakes basin became Manhattan's hinterland. Ports, then, were national concerns. Lighthouses kept ships engaged in the extensive interstate coastal trade from running ashore. So they too, like the breakwater in Delaware Bay where hundreds of ships annually took refuge from gale winds and ice, were indisputably national concerns.

The lives of our creator, Alexander Hamilton, and our potential destroyer, Andrew Jackson, were remarkably similar in numerous important respects. Born in 1767, Jackson was also literally a bastard and, by his early teens, an orphan. Jackson was too young to see combat in the Revolution, but he did run messages for the Patriots. Legend has it that a British officer struck him in the head with a sword because the youngster would not deign to clean his boots. A few years later, the British officer would have thought twice before offering such an insult; by 1788, at age twenty-one, Jackson stood six-foot-one, a towering figure for the day. His long, lean body, combined with his sharp features, intense blue eyes, and bristling red hair, made him an imposing, almost frightening, figure. That year, Jackson headed west, ending up in what eventually became Tennessee.

Like Hamilton, Jackson was a self-made man from a lowly background who eventually made a decent but not opulent living as a lawyer, eventually bought a small country estate, and married a comely rich girl, Rachel Robards. The Robards, in fact, were to Nashville what the Schuylers were to Albany, a leading family. By coincidence, Jackson's wife's name was Rachel and his mother's Elizabeth; Hamilton's mother's name was Rachel and his wife's Elizabeth.

Although Jackson missed fighting in the first War for Independence, he seized the opportunity presented by the second, the War of 1812, to establish his military fame. Like Hamilton, Jackson eventually rose to the rank of general. Also like Hamilton, Jackson often took bold military and political risks and reaped the rewards of his many colorful and successful exploits.

In the sphere of personal finance, similarities between Hamilton and Jackson abound. Neither one ever made, and held, a fortune. According to some sources, Jackson made a mint in land speculation, buying up large tracts on the cheap, holding them until prices increased, then selling them. Unfortunately, however, Jackson often sold on credit rather than for cash and ended up losing a lot of his paper profits when buyers, like Philadelphian David Allison, went bust and defaulted on their notes and mortgages. Those defaults, in turn, strained Jackson's finances.

Both men were lawyers with private practices, Jackson eventually even becoming a judge on Tennessee's highest court. In 1804, however, he resigned his judgeship and turned to storekeeping, horse racing, cotton ginning, and private legal practice as a means of reducing his indebtedness. With help from his beloved wife, Jackson eventually regained his financial solvency, only to lose it again in the wake of the Panic of 1819, an economic downturn brought about in part by mismanagement of the second Bank of the United States. Both experiences left an emotional scar and a deep distrust of leverage, or in other words running a business on borrowed money.

Here, Hamilton and Jackson parted ways, but not so much so that at least one of Hamilton's sons could not later become an ardent Jacksonian. At the behest of fellow Jacksonian New Yorker Martin Van Buren, James A. Hamilton visited Nashville at the height of the 1828 presidential campaign to aid the Old Hero. The young Hamilton, who later briefly served as Jackson's interim secretary of state, also helped Jackson to draft the bank-related portion of his 1829 State of the Union address. As his father had done some four decades earlier, Hamilton pulled an all-nighter, but in this case to fire the first salvo in a Bank War, not to have the last word in a gentlemanly debate. The young Hamilton wrote that "both the constitutionality and the expediency of the law creating the bank are well questioned by a large portion of our fellow-citizens." That assertion may very well have been correct. But Hamilton's next claim was such an outrageous falsehood that scholars have generally dismissed the entire Bank-related part of the message as hyperbole. "It must be admitted by all," Hamilton wrote, "that it has failed in the great end of establishing a uniform and sound currency." In fact, the Bank had done much to keep state bank issues in check and to reduce and regularize the cost of remitting sums to different parts of the Union. None other than Albert Gallatin argued that "we know from the experience of nearly forty years, that so long as the Bank of the United States has been in operation we have had a sound currency." (Almost all serious scholarly studies written since have demonstrated the veracity of Gallatin's claim.)

James A. Hamilton was not his father. But one wonders if Alexander Hamilton had lived to a ripe old age what his relationship with Jackson would have been like. Ostensibly, by the 1830s Hamilton would have seen government debt crowding out private capital investment and hence backed Jackson's decision to pay off the national debt. In the 1790s, federal bonds were unique and important assets because they were perfectly safe and highly liquid. In a pinch, investors could remit them to Europe in lieu of specie or good bills of exchange. By the 1830s, states, cities, and business corporations had learned that they could raise money in national and even international capital markets. New York's canal bonds, for instance, were a good proxy for the federal debt because they were just as safe and just as much in demand. It is difficult to believe that Hamilton would have opposed shifting funds from the national debt to positive net present value projects like the Grand Canal.

It is virtually impossible to see Hamilton agreeing with Jackson on the bank issue. Jackson once told James A. Hamilton: "Colonel, your Father was not in favor of the Bank of the United States." The comment, which on the face of it is absurd, left the young Hamilton speechless. But it is remotely possible that what Jackson meant was that Alexander Hamilton would *no longer* favor the Bank. It is indeed difficult to see our creator as a destroyer of the Bank. But might Hamilton have used the opportunity presented by the Bank War to create a new, more modern institutional structure? Had he lived, presumably Hamilton would have continued his intense interest in finance and would have interacted extensively with the new nation's best political economists and financial theorists. Men like Isaac Bronson, Mathew Carey, Albert Gallatin, Alexander Bryan Johnson, Thomas Law, Eleazar Lord, John McVickar, Condy Raguet, and Daniel Raymond. Those men all had fine minds, but often times rather divergent views. And none had Hamilton's combination of genius, reputation, and intense logical analysis. Even an aged Hamilton may have been able to focus the debate and drive it to a higher plane.

Thanks in large measure to Hamilton's efforts, the financial system that Jackson inherited was vastly larger and more efficient than that facing Hamilton himself in the early 1790s. A handful of commercial banks had become hundreds. Life, fire, and marine insurance companies were now ubiquitous. Savings banks had emerged and the building and loan industry was just being born. Literally thousands of corporations had popped up, the vast majority of which tapped the capital markets through the sale of equities. Some had even issued negotiable bonds. Financial education, though still rudimentary, had suffused all levels of society. Indeed, by the early nineteenth century even girls' grade school primers discussed the basics of stocks, bonds, and interest.

All that finance fueled a dynamic, growing economy. Turnpikes, canals, improved rivers, and the new railroads moved raw materials like coal and timber, agricultural produce like wheat and cotton, and partially manufactured products like flour and pig iron from their sources to factories, urban markets, and seaports. Those same improvements moved people, the latest fashions, and finished manufactured products back to the nation's frontiers and hinterlands. And throughout the nation, it was thanks to the financial system that people could turn wheat seed into bread, iron ore into plows, standing timber into houses, barns, and factories.

While Hamilton would never have denied the federal government's right to charter a bank, it is possible that he may have realized that by the 1830s a privately owned national bank was no longer a necessity. Hamilton, after all, was a pragmatic realist, and in point of fact the country no longer *needed* a central bank. With the start provided by the Bank and the funding system in the 1790s and early 1800s, private enterprise had kicked into high gear. And by the 1830s, what a magnificent sight the financial system was to behold. Even biased British travelers could not help but be struck by the amazing differences between Canada and the U.S. We speak here not of the differences between Georgia and the Yukon, which for obvious climatic reasons are not readily comparable. Rather, we refer to the differences between western New York and Ontario's Niagara Peninsula. The two regions shared a climate and the same basic flora, fauna, and (in)fertility of land. But the east side of the Niagara River had Hamiltonian financial markets and the west side had none. The east side, the travelers pointed out, flourished while the west side lay languid and undeveloped. To this day, the west side is an underpopulated vacation area for New Yorkers and remains a watering hole for the east side's eager, thirsty college students.

Readers should also recall that Hamilton ultimately based his argument for the constitutionality of the Bank on its expediency. The Bank was constitutional because its existence was necessary for the government to exercise its sovereignty. The federal government, he persuasively argued, needed the Bank. But did it still need it in the 1830s? Or perhaps more to the point, the Bank was the optimal institution for the 1790s, when the new government was weak, specie scarce, and finance in America still in its infancy. But was it still the optimal policy choice in the 1830s, by which time the national government was considerably stronger, the per capita specie supply larger, and banking and finance now much better understood?

To better answer that question, we must turn to Nicholas Biddle, the Second Bank's longtime president. Valedictorian of his class at Princeton at the age of fifteen, Biddle was the scion of a Philadelphia family distinguished for its wealth and financial acumen. Stately, intelligent, polished, almost aristocratic in bearing, he was as much an intellectual as a banker. He was such a serious and diligent lad that his fellow classmates at Princeton dubbed him "Grammaticus." (He was so studious that he soon picked up a master's degree from Princeton as well.) Initially a staunch Federalist, Biddle prepared himself for life in the mercantile, legal, and political arenas. In 1804, he accepted an unpaid clerkship under U.S. minister to France John Armstrong. A handsome, even dashing young man at the time, Biddle found the three-year stint in war-torn Europe an enticing experience, to say the least. Despite his formal duties, Biddle found ample time to tour the continent. He was especially fond of its numerous museums and, of course, its young ladies. He traveled as far east as Greece before returning to Philadelphia after a brief stint as a clerk for James Monroe, the U.S. ambassador in London.

Upon his return to Philadelphia, Biddle set himself up as an attorney and a frequent contributor to the literary magazine the *Port Folio*. Within a few years Biddle was serving in the Pennsylvania legislature, editing the journals of the Lewis and Clark Expedition, and courting seventeen-year-old beauty Jane Craig *and* her mother, the recently widowed Margaret Craig. He flirted with both extensively, but the lure of youth he preferred over the attraction of maturity. After a short engagement and a prenuptial agreement designed to protect Jane's share of her father's estate for herself and her unborn children, the pair wed. The Craigs like the Biddles were well off; the marriage allowed Biddle to end his legal career and concentrate on politics, family life, literary affairs, the family farm at Andalusia, and Mrs. Craig's business.

After election to the state legislature, Biddle took concrete steps to further ensure the freedom and equality of all Americans by pushing forward proposals to establish free schools throughout the Commonwealth. Pennsylvania's constitution paid lip service to universal education, but the legislature had done nothing to encourage it. Biddle, who had studied the public education systems of New England and Europe, hoped to change that. His fellow legislators were unwilling to pay the political price of raising the necessary taxes, so Biddle's plan languished for a quarter of a century before Thomas H. Burrows was able to draw upon it. The same forces quashed Biddle's attempts to save Philadelphia's trade from the inroads made upon it by New York and Baltimore.

But perhaps his greatest effort Biddle extended on behalf of the first Bank of the United States. In 1811, his pro-Bank speech, which ran for three hours, established him as a leading authority on banking, currency, and government finance. Given in the Pennsylvania legislature, the speech had little bearing on the decision by Congress to squelch the Bank. But it did serve to expose the purely political reasons underlying the Bank's destruction because Biddle argued persuasively that banks were the saviors of the poor, not their oppressors. Bank credit, he argued, went to those most deserving of it and hence assured the intelligent and entrepreneurial that they could obtain the financing their businesses needed, regardless of their lowly social standing or lack of rapport with wealthy individuals. He also argued that it would be much easier for a cabal of wealthy gentry to corner the markets for gold and silver than for them to control the volume of banknotes. He pointed out that the convertible banknote system created a money supply more elastic than one based solely on the precious metals, and one much less prone to inflation than fiat government notes. But that very elasticity left unchecked by a powerful national institution would leave state banks free to issue too many notes on too little a reserve of specie. The results, he correctly predicted, would be disastrous. In a final blow, Biddle noted that the government was also stripping itself of its lender of last resort and its primary agent for making payments. Biddle the banker had arrived, but more than a decade of financial disarray would ensue before he had the opportunity to again demonstrate his profound understanding of money and finance.

In the meantime, during the War of 1812 and its aftermath, Biddle proved himself an outstanding gentleman farmer unafraid to attempt to increase the productivity of his land through extensive capital investment in tools and fertilizer. His strategy of intensive, "scientific" cultivation worked well, partly because of his farm's proximity to Philadelphia. Transportation costs were slight and prices for his vegetables, pigs, cows, and milk were relatively high and predictable.

At the war's end, Biddle broke with the Federalist Party over the Hartford Convention, a meeting of disgruntled Federalists who hinted that New England might best go it alone. He was far too staunch a nationalist to espouse secession. Accordingly, he fell in with the National Republican faction, the more commercial, nationalistic wing of Jefferson's party. The other, moderate states' rights wing of the party thought the Bank of the United States unconstitutional and hence blocked its recharter in 1811. The government's fumbling efforts to finance the War of 1812, however, proved to many that a national bank was, if not entirely constitutional, at least highly expedient. Moreover, Madison, who felt the matter had been determined by precedent, had more nationalist leanings than his good friend Jefferson did. Madison as a congressman voted against the first bill that would have established a national bank in 1791, but more for political reasons than constitutional scruples. As president, he signed a second bill in 1816 establishing a national bank because he hoped that his party would control the new institution.

Indeed, Jeffersonian Republicans did at first control the Second Bank. They botched up though by appointing an alcoholic political crony and former naval officer by the name of William Jones to run the enormous institution. Under Jones's inebriated leadership, the Second Bank played a major role in fomenting the Panic of 1819, then exacerbating the ensuing recession. Biddle of course applauded the formation of the Second Bank but lamented the choice of William Jones as its president. He grew yet more concerned when Stephen Girard, one of the government's directors, refused to serve another term in protest of the Bank's lax management under the drunken mariner. Biddle became livid when financial defalcations at the Bank's Baltimore branch became public and when it became clear that a group of speculators had almost broken the institution. Biddle therefore heartily welcomed his appointment as one of the Bank's public directors in January 1819. For the next twenty years, the fate of Biddle and the Bank became increasingly intertwined.

Biddle at this stage was merely a director, one of several score of men who helped the institution's new president, Langdon Cheves of Charleston, South Carolina, to rescue the Bank from insolvency. They did so by severely restricting the Bank's loans. That sudden curtailment of credit saved the Bank but brought on a financial panic that ruined the economy and the economic well-being of many Americans, including General Jackson, for several years.

Cheves was clearly the right man to save the Bank, but he was just as clearly not the man to make it grow and thrive. He sought to keep the Bank's balance sheet as small as possible, keeping a tight lid on the Bank's loans and other investments. The result was a very safe yet unprofitable institution with a small supply of notes in circulation. After the initial crisis passed, Biddle argued that by buying inland exchange orders for the domestic transfer of money of account in the west and selling them in the east, the Bank could easily provide the nation with an extensive yet safe currency based largely on the Bank's own account books. Cheves disagreed and kept credit tight, much to the chagrin of businessmen. Biddle spent most of his time on his farm and little in the boardroom.

The Bank's stockholders grew impatient for dividends, which the Bank had stopped paying in 1818. Cheves buckled, announcing in January 1821 a 1.5 percent dividend. Biddle was outraged because he believed that the Bank had not yet made back the money it had lost during the crisis. Nobody appreciated Biddle's comments. When his commission expired at the end of 1821, it looked like Biddle's banking career was at an end. But within a year he managed to become president of the institution.

By late summer 1822, Cheves had had enough and announced that he would not seek reelection at the stockholder meeting that November. Nominations for Cheves's successor were immediately solicited, and Biddle's name was among those mentioned, but the former director remained a dark horse candidate at best. But as so often happens in politics, early front runners knocked each other out of the race. Then President James Monroe and Secretary of the Treasury William Crawford let it be known that they backed Biddle. That was enough for the stockholders, who obligingly voted in a slate of directors who promised to appoint Biddle to the Bank's top post.

Biddle, who had been looking for a major point of entry into public life, heartily accepted and immediately set to work introducing the reforms that Cheves had rejected just a year before. The Bank extended its discounts and used its extensive system of branches to reduce the cost of both domestic and foreign exchange. Within six months of his taking office, the price of inland exchange had fallen considerably, credit loosened, and the economy experienced a much needed expansion.

Under Biddle, the Bank's branches functioned like a giant clearinghouse, based in part on the Bank's own internal bookkeeping and in part on its dealings of bills of exchange and inland drafts. In Mississippi in 1832, the heyday of Biddle's system, one could purchase a draft on just about any location in the United States for at most a 1 percent premium. (After the destruction of the Bank, inland or domestic exchange, the price of making payments in distant domestic places, soared to as high as a 10 percent premium and at times could not be obtained at all, making one wonder if purely self-interested opposition to the Bank may have come from exchange arbitrageurs throughout the nation as well as Wall Street bankers!)

Biddle's Bank, as the Second Bank came to be called because of Biddle's almost complete control of the institution for over a decade, essentially regulated the national money supply. The Bank soon became the nation's largest dealer in bills of exchange. It used its large overseas credit lines to keep exchange rates below that which would induce merchants to remit specie instead of bills of exchange. Keeping specie in the nation's bank vaults prevented rapid decreases in the money supply that could lead to spikes in real interest rates and financial panics.

Similarly, by promptly redeeming notes at the institution of issue, the Bank kept state banks in check. When the Bank's branch at Natchez, Mississippi opened in 1831, for instance, Mississippi's only state bank had to cease lending operations. Each day a representative of the Bank showed up at its counters, a fistful of the state bank's notes in one hand, the other hand outstretched in anticipation of a golden reward—actual gold coins from the bank's vault. Soon, the state bank's stockholders voted to liquidate the concern rather than slowly go broke at the hands of the much larger and more efficient national bank that could deplete its vaults of its small amount of gold.

By the 1830s, the Bank was *the* major financial force in the Mississippi Valley, and that mighty drainage system was *the* major economic influence on the Bank. Its New Orleans branch was its most important; the branch at Natchez was larger than that of Boston. (Purportedly, more millionaires graced Natchez in the 1830s than any other city in America. Of course by later standards it was all tainted wealth.) In East Coast cities, including Philadelphia, the Bank was a major but not dominant player. In contrast, it pretty much ruled the money, exchange, and credit markets of the vast West. Planters, cotton factors, and exchange dealers relied heavily on the Bank's branches to fund their operations. When the Bank began to withdraw capital from the West following Jackson's veto in 1832, the Mississippi Valley suffered most.

Though head and shoulders above his predecessors in the Second Bank, Biddle was far from perfect and probably inferior to Thomas Willing and David Lenox, presidents of the First Bank. Biddle failed to see that each branch had to conduct its business a little differently in order to meet local conditions. He also sometimes misunderstood the nature of certain financial instruments. His shortcomings all stemmed from the fact that his understanding of banking was largely theoretical, and not based on job experience or personal inspection of his Bank's numerous branches. His relative lack of mercantile experience, a deficiency noted at the time of his election, was mostly to blame for his mistakes.

But the strengths of Biddle and his Bank outweighed their weaknesses. One of the Bank's major strengths was its ability and willingness to act as a lender of last resort. By lending freely at the outset of a crisis, it averted the financial panic that ensued when interest rates appeared poised to surge uncontrollably upward. Such spikes caused businesses to go bankrupt and reduced the market price of all assets, financial and tangible. Biddle understood that interest rates had to be brought to heel or they would send the economy spiraling downward as in the years after 1819.

Biddle, as Willing had done, used his Bank's power to serve the greater good. As John Sergeant noted at the last meeting of the Bank's stockholders: "When danger threatened, when credit was trembling, when confidence was shaken, whenever, in a word, a revulsion was threatened with its disastrous train of circumstances, this Bank, strong in its power, stronger in its inclination to do good, anticipated and averted the crisis." Biddle himself had often noted that the Bank had "to keep itself in such an attitude that at a moment's warning, it may interpose to preserve the state banks and the country from sudden dangers." Biddle and his Bank met their most difficult challenge in late 1825 when the Bank of England poked a hole in a speculative bubble. Britain lost 104 banks in the ensuing credit crunch, which also took down thousands of other British businesses.

Protested bills of exchange that brought about the failure of several New York and New Orleans merchants portended a spread of the contagion to America's shores. In a brilliant move, Biddle authorized the New York branch to increase discounts $50,000. Though small, the increase eased tensions. Like Alan Greenspan would do in 1987, Biddle used the power and prestige of his bank to stave off panic without actually doing much of anything other than signaling his intentions to infuse the system with funds if required. Even Hezekiah Niles, a foe of the Bank, praised Biddle for having the "great good sense" to extend the Bank's discounts in the community's hour of need. Thanks to Biddle, the Panic of 1825 barely grazed the golden goose or the nation's economy.

So Biddle's Bank, as Willing's had been, was a central bank because it implemented monetary policy and served as a lender of last resort. Unlike most modern central banks, however, it was a private institution. And that is why in Jackson's eye it had to die. Biddle, Hamilton, and Jackson all understood that a constitution was merely a piece of paper. What mattered was the implementation of a constitution's rules and its checks and balances. Where Biddle and Hamilton differed from Jackson was over the role of the Bank.

To Jackson, the Bank's enormous positive influence on the economy mattered not at all. The nation, he believed, was but a babe playing with fire. The federally sponsored turnpikes and canals that many desired would also have had a salubrious effect on the economy. But the price of that prosperity, the destruction of the Constitution as he understood it, Jackson believed to be far too high.

Moreover, Jackson was a fighter, and his blood was up. And as we know, he was no friend to banks. He had been burned in the recession that followed the Panic of 1819 because he was over-leveraged. Like many failed businessmen in the era, he blamed his creditors, including his bankers, for his lack of business luck and financial prowess. He also disliked banknotes and wished to see the money stock composed mostly of specie, with credit instruments like banknotes and bank deposits relegated to large business transactions only. Most importantly, he distrusted the influence of banks in elections. As we saw "In the Beginning," the Manhattan Bank was responsible, at the margin, for Jefferson's election to the presidency. Banks played influential roles in many state elections as well. Worst of all, Jackson believed that some branches of the Second Bank had expended considerable sums in favor of John Quincy Adams in the 1828 presidential election.

Jackson was above all a democrat. Almost all Americans sought material prosperity. A majority favored banks. Indeed before 1832 a majority favored the rechartering of the Second Bank. But when push came to shove, they wanted

Jackson more than the Bank. In the 1832 presidential election, Americans voted overwhelmingly for Jackson and, by explicit extension, against the Bank. The Bank's charter would not officially expire until 1836, but for all intents and purposes, Jackson's reelection sealed its fate.

The Bank was in some ways a victim of its own success. Under Biddle, the Bank became an extremely efficient financial machine that helped to drive a decade of almost uninterrupted economic growth and financial development. Things were running so smoothly that it was not unreasonable to think that perhaps the Bank could be replaced, with a more constitutional national institution or maybe a phalanx of state banks, without causing much if any damage to the economy. Indeed, in his first annual address to Congress, Jackson wondered aloud if a government-owned bank "might not be devised which would avoid all constitutional difficulties, and at the same time secure all the advantages to the Government and country that were expected to result from the present bank." Jackson openly told Biddle that he did not believe that "the power of Congress extends to charter a Bank out of the ten mile square" (i.e., Washington, D.C.). Again in his second annual address to Congress, Jackson noted that "it becomes us to inquire whether it be not possible to secure the advantages afforded by the present bank through the agency of a Bank of the United States so modified in its principles and structures as to obviate Constitutional and other objections."

Biddle had taken a gamble and, like all of Jackson's foes, lost. Jackson had explicitly warned him not to make the Bank an issue in the 1832 presidential election. But Biddle took the warning as a sign of weakness and pressed the attack. Enraged at Biddle's audacity, Jackson played the class card. He made clear that he saw little difference between the Bank and the numerous local internal improvement projects that he had nixed because both unfairly enriched the few at the expense of the many. The Old Hero made clear that could not occur. In his Bank Veto message, Jackson regretted "that the rich and powerful too often bend the acts of government to their selfish purposes." "Every man," he argued, "is equally entitled to protection by the law; but when the laws undertake to add to these natural and just advantages artificial distinctions, to grant titles, gratuities, and exclusive privileges, to make the rich richer and the potent more powerful, the humble members of society—the farmers, mechanics and laborers— who have neither the time nor the means of securing like favors to themselves, have a right to complain of the injustice of their Government." A powerful man in a powerful position looking out for the little guy's interests. In an era when firms grew ever larger (though still small by today's standards) and workers were emerging as a distinct class, rather than a life-cycle phase, that was just what many Americans wanted to hear.

A struggle between two uncompromising, implacable foes, the Bank War was a contest that Nicholas Biddle and his Bank never had a chance to win. Jackson, like Jefferson, thought the Bank unconstitutional. Unlike Washington, Jackson could not be swayed by the logic of Hamiltonian nationalists, especially now that the Bank's necessity was empirically in doubt. Nor did the initial popularity of the Bank influence him. The Constitution did not expressly allow the federal government to establish a corporation national in scope. The government did need a fiscal agent, but not necessarily one in the form taken by Hamilton's bank or its successor. After all, Jackson was not opposed to central banking in principle. Had events played out slightly differently, he might have supported the creation of a new, federally chartered bank located in Washington. That bank might even have had branches where requested by state governments. But that outcome was not to be.

Certain that he was right, and that the American people had spoken, Jackson moved in for the kill, as he had done so many times before. He ordered the Treasury Department to withdraw the national government's deposits from the Second Bank and place them in so-called "pet banks," state-chartered banks loyal to the Jackson administration. He also ordered the federal government to accept only gold and silver coins in return for its lands. Both of those sudden drastic commands shocked the economy.

Biddle should have responded as he had in 1825, adding liquidity to the system to calm investors' nerves. But he stopped acting as the nation's central banker, seeking only to save himself and his institution. Instead of extending credit, he curtailed it drastically, hoping to induce a recession that would force Americans, and Jackson, to beg for mercy. The golden goose was caught in the crossfire. But it proved more durable than both the arrogant Biddle and the irascible Jackson.

After the war between Biddle and Jackson, the U.S. economy entered into six years of the worst economic conditions that it had seen since the darkest days of the American Revolution. Some scholars deny any direct causal connection between Jackson's policies and the depression, placing blame instead on the actions of the Bank of England, international gold flows, a decline in cotton prices, and an overextension of credit during the heady days of the 1830s. In short, they point to the business cycle and the notion that an economic boom must be followed by a bust. But many scholars, even in some cases those otherwise favorable to Jackson, lay blame for the depression squarely on the shoulders of Jacksonian economic and bank policies, an interpretation first hatched by Jackson's political enemies. Truth be told, Biddle was as much to blame. Out of the ruins of the Second Bank he created a new institution, the United States Bank of Pennsylvania. He quickly ran his new bank into bankruptcy, dragging a slew of other companies with it. The debacle undoubtedly deepened the depression.

The controversy surrounding the causes of the depression of 1837–43 cannot be settled here. There is general agreement, though, that the depression was a deep one. By one estimate, the nation's gross domestic product (GDP—the market value of goods and services produced) peaked at $1.84 billion in 1836, but dropped 12.5 percent to $1.61 billion by 1843. Not until 1846 did it top the $2 billion mark. Moreover, because the nation's population was growing quickly in those years, analysis of per capita GDP paints an even bleaker picture. In 1836, each American produced on average $119 of goods and services. By 1843 that figure had plummeted to $85, a decrease of over 28 percent. Not until 1853 did per capita income exceed the record set in 1836, but growth thereafter was extremely rapid, with per capita income reaching $153 in 1857 before a sharp but mercifully short recession again sent incomes downward.

The depression's effects on different regions of the country are more difficult to ascertain with any degree of precision. The Bank's exit from the Mississippi Valley, where it was a major force, certainly hurt westerners at first, but state-chartered banks soon cropped up from Ohio to Louisiana. Jackson's policies did not permanently destroy any bank capital but rather encouraged it to shift to local banks. In some states, the transition proceeded quickly and easily. In others, it did not, usually because local political factions opposed banking. From the point of view of Jackson and other advocates of states' rights, that was a good outcome because important decisions about political economy were made where they should have been—in state capitals, not Washington.

Such dire trials threatened to bring Hamilton's financial system to an ignominious end. But the golden goose had grown from gosling to magnificent bird. Though damaged by the Bank War, it was mature enough to survive the carnage. It soon recovered and again drove the engines of economic growth. For example, though shorn of both the first and second Bank of the United States (as institutions—their marble edifices stand to this day), the Philadelphia region continued to grow and develop, fueled by its banks and securities markets. By 1850 Philadelphia, though sailing ships and steamers still used its Port Richmond docks, had essentially been transformed into an industrial center.

Through stocks, bonds, and bank loans, the credit markets financed Philadelphia's metamorphosis. Breweries, icehouses, and a large variety of mills, all made possible by our creator's financial and legal innovations, dotted the city and the surrounding countryside. Infrastructure, much of it privately owned and all of it financed by the golden goose, tightly bound together the regional economy. Railroads leading far into the interior flanked both sides of the canalized Schuylkill River. Bridges spanned the Schuylkill and the narrower parts of the Delaware; ferries and steamers handled the rest. Private roads known as turnpikes crisscrossed the Delaware valley, connecting city to hinterland, river to river, and market to market. Finished goods of considerable variety and value traversed those sundry avenues of commerce.

Just northwest of the city, Manayunk's industrialists, with help from the financial markets, tapped both upstate coal deposits and the Schuylkill River to power mills that produced cottons and woolens, flour, and paper. The district, which grew rapidly after 1819, was home to some seven thousand persons, almost all of whom found employ in the mills or in the furnaces and machine shops that helped to keep them running. Beyond Manayunk lay the limestone deposits and marble quarries of the Spring Mill area. Next came Conschocken, with its sheet iron mill, anthracite furnaces, and marble mill. To the northeast of that industrial town lay Montgomery County, "one of the richest and most favorably situated counties in Pennsylvania," according to one contemporary. By 1850 that county boasted of 30 merchant mills, 20 paper mills, 35 oil mills, 12 clover mills, 8 marble mills, 12 powder mills, some 15 iron works, 25 cotton factories, 10 woolen factories, 35 tanneries, and 12 fulling mills. Devoid of major rivers, several turnpikes, counted among the best in the nation, linked its farms and factories to Philadelphia, New York, and the world.

In the decades between the War of 1812 and the Civil War, similar transformations occurred throughout the North and in some parts of the South. Thanks to the rapidly maturing financial system, Americans could loosen nature's constraints in innumerable ways. They could cut artificial rivers over vast distances, build roads over, around, or through mountains, bring scattered raw materials together in one centralized place for processing and assembly, and sell the finished products across town or on the other side of the world. The financial system ensured that, more often than not, profitable projects got funding and unprofitable ones did not.

America would be a little richer today if the economy had not suffered such a major setback between 1837 and 1843 and everything else had remained the same. We will never know, though, if Biddle and his Bank could have staved off depression, or at least ameliorated the downturn. We will also never know if recharter of the Bank would have increased the odds that America would have experienced significant class upheaval in the nineteenth century. Compared to most Western European countries, the United States did not have a viable socialist political party or a strong social safety net. Attempts to explain those cru-cial facts abound, but we believe that Jackson's victory in the Bank War was a major contributor to the country's relatively tight embrace of free market capi-talism. The veto took place at a critical period in the country's economic devel-opment, after the shackles of tradition had been removed but before new mores and institutions had crystallized. Unlike many other peoples, Americans acqui-esced in economic modernization relatively quickly and quietly. They did so, we believe, because they thought that the country's institutions had created a level playing field where rewards went to the best and the brightest, not the best con-nected.

In the 1830s, the one glaring exception, the one area where the playing field looked to slope steeply upward in front of Americans aspiring to better their condition, was the Bank of the United States. The Bank was by far the largest and most powerful institution in the country. Worse, it was the creature of a rela-tively distant, aloof government in Washington. Unlike the country's political president, its monetary president was arrogant and "aristocratical." Worse, he showed himself capable of trying to use the power of his institution to influence both the electorate and the economy. Though not the many-headed hydra dreamed up by Jackson's propagandists, the Bank clearly menaced many Amer-icans, if only in their imagination.

Were the benefits provided by the Bank worth the political risk it posed? Maybe, maybe not. The United States was after all on a specie standard, a self-equilibrating (self-righting) system largely inimical to discretionary monetary policy. The Bank certainly decreased the cost of inland exchange and made the market for foreign exchange in the United States more efficient. Those were im-portant functions, but ones largely outside the national government's purview. The Bank also managed the government's payments and when necessary lent to it. But after the Bank's demise the government showed that it no longer needed the Bank; the Treasury could manage payments itself and raise funds by selling notes and bonds directly to investors. The virtual elimination of the national debt during Jackson's administration made it that much easier to dispense with the Bank's payment services. The Treasury still used banks and brokers when convenient to do so, but it no longer needed a giant federally chartered bank. Even in wartime, as the experiences of the Mexican and Civil wars demon-strated, the Treasury no longer needed a central bank.

Our relatively harsh criticism of Jefferson compared to Jackson is therefore no mistake. Both were leaders of nominally the same party, but there the simi-larities end. Jefferson wanted to the kill the Bank, and the rest of the financial system, at such an early stage that his success would have meant an abrupt end to the American economic miracle. Jefferson was also on much shakier legal ground because in the late eighteenth and early nineteenth centuries the Bank was clearly expedient—the financial debacle that occurred during the War of 1812 was ample proof of that—and hence constitutional. Moreover, his own finance minister, Albert Gallatin, made it clear that the Bank was a necessity. Finally, Jefferson's interpretation of the Constitution was inconsistent. He espoused a strict construction of the Constitution on the Bank issue, for example, but later maintained a loose construction on the Louisiana Purchase.

Jackson's view of the Constitution, in contrast, was entirely consistent. In addition to opposing the Bank, Jackson greatly reduced federal investments in private corporations and purely intrastate internal improvements. Yet, he was no advocate of a weak national government, greatly expanding what he saw as the legitimate ends of the federal government, including investment in ports, harbors, and lighthouses. He also battled Nullifiers, the Supreme Court, and others who sought to limit the power of the national government and especially its executive branch. Critics labeled him King Andrew, but unlike Biddle he was duly elected to office by the American people. His policies may not have been optimal, but they were consistent and had the support of a large number of Americans eager for a signal that they, and not the rich, really ran the country. That is why, in his own way, Jackson was one of our financial founding fathers, one of the men who helped to make America rich.

America owes its industrial might, the economic strength that ended slavery in the nineteenth century and saved democracy not once (World War I), not twice (World War II), but thrice (Cold War) in the twentieth century, to the financial founding fathers. The creative vision of Alexander Hamilton and Robert Morris, the administrative skill and economic insights of Tench Coxe, the sound and steady habits of Thomas Willing and Stephen Girard, the saving graces of Albert Gallatin, and the grasping, self-interested machinations of William Duer mixed, collided, competed, and, finally, harmonized to create the world's strongest and most beautiful financial system. While scholars and pundits debate the Bank War's impact on the U.S. economic and financial systems, we know that the struggle between Jackson and Biddle did not signal the end of the story of finance-led U.S. economic growth. The basis laid by our creator, our savior, our angels, our saint, and yes, even our sinner was simply too strong, too efficient, too important.

Apocalypse? No.

CONCORDANCE
Terms, People, and Timeline

TERMS

Assumption: Many of the debts the Patriots incurred during the Revolution were at first the responsibility of the state governments. As part of his financial program, U.S. Treasury Secretary Alexander Hamilton suggested legislation, eventually enacted by Congress, that allowed the federal government to "assume," or take responsibility for, the sundry state debts. In return for the old state obligations, the federal government issued three new bonds, "Sixes," which paid 6 percent interest in quarterly installments, "Threes," which did likewise but at the rate of 3 percent per annum, and "Deferreds," which paid no interest until 1801. "Assumption" greatly reduced the number of bonds and their risk of default (i.e., nonpayment), and hence proved a great boon to America's nascent securities markets. The process also served to unite the nation politically by creating incentives to strengthen the federal court, taxation, and infrastructure systems.

Banknotes: Bearer promissory notes, usually composed of engraved paper signed by at least the president and/or the cashier of the bank, redeemable in specie at the bank of issue. After about 1790, banknotes, bank deposits, and coins (mostly foreign until the 1850s) composed the bulk of the U.S. money supply.

Bills of credit: See paper money.

Discounts: A loan where the interest is deducted at the beginning of the loan term. For example, a merchant who successfully sought a $100 loan for 30 days would receive $99.52, the present value of the loan at 6 percent, today in exchange for his promise to pay to the bank $100 in 30 days. The equation used was simply the present value formula, or in other words: present value = future value$/(1 + $ interest rate$)^{\text{loan maturity}}$, or in this case $100/1.06^{.083333} = \$99.52$.

Federalist Party: The nation's first "conservative" political party espoused a broad interpretation of the U.S. Constitution that strengthened the power of the federal or national government. Most Federalists favored Hamilton's financial reform program and close commercial ties with Great Britain.

Golden goose: A metaphor for the financial system, the institutional financial intermediaries (banks and insurers) and markets (for equity and debt) that made the nation and its inhabitants rich by efficiently matching entrepreneurial energy to investor savings.

National bank: Depending on the context, this term may refer to the Bank of the United States (1791–1811), which we also occasionally refer to as the First Bank. Or, it may refer to the Bank of the United States (1816–36), a.k.a. the Second Bank, or Biddle's Bank.

The appellation "national" stems from the facts that both banks received their charters from the U.S. national (federal) government, not from a state government or governments, and that both banks established a network of branches in major commercial and political centers throughout the nation.

Paper money: Was a term applied to money issued or emitted by colonial or state governments. Like today's Federal Reserve Notes (the greenish bills in your wallet or purse), those paper IOUs or "bills of credit" paid no interest. But they were convenient to carry and spend and could be used to pay taxes. When a government issued too many of them, more than was necessary for everyday transactions, the paper bills lost value. Early Americans, who also could pay their obligations with coin or banknotes, saw this as "depreciation" of the paper money. In the 1970s, when the government again emitted too much money but there were no ready substitutes, Americans felt the effects as "inflation," or increases in the general price level.

Republican Party: Grew in the early 1790s in response to Hamiltonian Federalist policies. Most Republicans favored closer ties with France and a strict interpretation of the Constitution that favored the power of state governments over the national government. The party was composed of two wings or factions, the "Old" or "radical" Republicans, who believed in an agricultural economy with a limited need for institutional financial intermediation, and the "commercial" Republicans, who differed from Federalists mainly over foreign affairs. By 1815 or so, the Republican Party had almost entirely defeated the Federalist Party. During the ensuing "Era of Good Feelings," the Republican Party cleaved into two new parties, Andrew Jackson's Democrats and Henry Clay's National Republicans. Within a decade, the latter party morphed into the Whig Party, which on the eve of the Civil War planted the seeds for the modern Republican Party. So the early Republicans were what we would today call Democrats, and the Federalists joined with more conservative Republicans to form today's Republican Party.

Specie: Full-bodied gold and silver coins. Banks exchanged such coins for their notes and deposits upon the demand of the holder or owner. Specie circulated both domestically and internationally.

State bank: A bank that received its charter or act of incorporation from a state government, as opposed to the federal or national government.

PEOPLE

Adams, John (1735–1826) was a Massachusetts Federalist who served as second president of the United States. A learned, portly gentleman, Adams was one of the few Federalists who opposed Hamilton's financial reforms.

Adams, John Quincy (1767–1848) was the son of President John Adams and sixth president of the United States. Adams was a National Republican, or in other words a member of the conservative wing of the Republican Party that eventually mutated into the Whig Party.

Ames, Fisher (1758–1808) was a Federalist Party leader and member of Congress from Massachusetts. A renowned, Harvard-educated orator and essayist, Ames was one of Hamilton's staunchest defenders.

Arnold, Benedict (1741–1801) was the son of a Connecticut merchant. A veteran of the French and Indian War, Arnold was a leading Patriot general until the lure of gold induced his infamous act of treachery, compromising the key U.S. stronghold at West Point, New York.

Biddle, Clement (1740–1814) was the son of Philadelphia merchant John Biddle. Clement, a liberal Quaker, followed in his father's mercantile footsteps but after the Revolution, particularly after Hamilton's financial revolution, he became increasingly involved in securities brokerage.

Biddle, Nicholas (1786–1844) is best known for his long, largely successful term as president of the second Bank of the United States. But the Philadelphian, valedictorian of his class at Princeton, was also a capable diplomat and *literatus*. After the demise of the Second Bank, Biddle headed its corporate successor, the United States Bank, a state-chartered bank that he quickly ran into bankruptcy with the help of a severely worsening economy and his own hubris.

Bingham, William (1752–1804) was the son of a Philadelphia saddler of the same name. He graduated cum laude from Penn in 1768, then embarked on a highly successful commercial career. During the Revolution, Bingham traveled to French Martinique where he helped the rebels to import war materials and other contraband. In 1780 he returned to Philadelphia and married Anne Willing, daughter of Thomas Willing. Soon after, Bingham, a staunch nationalist and Federalist, became one of the largest stockholders in the Bank of North America. He later played a major role in the construction of the important and highly profitable Philadelphia and Lancaster Turnpike. Shortly before his death, successful land speculations may have made him the richest man in America.

Boudinot, Elias (1740–1821) was a Federalist Delaware Valley attorney, friend of Hamilton, and third director of the U.S. Mint.

Breck, Samuel (1771–1862) was born in Boston but moved to Philadelphia in 1792. A corporal in the federal army during the Whiskey Rebellion, Breck was later a merchant and politician. He was one of the most important directors of the first Bank of the United States.

Burr, Aaron (1756–1836) killed Alexander Hamilton in a duel in July 1804. In 1800, the consummate commercial Republican ironically had come close to indirectly killing Hamilton's financial system by using the discount window of his newly formed Manhattan Bank to persuade Manhattan's artisans to vote Republican. Though he tied with Jefferson in the electoral college, Burr, a former Revolutionary War soldier, Princeton grad, attorney, and U.S. senator, eventually lost the runoff election in the House and had to settle for the vice presidency. Soon after killing Hamilton, he engaged in a series of near treasonous acts in the western territories. Though acquitted of treason, he nevertheless fled the country.

Calhoun, John C. (1782–1850) enjoyed a long, distinguished career in public service that included stints as U.S. vice president, senator, and secretary of state. The illustrious South Carolinian began his career as a nationalist but ended it as a supporter of an extreme states' rights doctrine known as Nullification.

Cheves, Langdon (1776–1857) was born in South Carolina. A lawyer and congressman, he is best remembered for saving the Second Bank from the drunken clutches of William Jones and passing the important national institution on to Nicholas Biddle in good shape.

Constable, William (1752–1803) was born in Dublin, Ireland, but migrated to upstate New York to engage in the fur trade. He later established a commercial, financial, and industrial empire based out of his Manhattan counting house. Like many immigrants, Constable was a Federalist and a supporter of Hamilton's financial reform program.

Coxe, Tench (1755–1824) is our Judas because he forsook the Federalist Party for the commercial wing of the Republican Party after Hamilton promoted Oliver Wolcott ahead of him. Coxe, who already had a reputation for vacillation because he joined the Patriot cause after initially supporting the Crown, later made an unsuccessful attempt to sunder the Republican Party. He is best known for his vehement support of the development of the American manufacturing sector.

Craigie, Andrew (1754–1819) began his career as a druggist but later became heavily involved in land speculation and securities brokerage in the important Boston market. Like Morris, his financial fortunes waxed during the Revolution but waned thereafter. Craigie never made it to debtors' prison, but his young widow subsisted in straightened circumstances for decades.

Dickinson, John (1732–1808) was born in Maryland but he resided in Delaware and Pennsylvania most of his life. This British-educated attorney was in the colonial period a highly influential statesman and political pamphleteer, best known for *Letters from a Farmer in Pennsylvania,* which warned of British encroachments upon the liberties of Americans. He fell out of favor, however, when he proposed that Americans follow a more moderate path than that offered by the Declaration of Independence. By the final years of the Revolution, he was again popular enough to serve as the "president" of both Delaware and Pennsylvania. He supported adoption of the Constitution but later drifted into the Republican camp.

Duer, William (1743–99) was born in England, but our sinner was in many ways the quintessential American. Though heir to a considerable inheritance, Duer never felt rich enough. Nominally a Hamiltonian Federalist, Duer in the end proved to be out only for himself. Fittingly, he spent most of his final years in debtors' prison.

Gallatin, Albert (1761–1849), our savior, was the fourth Secretary of the Treasury, a diplomat, and later a commercial banker. Born in Geneva, Switzerland, Gallatin was a member of the commercial wing of the Republican Party. As Treasury secretary he staved off attempts by the radical or agrarian wing of the party to kill Hamilton's financial program, the golden goose.

Girard, Stephen (1750–1831) was born in France but he later moved to Philadelphia, where his successful mercantile and banking pursuits made him America's richest man. He is our saint because he cared for those afflicted with the yellow fever and because he bequeathed his vast fortune to Philadelphia's orphans, who to this day benefit from his largess.

Greene, Nathanael (1742–1786) was a Rhode Islander who, though of Quaker parentage, served with distinction as a general in the American Revolution. Washington instructed that Greene, probably the American side's most brilliant military strategist, should replace him as commander-in-chief should he die in battle.

Hamilton, Alexander (1755–1804) was the first Secretary of the Treasury and our creator. Born a bastard and soon orphaned, Hamilton emigrated to New York from his native West Indies on the eve of the Revolution, in which he fought with distinction. After the Revolution he trained himself quickly for the law, a profession well suited to his intense, logical mind. After putting his adopted country on the path to untold riches by helping it to establish a modern financial sector, Hamilton remained active in Federalist politics. What he would have accomplished had Burr not cut him down in his prime, only the real Creator knows with certainty.

Hillegas, Michael (1729–1804) was a Philadelphia merchant and Pennsylvania assemblyman. He served as Pennsylvania's treasurer and later as treasurer of the United States under the Articles of Confederation, in which post he aided Robert Morris. Like most businessmen of the era, Hillegas dabbled in many endeavors, including land and securities speculation, iron forging, retailing, and wholesaling.

Jackson, Andrew (1767–1845) hailed from South Carolina. After moving around for decades as a land speculator, horse race enthusiast, and duelist, Jackson's big break finally came during the War of 1812, when he had the opportunity to lead armies that slaughtered thousands of hardened Indian warriors and thousands of crack British troops. Always happy with winning generals, Americans almost voted the Old Hero into the presidency in 1824. They succeeded in 1828 and 1832. Jackson used his two terms in office to pay off the national debt and to kill the Second Bank's bid for Treasury Department. But he did not succeed in killing the golden goose, which had matured since Jefferson had tried to strangle it earlier in the century.

Jay, John (1745–1829) was the son of a Manhattan merchant. Rather than following his father in the commercial line, Jay became a lawyer. He is best known for the treaty that bore his name and that caused him to be burned in effigy, but Jay is also remembered for serving as the first chief justice of the U.S. Supreme Court, for drafting New York's first constitution, and for contributing to the famous *Federalist Papers*.

Jefferson, Thomas (1743–1826) has inspired more books than all of the other Founding Fathers combined. Jefferson was a genius in some fields, a champion of the farmer, and had vocal opinions on most subjects, including finance, which admittedly was not his strongest suit. Paradoxes often abounded with this fascinating founding father: he authored the Declaration of Independence yet remained a committed member of the slavocracy that eventually fomented the Civil War; he ran the nation for eight years but kept Monticello, his main plantation, afloat only with great difficulty; he was a committed bachelor, but DNA evidence suggests he could have fathered offspring with Sally Hemmings, one of his slaves.

Jones, William (1760–1831) was a Philadelphia-born merchant and Republican Party hack. He served in the Revolution with distinction and was Secretary of the Navy during the War of 1812. According to one historian, "Jones was a vigorous and efficient secretary." That may have been, but by the time he became president of the Second Bank, Jones was a drunk who nearly ruined the Bank with his unsound business practices. Jones had served as interim Treasury secretary from May 1813 to February 1814, but he had shown little flair for the field of finance during his tenure.

Kent, James (1763–1847) a conservative New York jurist, long chief justice of the Empire State's Supreme Court and later its chancellor, was most famous for his *Commentaries on American Law.*

King, Rufus (1755–1827) was born in Maine (then Massachusetts) and graduated from Harvard at the head of his class in 1777. The staunch Federalist moved to New York shortly after representing Massachusetts at the Constitutional Convention. He served as a diplomat and U.S. senator and was always a firm supporter of Hamilton's policies. King served as Charles C. Pinckney's running mate in 1804 and 1808 and was soundly defeated both times.

Knox, Henry (1750–1806) was born in Boston. A general during the Revolutionary War, he served as Secretary of War during the Confederation and the Washington Administration. He played little role in the Whiskey Rebellion or the Quasi-War with France because he disliked Hamilton and refused to serve under him. Knox was a large man, tipping the scales at 280 pounds. He died from an infection he acquired from swallowing a chicken bone.

Lee, Charles (1731–82) was born in England but served as a general in the Patriot army during the Revolution. A highly educated aristocrat, Lee soon came to denigrate both Washington and his ragtag army. When Washington lambasted him for cowardice during the Battle of Monmouth (June 28, 1778), Lee demanded court-martial proceedings to clear his name. He lost and was suspended for a year. Later, he was cashiered outright.

Lee, Charles (1758–1815) was a Virginia lawyer and U.S. attorney general. The younger brother of "Light-Horse Harry" (Henry) Lee, Charles Lee graduated from Princeton with honors in 1775. A committed Federalist, it fell to Lee as attorney general to enforce the infamous Alien and Sedition Acts. Later, as a private attorney, Lee was counsel in some famous legal cases, including *Marbury v. Madison,* the impeachment trial of Samuel Chase, and the treason trial of Aaron Burr.

Livingston, Brockholst (1757–1823) part of a large clan of Livingstons that dominated New York and New Jersey politics and business for several generations, first saw the light of day in New York City. Christened Henry Brockholst, he dropped his all-too-common first name so his identity would not be confused with those of his many cousins and nephews. Like Tench Coxe he was a Federalist turned Republican. Livingston was primarily a lawyer. Given his family connections and his Princeton degree, it is not surprising that he eventually landed himself a seat on the U.S. Supreme Court.

Livingston, Walter (1740–97) was born in Albany, part of the same great clan as Brockholst Livingston. Indeed, they were first cousins. In addition to his speculations, Walter found time to serve in the New York state assembly and the Continental Congress. Like Hamilton, Gallatin, and many other famous early New Yorkers, he is buried in Trinity Churchyard at the top of Wall Street.

Ludlow, Daniel (1750–1814) was born in Manhattan but educated in Holland. A commercial Republican, he became a successful merchant, insurer, and banker.

Maclay, William (1737–1804) was born and raised in Pennsylvania. At 6 foot 3 inches, Maclay was an imposing figure during both his colonial military and subsequent political career, which began late in the Revolutionary War with his election to the Pennsylvania assembly. Nominally a member of the Federalist Party, his political views were idiosyncratic. Unlike most Federalists, for instance, as a U.S. senator he strongly opposed Hamilton's financial reform program. Unsurprisingly, by 1796 he joined Tench Coxe in the ranks of apostate Federalists. He left posterity a very important and often-cited diary that details his view of events political, social, and economic.

Madison, James (1751–1836) was "the father of the Constitution" and fourth president of the United States. A Virginian, he soon split with the Washington administration and joined Jefferson's emerging Republican Party.

Monroe, James (1758–1831) was a Republican slaveholder and the fourth Virginian to serve as president of the United States. He fought with distinction in the Revolution, studied law under Thomas Jefferson, and slowly built up a political resume that made him Madison's heir apparent during the War of 1812.

Morris, Gouverneur (1752–1816) was not related to Robert Morris but the two often saw eye-to-eye on financial and business matters. Born near Manhattan, Morris came from a fairly well-to-do family with rich political connections in both New York and New Jersey. A Federalist, Morris suffered several major accidents, one of which cost him his left leg below the knee. He is also credited with editing the final draft of the Constitution.

Morris, Robert (1735–1806) was born in England but he helped to finance the closing days of the Revolution. A long-time partner of Thomas Willing, Morris is our fallen angel be-

cause his career followed a downward trajectory. After saving the Revolution and establishing the important Bank of North America, Morris eschewed his traditional mercantile pursuits in a quest for the holy grail of unparalleled riches. His luck and skill gave out
by the mid-1790s, however, so he had to take up residence in Philadelphia's debtors'
prison.

Necker, Jacques (1732–1804) was France's finance minister from 1776 to 1781 and 1788 to
1790. This was no mean feat given that he was a Protestant and that he came into life and
went out of it in Switzerland. Contemporaries widely regarded Necker as a financial
genius.

Pinckney, Charles C. (1745–1825) was a lawyer and planter from South Carolina. A Federalist who attended the 1787 Constitutional Convention in Philadelphia, Pinckney is best
remembered for his involvement in the infamous XYZ Affair, the attempted bribery of
U.S. diplomats by French schemers. Upon his return to America, he became third in
command of the U.S. army behind Washington and Hamilton. The Federalist Party officially nominated him for president in 1804 and 1808, but electors, even those in South
Carolina, favored Virginians over the South Carolinian.

Randolph, Edmund (1753–1813) served as governor of Virginia and U.S. attorney general
and secretary of state. A graduate of William and Mary and an attorney, Randolph, like
most Virginia planters, was a Republican.

Robespierre, Maximilien (1758–94) came to personify the bloody excesses of the French
Revolution. Responsible for the deaths of thousands of innocents, the not-so-innocent
Robespierre lost his head, literally, in July 1794.

Rush, Benjamin (1746–1813) was a physician, a professor of chemistry and of medicine, and
a social reformer. Born in Byberry, now a northern suburb of Philadelphia, he graduated
from Princeton in 1760 at age fourteen. Clearly gifted, Rush obtained in Scotland and
England what passed for advanced medical training. A delegate at Pennsylvania's ratifying convention, he pushed for adoption of the Constitution. Later, he also urged Pennsylvanians to adopt a less radical state constitution. Ironically, Rush's politics were
sounder than his medical theorizing, which led him to the conclusion that all physical
and mental maladies stemmed from the same cause and could be cured with the same
treatment, bloodletting and mercury purges. He later served as treasurer of the U.S.
Mint, an institution whose anemic condition predated Rush's arrival on the scene.

Salomon, Haym (c. 1740–85) was a New York financier and patriot presumably born in
Lissa, Poland, of Jewish parents. His efforts to finance the Revolution were second only
to those of Robert Morris. Had he lived, he likely would have headed one of the early nation's most important securities brokerage firms.

Schuyler, Philip John (1733–1804) was born in Albany, New York. A general during the
Revolution and an important New York politician, Schuyler is perhaps best known as
the father-in-law of Alexander Hamilton.

Smilie, John (1742–1812) was born in Ireland. He emigrated to Lancaster County, Pennsylvania in 1760 and of course took great joy in fighting the British during the Revolution. He moved further west at the end of the Revolution and was soon serving western interests in various political posts, including the state legislature. A foe of the Bank of North America and the U.S. Constitution, Smilie favored retention of Pennsylvania's radical constitution of 1776. Unsurprisingly, he became a Jeffersonian Republican in the early 1790s and upheld the Republican standard the rest of his days.

Smith, Adam (1723–90) was a famed Scottish political economist best known for his seminal treatise, *An Inquiry into the Nature and Causes of the Wealth of Nations* (1776), a brilliant defense of the efficacy of markets unfettered by commercial monopolies or government fiat.

Swanwick, John (1759?–1798) was born in Liverpool, England. Around 1770 his family settled in Pennsylvania. Swanwick, who joined the Patriot cause despite the fact that his father remained a Loyalist, became a merchant, banker, and congressman of the commercial Republican persuasion.

Troup, Robert (1757–1832), a Federalist land agent, attorney, and close companion of our creator, took his first breath in Elizabethtown, New Jersey. He inherited a fortune from his father, a sea captain and privateer who earned much booty and glory in America's colonial wars. Though orphaned at age eleven, Troup graduated from King's College (Columbia) in 1774. He died in New York City a rich man, but land speculations almost broke him in 1798.

Van Buren, Martin (1782–1862) was nicknamed the "Little Magician" by friends due to his diminutive physique but outsized political skills. Those skills eventually earned him a single term as president of the United States, the first New Yorker awarded that honor. The economic woes that the nation endured during most of his presidency, however, ensured that he would not be returned to office.

Wadsworth, Jeremiah (1743–1804) was a Connecticut-born merchant, Revolutionary War commissary, and Federalist congressman. He was also a securities speculator, banker, insurer, and manufacturer.

Washington, George (1732–99) was made first president of the United States in recognition of his services as Commander-in-Chief of the Continental Army during the Revolution. Unlike most slaveholding Virginia planters, Washington was a fervid nationalist, the titular head of the Federalist Party. Not by coincidence, he was also a skilled businessman and an avid investor.

Webster, Noah (1758–1843) was a Connecticut Federalist. The Revolution cut short his studies at Yale but that did not stop him from earning the appellation "The Schoolmaster of America" for his textbooks, including one that eventually sold over sixty-two million copies. He later compiled a dictionary that did even better.

Webster, Pelatiah (1725–95) is best known as a Federalist political economist. A Connecticut-born graduate of Yale, Webster moved to Philadelphia in the 1750s where he amassed a small fortune, most of which he lost assisting the rebel cause during the Revolution.

White, William (1748–1836) was a prominent, Philadelphia-born Episcopal bishop. A Penn graduate, White studied theology with William Smith, the college's provost and a leading liberal Anglican.

Willing, Thomas (1731–1821), our risen angel, was America's banking pioneer. Born in Philadelphia but educated in England, Willing was a prominent merchant, politician, and judge in colonial Pennsylvania. Long-time partner of Robert Morris, Willing fell out of political favor when he remained in British-occupied Philadelphia. He redeemed himself, however, by successfully steering the Bank of North America and the First Bank for two and a half decades. He died happy, the head of a large, beautiful, wealthy family.

Wilson, James (1742–98) was born in Scotland, where he attended university before sailing for America in 1765. After picking up a master's degree at the University of Pennsylvania, he studied law under John Dickinson. His education served him well in his later career as a Philadelphia lawyer, merchant, and Federalist politician.

Wolcott, Oliver (1760–1833) succeeded Hamilton as Secretary of the Treasury. A Yale-trained Federalist lawyer, he later served as governor of Connecticut, his home state. (He should not be confused with his father, Oliver Wolcott Sr, a signer of the Declaration of Independence who also served as governor of Connecticut.)

TIMELINE

1731: Thomas Willing born in Philadelphia.

1735: Robert Morris born in Liverpool, England.

1743?: William Duer born in Devonshire, England.

1750: Stephen Girard born in Bordeaux, France.

1754: Willing takes over family mercantile business when his father dies.

1755: Alexander Hamilton born in Nevis; Tench Coxe born in Philadelphia.

1757: Willing and Morris join in a partnership that soon becomes a leading mercantile firm in Philadelphia.

1761: Albert Gallatin born in Geneva, Switzerland.

1767: Andrew Jackson born in the Waxhaw settlement on the border of North and South Carolina.

1775: War commences; efforts to finance the rebellion begin in earnest.

1776: Americans declare their independence from Britain.

1777: British occupy Philadelphia (late summer) until mid 1778; Willing remains in the city; Coxe returns to the city with the British as a Loyalist.

1781: Continental Congress appoints Morris superintendent of finance (Feb.); Morris takes oath of office (June); creation and funding of the Bank of North America (summer to late fall); charter of Bank of North America granted by Continental Congress (Dec.).

1782: Bank of North America commences operations (Jan.); Willing named president.

1783: War for Independence ends with British evacuation of New York City.

1784: Creation of the Bank of New York. Hamilton writes the articles of incorporation; Morris resigns as superintendent of finance (Nov.).

1785: Duer appointed Secretary of the Treasury Board (Jan.).

1786: Biddle born in Philadelphia.

1789: Hamilton appointed Secretary of the Treasury (Sept.); Duer becomes second in command to Hamilton (fall).

1790: Hamilton's *Report on Public Credit* (Jan.) becomes public; Duer leaves the Treasury Department (April); Coxe joins the Treasury Department to replace Duer (May); the national government moves from New York to Philadelphia (completed by fall); Hamilton's *Report on the Bank* (Dec.) is made public.

1791: Hamilton's *Report for the Establishment of a Mint* (Jan.) is issued; Washington signs the bill to create the first Bank of the United States with a twenty-year charter (Feb.); Bank stock receipts (scripts) commence trading and rise 50 percent in one month (July); creation of the Society for the Establishment of Useful Manufactures (winter); first Bank opens for business in Philadelphia (Dec.) with Willing as president; Hamilton's *Report on Manufactures* (Dec.) becomes public.

1792: Panic of 1792—large defaults including Duer (March); first Bank of the United States opens branches for business in Baltimore, Boston, Charleston and New York (early spring); Washington signs the bill to create a mint (April).

1793: Yellow fever strikes Philadelphia and other cities (fall); Girard remains in the city.

1794: Whiskey Rebellion (summer, fall); Willing and Morris dissolve their longstanding partnership.

1795: Hamilton resigns as Treasury secretary (Jan.), and Wolcott replaces him.

1797: Wolcott dismisses Coxe from Treasury Department (Dec.).

1798: Morris, now bankrupt, enters debtors' prison.

1799: Duer dies after release from debtors' prison.

1800: Transfer of the government from Philadelphia to Washington, D.C. (completed by June 1801).

1801: Gallatin appointed Secretary of the Treasury (May); Morris released from prison (Aug.).

1804: Hamilton dies from a wound inflicted by Aaron Burr in a duel; he is buried on the grounds of Trinity Church at the top of Wall Street.

1806: Morris dies in Philadelphia.

1811: Congress votes not to renew the charter of the first Bank of the United States (Feb.); the bank closes its doors (March).

1812: Bank of Stephen Girard begins operation in the building formerly used by the first Bank of the United States (May); war breaks out with Great Britain (June).

1813: Girard and other bankers underwrite U.S. government bonds when the Treasury Department under Gallatin is unable to raise funds (through 1814).

1814: Gallatin leaves Treasury (Feb.); British forces sack Washington, D.C. (Aug.).

1815: War concludes with the Treaty of Ghent; Gallatin is one of three U.S. negotiators.

1816: Congress charters the second Bank of the United States for twenty years (Apr.).

1819: Biddle becomes a director of the second Bank of the United States; nationwide financial panic results in economic recession.

1821: Willing dies in Philadelphia.

1822: Biddle appointed president of the second Bank of the United States.

1824: Coxe dies in Philadelphia.

1829: Jackson sworn in as president and commences initial skirmishes in metaphorical Bank War.

1831: Girard dies in Philadelphia.

1832: Bank issue on forefront of politics as Biddle asks for renewal of charter (summer); Jackson vetoes an extension.

1833: Jackson orders the transfer of the government's money out of the Second Bank to so-called "pet banks" loyal to the Jackson administration; Biddle responds by restricting credit; the economy suffers.

1836: Second Bank of the United States closes its doors as charter is not renewed.

1844: Biddle dies in Philadelphia.

1845: Jackson dies at the Hermitage, near Nashville, Tennessee.

1849: Gallatin dies in Astoria, Long Island, and is buried on the grounds of Trinity Church but on the opposite side of the church from Hamilton.

INSPIRATION

To write this book, we analyzed literally thousands of sources, many of them primary (original) sources like financial ledgers, newspapers, diaries, account books, and sundry government records. We also consulted hundreds of books and articles written by historians and economists. We present here only the most important, most widely available sources that aided our story.

1. IN THE BEGINNING

The best overview of the colonial economy is John J. McCusker and Russell Menard, *The Economy of British America, 1607–1789* (Chapel Hill: University of North Carolina Press, 1985). Those looking for a quicker read can consult Edwin J. Perkins, *The Economy of Colonial America*, 2d ed. (New York: Columbia University Press, 1988).

Two major and relatively recent surveys of the founding period with good bibliographies are Stanley Elkins and Eric McKitrick, *The Age of Federalism: The Early American Republic, 1788–1800* (New York: Oxford University Press, 1993) and Bernard Bailyn et al., *The Great Republic: A History of the American People*, 4th ed. (Lexington, Mass.: D.C. Heath and Co., 1992).

Readers interested in the European antecedents of the U.S. financial system should consult Larry Neal, *The Rise of Financial Capitalism: International Capital Markets in the Age of Reason* (New York: Cambridge University Press, 1990) and James Macdonald, *A Free Nation Deep in Debt: The Financial Roots of Democracy* (New York: Farrar, Straus and Giroux, 2003).

Regarding the election of 1800, see Robert E. Wright, *Hamilton Unbound: Finance and the Creation of the American Republic* (Westport, Conn.: Greenwood, 2002) and Robert E. Wright, "Artisans, Banks, Credit, and the Election of 1800," *Pennsylvania Magazine of History and Biography* (July 1998), 211–39.

Important aspects of the growth of manufacturing in the early U.S. are chronicled in three recent books, Sean Patrick Adams, *Old Dominion, Industrial Commonwealth: Coal, Politics, and Economy in Antebellum America* (Baltimore: Johns Hopkins University Press, 2004), Doron S. Ben-Atar, *Trade Secrets: Intellectual Piracy and the Origins of American Industrial Power* (New Haven: Yale University Press, 2004) and Lawrence A. Peskin, *Manufacturing Revolution: The Intellectual Origins of Early American Industry* (Baltimore: Johns Hopkins University Press, 2003). For the rapid growth of American manufacturing output, see Joseph H. Davis, "A Quantity-Based Annual Index of U.S. Industrial Production, 1790–1915: An Empirical Appraisal of Historical Business-Cycle Fluctuations," Ph.D. diss., Duke University, 2002.

The classic treatments of early U.S. economic growth and industrialization are Stuart Bruchey, *The Roots of American Economic Growth, 1607–1861* (New York: Harper and Row, 1965), Thomas Cochrane, *Frontiers of Change: Early Industrialism in America* (New York: Oxford University Press, 1981), Brooke Hindle, *Engines of Change: The American Industrial Revolution, 1790–1860* (Washington, D.C.: Smithsonian Institution Press, 1986), and Douglass North, *The Economic Growth of the United States, 1790–1860* (Englewood Cliffs, N.J.: Prentice-Hall, 1961).

The best recent surveys of the financial-led growth hypothesis—the notion that banks, securities markets, insurance, and other aspects of finance play a crucial role in promoting economic growth—are by Ross Levine: "More on Finance and Growth: More Finance, More Growth?" *Federal Reserve Bank of St. Louis Review* (July/August 2003) and "Finance and Growth: Theory and Evidence," in *Handbook of Economic Growth* (forthcoming).

On debtors and Indians, see Woody Holton, *Forced Founders: Indians, Debtors, Slaves, and the Making of the American Revolution in Virginia* (Chapel Hill: University of North Carolina Press, 1999). Catherine Allgor, *Parlor Politics: In Which the Ladies of Washington Help Build a City and a Government* (Charlottesville: University Press of Virginia, 2000) and Cokie Roberts, *Founding Mothers: The Women Who Raised Our Nation* (New York: HarperCollins, 2004) are good places to start for more information regarding women and early politics. A good overview of slavery is Donald Wright (no relation), *African Americans in the Early Republic, 1789–1831* (Arlington Heights, Ill.: Harlan Davidson, 1993). For the economics of slavery, readers should consult Robert William Fogel, *Without Consent or Contract: The Rise and Fall of American Slavery* (New York: W. W. Norton, 1989) and Fred Bateman and Thomas Weiss, *A Deplorable Scarcity: The Failure of Industrialization in the Slave Economy* (Chapel Hill: University of North Carolina Press, 1981).

The big classic works on early U.S. financial history are Davis Rich Dewey, *Early Financial History of the United States,* 12th ed. (New York: Longmans Green and Company, 1934) and E. James Ferguson, *The Power of the Purse: A History of American Public Finance, 1776–1790* (Chapel Hill: University of North Carolina Press, 1961). The classic broader text, which takes the story through World War II, is Paul Studenski and Herman Edward Krooss, *Financial History of the United States* (New York: McGraw-Hill Book Company, 1952).

Important works on early financial regulation and early corporate finance are, respectively, Stuart Banner, *Anglo-American Securities Regulation: Cultural and Political Roots, 1690–1860* (New York: Cambridge University Press, 1998) and Jonathan Barron Baskin and Paul J. Miranti Jr, *A History of Corporate Finance* (New York: Cambridge University Press, 1997).

J. Van Fenstermaker, *The Development of American Commercial Banking: 1782–1837* (Kent, Ohio: Kent State University, 1965) and George Heberton Evans, *Business Incorporations in the United States, 1800–1943* (New York: National Bureau of Economic Research,

1948) are classic sources for the number of commercial banks and the number of corporations, respectively. On binding the interests of the state to that of early corporations through taxation, see Richard E. Sylla, John B. Legler, and John J. Wallis, "Banks and State Public Finance in the New Republic, 1790–1860," *Journal of Economic History* (June 1987), 391–403.

David J. Cowen, *The Origins and Economic Impact of the First Bank of the United States, 1791–1797* (New York: Garland Publishing, 2000) and Walter Buckingham Smith, *Economic Aspects of the Second Bank of the United States* (Cambridge: Harvard University Press, 1953) provide the best analyses of the nation's two early central banks.

An excellent recent study of early American religiosity and government formation is Gregory John Edwards, "'Righteousness Alone Exalts a Nation': Protestantism and the Spirit of the American Revolution," Ph.D. diss., SUNY Buffalo, 2002. Classic discussions of religion and economic growth include R. H. Tawney, *Religion and the Rise of Capitalism: A Historical Study* (New York: Harcourt, Brace, 1926) and Max Weber, *The Protestant Ethic and the Spirit of Capitalism* (New York: Scribners, 1958).

The term "golden goose" has been used by various writers in connection to financial systems or economic growth, most notoriously by Louis Brandeis, *Other People's Money and How the Bankers Use It* (New York: Frederick A. Stokes Company, 1932), 17, and most recently by Nobel laureate Douglass C. North, *Understanding the Process of Economic Change* (Princeton: Princeton University Press, 2005), 132.

This book owes its title to Joseph J. Ellis's *Founding Brothers: The Revolutionary Generation* (New York: Alfred A. Knopf, 2001).

2. THE CREATOR: ALEXANDER HAMILTON
Important biographies of Hamilton include Broadus Mitchell, *Alexander Hamilton: The National Adventure, 1788–1804* (New York: Macmillan, 1962), Forrest McDonald, *Alexander Hamilton: A Biography* (New York: W. W. Norton and Company, 1979), Harvey Flaumenhaft, *The Effective Republic: Administration and Constitution in the Thought of Alexander Hamilton* (Raleigh, N.C.: Duke University Press, 1992), Willard Randall, *Alexander Hamilton: A Life* (New York: HarperCollins, 2002), Richard Brookhiser, *Alexander Hamilton: American* (New York: Free Press, 2000), John C. Miller, *Alexander Hamilton: Portrait in Paradox* (New York: Harper and Brothers, 1959), and Louis M. Hacker, *Alexander Hamilton in the American Tradition* (New York: McGraw-Hill, 1957).

Far and away the best recent biography of Hamilton is Ron Chernow, *Alexander Hamilton* (New York: Penguin, 2004). Harold Syrett et al., eds., *The Papers of Alexander Hamilton* (New York: Columbia University Press) is the best source for original documents relating to Hamilton.

For more about Federalism, see Leonard White, *The Federalists: A Study in Administrative History* (New York: Macmillan, 1948). A great study of the founding period is Forrest McDonald, *E Pluribus Unum: The Formation of the American Republic, 1776–1790*, 2d ed. (Indianapolis: The Liberty Fund, 1979). Curtis Nettels, *The Emergence of a National Economy 1775–1815* (New York: Holt Rinehart and Winston, 1962) is a good, if somewhat dated, introduction to the basic economic history of the era. Readers should also consult Edwin J. Perkins, *American Public Finance and Financial Services, 1700–1815* (Columbus: Ohio University Press, 1994). Robert E. Wright, *The Origins of Commercial Banking in America, 1750-1800* (Lanham, Md.: Rowman and Littlefield, 2001) details the early history of U.S. banking and also contains an extended discussion of ground rents, on which topic see also Robert E. Wright, "Ground Rents Against Populist Historiography: Mid-Atlantic Land Tenure, 1750–1820," *Journal of Interdisciplinary History* (Summer 1998), 23–42.

Max M. Edling's book, *A Revolution in Favor of Government: Origins of the U.S. Constitution and the Making of the American State* (New York: Oxford University Press, 2003), puts Hamilton's Constitutional and fiscal (tax) achievements into international perspective.

Robert E. Wright overviews the history of the U.S. national debt in his series, *The U.S. National Debt, 1785–1900,* 4 vols. (London: Pickering and Chatto, 2005).

The two best studies of financial panics and securities speculation are Charles Kindleberger, *Manias, Panics, and Crashes: A History of Financial Crises,* 4th ed. (New York: John Wiley and Sons, 2000) and Edward Chancellor, *Devil Take the Hindmost: A History of Financial Speculation* (New York: Plume, 1999).

A classic biography of Hamilton's arch nemesis, Thomas Jefferson, is Dumas Malone, *Jefferson and His Time: Jefferson and the Rights of Man* (Boston: Little Brown and Company, 1951). For the stark ideological differences within the Republican Party, see Richard E. Ellis, *The Jeffersonian Crisis: Courts and Politics in the Young Republic* (New York: W. W. Norton and Company, 1971).

For more about Philadelphia and its important role in the early U.S. financial system, see Robert E. Wright, *The First Wall Street: Chestnut Street, Philadelphia, and the Birth of American Finance* (Chicago: University of Chicago Press, 2005).

Billy Smith, ed., *Life in Early Philadelphia: Documents from the Revolutionary and Early National Periods* (University Park: The Pennsylvania State University Press, 1995) contains vivid descriptions of life in Philadelphia in the era under study.

For a discussion of the dearth of "true" divorce laws in eighteenth and nineteenth century Anglo-America, see Lisa Wilson, *Life After Death: Widows in Pennsylvania, 1750–1850* (Philadelphia: Temple University Press, 1992).

For details about the business incorporation process, see Ronald Seavoy, *The Origins of the American Business Corporation, 1784–1885: Broadening the Concept of Public Service During Industrialization* (Westport, Conn.: Greenwood, 1982). For general background on the Mint, see Robert E. Wright, *The First Wall Street.* A more technical discussion of the crucial distinction between the unit of account and the medium of exchange can be found in Ron Michener and Robert E. Wright, "State 'Currencies' and the Transition to the U.S. Dollar: Clarifying Some Confusions," *American Economic Review* (June 2005), 682–703.

3. THE JUDAS: TENCH COXE

The best two biographies of Coxe are Jacob E. Cooke, *Tench Coxe and the Early Republic* (Chapel Hill: University of North Carolina Press, 1978) and Harold Hutcheson, *Tench Coxe: A Study in American Economic Development* (Baltimore: The Johns Hopkins University Press, 1938). We drew heavily on the former because Cooke, a former editor of the *Papers of Alexander Hamilton,* deeply understood the thought of both Coxe and the Creator.

Primary documents relating to Coxe are housed in the Historical Society of Pennsylvania and are available on microfilm. The life of this Judas, unlike the biblical one, is well documented. According to biographer Jacob Cooke, Coxe was "incapable of throwing away a single piece of paper," so the record he left historians is in many ways too fulsome (which we mean in both the modern and archaic sense), while those left by other Founders, particularly Willing, Morris, and Hamilton, are much too slim. Readers may prefer, therefore, to consult Coxe's published works instead, the most important of which was his 1794 effort, *A View of the United States of America in a Series of Papers Written at Various Times, in the Years between 1787 and 1794,* which was widely reprinted in the twentieth century.

For more about the Constitution as a solution to agency problems, see Robert E. Wright, *Hamilton Unbound: Finance and the Creation of the American Republic.* Early technological espionage is the subject of Doron Ben-Atar's "Alexander Hamilton's Alternative: Technology Piracy and the Report on Manufactures," *William and Mary Quarterly* 52 (1995), 389–414 and his *Trade Secrets: Intellectual Piracy and the Origins of American Industrial Power* (New Haven: Yale University Press, 2004). The best source on the SEUM remains Joseph S. Davis, *Essays in the Earlier History of American Corporations* (New York: Russell and Russell, 1917). On the growth of manufacturing in the Philadelphia region in the early nineteenth century, be certain to read Diane Lindstrom, *Economic Development in the Philadelphia Region, 1810–1850* (New York: Columbia University Press, 1978). A vivid primary source on the same topic is Eli Bowen, *The Pictorial Sketch-Book of Pennsylvania* (Philadelphia: William Bromwell, 1853). Lawrence A. Peskin, *Manufacturing Revolution: The Intellectual Origins of Early American Industry* (Baltimore: Johns Hopkins University Press, 2003) describes the early ideological underpinnings of industrialization.

On the securities regulations that forced Coxe and other Treasury officials to give up private business pursuits while in office, see Stuart Banner's *Anglo-American Securities Regulation: Cultural and Political Roots, 1690–1860* (New York: Cambridge University Press, 1998). On the economic inefficiency of slavery, see Robert E. Wright "Bound and Unbound Labor: Socioeconomic Decision-Making," in James Mueller, ed. *Against Slavery: Systems and Institutions of Immediacy* (Philadelphia: University of Pennsylvania Press, forthcoming).

Benedict Arnold is the subject of James Kirby Martin's *Benedict Arnold, Revolutionary Hero: An American Warrior Reconsidered* (New York: New York University Press, 1997).

4. THE SINNER: WILLIAM DUER

The best studies of Duer's life and career are Robert Jones, *"The King of the Alley" William Duer: Politician, Entrepreneur, and Speculator, 1768–1799* (Philadelphia: American Philosophical Society, 1992) and Joseph S. Davis, *Essays in the Earlier History of American Corporations*. Davis is also an excellent source of information regarding early U.S. corporations and IPOs.

For more sympathetic treatments of Duer, see Cathy Matson, "Public Vices, Private Benefit: William Duer and His Circle, 1776–1792," in *New York and American Capitalism* (New York: New York Historical Society), 72–123 and the anonymous tract "Colonel William Duer," *The Knickerbocker* (August 1852), 96–103.

A superb treatment of bankruptcy in the period is Bruce Mann, *Republic of Debtors: Bankruptcy in the Age of American Independence* (Cambridge, Mass.: Harvard University Press, 2003). Readers interested in financial panics and stock speculation should read Charles Kindleberger, *Manias, Panics, and Crashes,* and Edward Chancellor, *Devil Take the Hindmost: A History of Financial Speculation.*

For more about the British Empire and the important role that finance played in its establishment and perpetuation, see Niall Ferguson, *Empire: The Rise and Demise of the British World Order and the Lessons for Global Power* (New York: Basic Books, 2002), Niall Ferguson, *The Cash Nexus: Money and Power in the Modern World, 1700–2000* (New York: Basic Books, 2001), and John Brewer, *The Sinews of Power: War, Money, and the English State, 1688–1783* (New York: Alfred A. Knopf, 1989).

The best recent biography of Gouverneur Morris is Richard Brookhiser's *Gentleman Revolutionary: Gouverneur Morris, the Rake Who Wrote the Constitution* (New York: Free Press, 2003).

5. THE SAVIOR: ALBERT GALLATIN

The late 1950s witnessed the publication of several strong biographies of Gallatin, including Raymond Walters Jr, *Albert Gallatin, Jefferson Financier and Diplomat* (New York: Macmillan, 1957), Frank Ewing, *America's Forgotten Statesman: Albert Gallatin* (New York: Vantage, 1959), and Alexander Balinky, *Albert Gallatin: Fiscal Theories and Policies* (New Brunswick: Rutgers University Press, 1958). We also found John Austin Stevens, *Albert Gallatin* (Boston: Houghton-Mifflin, 1883) useful. Printed primary source material of Gallatin's writings includes Henry Adams, *The Writings of Albert Gallatin* (Philadelphia: J. B. Lippincott, 1879) and E. James Ferguson, *Selected Writings of Albert Gallatin* (Indianapolis: Bobbs-Merrill, 1967). The most detailed treatment of Gallatin's relationship with the First Bank can be found in David J. Cowen, *Origins and Economic Impact of the First Bank of the United States.*

For more about banking in the antebellum era, see Bray Hammond, *Banks and Politics in America from the Revolution to the Civil War* (Princeton: Princeton University Press, 1957) and Howard Bodenhorn's *A History of State Banking in Antebellum America* (New

York: Cambridge University Press, 2000) as well as his *State Banking in Early America: A New Economic History* (New York: Oxford University Press, 2003).

For Jefferson's personal financial difficulties, see just about any of his biographies, but the definitive discussion is Herbert Sloan, *Principle and Interest: Thomas Jefferson and the Problem of Debt* (New York: Oxford University Press, 1995).

Little is known about what the common man thought about the financial system. It is not clear that William Manning was as common as his biographers let on. Moreover, a close study of Manning's book suggests that he disliked the funding system only because he was ignorant of some of its finer points. See Sean Wilentz and Michael Merrill, eds., *The Key of Liberty: The Life and Democratic Writings of William Manning, "A Laborer," 1747–1814* (Cambridge, Mass.: Harvard University Press, 1993).

Internal improvements is the subject of John L. Larson, *Internal Improvement: National Public Works and the Promise of Popular Government in the Early United States* (Chapel Hill: University of North Carolina Press, 2001). The best recent treatment of the Erie Canal (Grand Canal) is Peter L. Bernstein, *Wedding of the Waters: The Erie Canal and the Making of a Great Nation* (New York: W. W. Norton and Company, 2005). For Pennsylvanians' lust for turnpikes, see John Majewski, *A House Dividing: Economic Development in Pennsylvania and Virginia Before the Civil War* (New York: Cambridge University Press, 2000).

The development of central banking theory can be traced in Walter Bagehot, *Lombard Street: A Description of the Money Market* (New York: Scribner, Armstrong and Co., 1873), Bray Hammond, *Banks and Politics in America From The Revolution to the Civil War* (Princeton: Princeton University Press, 1957), Fritz Redlich, *The Molding of American Banking,* 2 vols. (New York: Johnson Reprint Corporation, 1968), and Lloyd Mints, *A History of Banking Theory in Great Britain and the United States* (Chicago: University of Chicago Press, 1945).

Good overviews of the War of 1812 are supplied by John C. Stagg, *Mr. Madison's War: Politics, Diplomacy, and Warfare in the Early American Republic, 1783–1830* (Princeton University Press, 1983), and Donald Hickey, *The War of 1812: A Forgotten Conflict* (Urbana: University of Illinois Press, 1989).

6. ANGELS RISEN AND FALLEN: THOMAS WILLING AND ROBERT MORRIS
Biographical information about Willing can be found in Robert E. Wright, "Thomas Willing (1731-1821): Philadelphia Financier and Forgotten Founding Father," *Pennsylvania History* 63 (1996), 525–60, and Eugene Slaski, "Thomas Willing: Moderation During the American Revolution," Ph.D. diss., Florida State University, 1971.

The classic Morris biography is Clarence Ver Steeg, *Robert Morris: Revolutionary Financier* (Philadelphia: University of Pennsylvania Press, 1954). But see also Eleanor Young, *Forgotten Patriot: Robert Morris* (New York: Macmillan Company, 1950), and Barbara Chernow, "Robert Morris and Alexander Hamilton: Two Financiers in New York," in

Joseph Frese and Jacob Judd, eds., *Business Enterprise in Early New York* (Tarrytown, N.Y.: Sleepy Hollow Press, 1979), 77–98. The best recent scholarly treatment of Morris, *The Papers of Robert Morris,* edited by E. James Ferguson, Elizabeth Nuxoll, and a host of others mostly concerns his tenure as superintendent of finance.

The stories of Morris and of Willing can also be viewed through the lenses of third parties, like business associates and in-laws such as William Bingham, the best biography of which is Robert C. Alberts, *The Golden Voyage: The Life and Times of William Bingham, 1752–1804* (Boston: Houghton Mifflin Company, 1969), and John Nicholson, whose life and times are chronicled in Robert Arbuckle, *Pennsylvania Speculator and Patriot: The Entrepreneurial John Nicholson, 1757–1800* (University Park: Pennsylvania State University Press, 1975).

Consult Laurens R. Schwartz, *Jews and the American Revolution: Haym Salomon and Others* (Jefferson, N.C.: McFarland and Co., 1987), and Samuel Rezneck, *Unrecognized Patriots: Jews in the American Revolution* (Westport, Conn.: Greenwood Press, 1975), for more about America's most important early broker.

See Robert E. Wright and George David Smith, *Mutually Beneficial: The Guardian and Life Insurance in America* (New York: New York University Press, 2004), for more about the development of American life insurance.

A fine recent treatment of the wartime economy is Richard Buel Jr, *In Irons: Britain's Naval Supremacy and the American Revolutionary Economy* (New Haven: Yale University Press, 1998). Buel also discusses the Bank of North America, which is the primary subject of George Rappaport's *Stability and Change in Revolutionary Pennsylvania: Banking, Politics, and Social Structure* (University Park: Penn State University Press, 1996).

For the early years of commercial banking more generally, see David Cowen, *The Origins and Economic Impact of the First Bank of the United States, 1791–1797,* and Robert E. Wright, *Origins of Commercial Banking in America, 1750–1800.* The latter source also discusses ground rents, as does Wright's "Ground Rents Against Populist Historiography: Mid-Atlantic Land Tenure, 1750-1820," *Journal of Interdisciplinary History* (Summer 1998), 23–42 and Wright's *The First Wall Street: Chestnut Street, Philadelphia, and the Birth of American Finance,* which also contains a chapter-length biography of Michael Hillegas.

The business strategies of Thomas Passmore are discussed in Robert E. Wright, "The First Phase of the Empire State's 'Triple Transition': Banks' Influence on the Market, Democracy, and Federalism in New York, 1776–1838," *Social Science History* 21 (Winter 1997), 521–58.

7. THE SAINT: STEPHEN GIRARD

The best biography of Girard is still Harry Emerson Wildes, *Lonely Midas: The Story of Stephen Girard* (New York: J. J. Little and Ives Company, 1943), while by far the best study of Girard's bank is Donald R. Adams Jr, *Finance and Enterprise in Early America: A Study of Stephen Girard's Bank, 1812–1831* (Philadelphia: University of Pennsylvania Press, 1978). J. H. Powell, *Bring Out Your Dead: The Great Plague of Yellow Fever in Philadelphia in 1793* (Philadelphia: University of Pennsylvania Press, 1949) details Girard's role in the yellow fever epidemic of 1793.

Consult Tamara Thornton, *Cultivating Gentlemen: The Meaning of Country Life Among the Boston Elite, 1785–1860* (New Haven: Yale University Press, 1989) for the practices of gentlemen farmers. For vivid descriptions of Philadelphia's antebellum economy, see Eli Bowen, *The Pictorial Sketch-Book of Pennsylvania* (Philadelphia, Willis P. Hazard, 1852).

A great discussion of the prices of bank notes in this period is Gary Gorton, "Reputation Formation in Early Bank Note Markets," *Journal of Political Economy* 104 (1996), 346–97.

The best recent discussion of the impact of Jeffersonian trade restrictions on the U.S. economy is Douglas Irwin, "The Welfare Costs of Autarky: Evidence from the Jeffersonian Embargo, 1807–1809," *Review of International Economics* (forthcoming).

The history of investment banking is the subject of Donald Adams's "The Beginning of Investment Banking in the United States," *Pennsylvania History* 45 (1978), 99–116, and Vincent Carosso's *Investment Banking in America: A History* (Cambridge, Mass.: Harvard University Press, 1970). The best history of the Rothschild banking empire is Niall Ferguson, *The World's Banker: The History of the House of Rothschild* (London: Weidenfeld and Nicolson, 1998), while that of J. P. Morgan is Ron Chernow's *The House of Morgan: An American Banking Dynasty and the Rise of Modern Finance* (New York: Atlantic Monthly Press, 1990).

For further study of early U.S. corporate finance and governance, readers should consult Robert E. Wright, ed., *The History of Corporate Finance: Development of Anglo-American Securities Markets, Financial Practices, Theories and Laws*, 6 vols. (London: Pickering and Chatto, 2003) and Robert E. Wright, Wray Barber, Matthew Crafton, and Anand Jain, eds., *History of Corporate Governance: The Importance of Stakeholder Activism*, 6 vols. (London: Pickering and Chatto, 2004).

No one knows for sure what America's aggregate output was in these early decades, but estimates are available in sources like Thomas S. Berry, *Estimated Annual Variations in Gross National Product, 1789 to 1909* (Richmond: Bostwick Press, 1968).

8. APOCALYPSE NO: ANDREW JACKSON AND NICHOLAS BIDDLE

Biographical information about Jackson can be found in Robert Remini, *The Life of Andrew Jackson* (New York: Harper and Row, 1988) and H. W. Brands, *Andrew Jackson: His Life and Times* (New York: Doubleday, 2005). The best narrative of the Bank War is still Robert Remini, *Andrew Jackson and the Bank War* (New York: W. W. Norton, 1967), but see also Bray Hammond, *Banks and Politics in America: From the Revolution to the Civil*

War (Princeton: Princeton University Press, 1957). Our interpretation of Jackson's views of the Constitution is based on Richard E. Ellis, *The Union at Risk: Jacksonian Democracy, States' Rights and the Nullification Crisis* (New York: Oxford University Press, 1987). The classic source on Jacksonian democracy is Arthur Schlesinger Jr, *The Age of Jackson* (Boston: Little, Brown and Company, 1945).

For more about the credit implications of dueling, and the role of banks in the election of 1800, see Robert E. Wright, *Hamilton Unbound: Finance and the Creation of the American Republic.* On the Bank's role in the Mississippi Valley, see Richard Kilbourne, *The Bank of the United States in Mississippi, 1831–1852: A Study of Exchange and Money Markets* (forthcoming). On Nicholas Biddle himself, see Thomas Govan, *Nicholas Biddle: Nationalist and Public Banker, 1786–1884* (Chicago: University of Chicago Press, 1959).

The best study of the Panic of 1819 and its aftermath is still Murray Rothbard, *The Panic of 1819: Reactions and Policies* (New York: Columbia University Press, 1962). For more on the global financial troubles in 1825, see Frank Griffith Dawson, *The First Latin American Debt Crisis: The City of London and the 1822–25 Loan Bubble* (New Haven: Yale University Press, 1990). The classic source on the Panic of 1837 and its aftermath is Peter Temin, *The Jacksonian Economy* (New York: Norton, 1969).

On the repayment of the national debt, see Robert E. Wright, ed., *The U.S. National Debt, 1785–1900.* For extended discussion of the finance-led growth hypothesis, see Ross Levine, "More on Finance and Growth: More Finance, More Growth?" *Federal Reserve Bank of St. Louis Review* (July/August 2003), and Ross Levine, "Finance and Growth: Theory and Evidence," in *Handbook of Economic Growth* (forthcoming).

CONCORDANCE

Robert E. Wright, "Banking and Politics in New York, 1784–1829," Ph.D. diss., SUNY Buffalo, 1997, and David J. Cowen, *The Origins and Economic Impact of the First Bank of the United States, 1791-1797,* contain extensive glossaries of financial terms and concepts.

Other sources of immense value for the study of financial history include: Rafael Bayley, *The National Loans of the United States,* 2d ed. (Washington: Government Printing Office, 1882), Jonathan Elliot, *The Funding System of the United States and Great Britain,* 2 vols. (Washington: Blair and Rives, 1845), Sidney Homer and Richard E. Sylla, *A History of Interest Rates,* 3d ed. rev. (New Brunswick: Rutgers University Press, 1996), John J. McCusker, *Money and Exchange in Europe and America, 1600–1775: A Handbook* (Chapel Hill: University of North Carolina Press, 1978).

On the development of U.S. political parties, see Richard Hofstadter, *The American Political Tradition and the Men Who Made It* (New York: Alfred Knopf, 1943).

The history of the early U.S. Supreme Court can be fruitfully investigated via G. Edward White's *The Marshall Court and Cultural Change, 1815–1835* (New York: Oxford University Press, 1991).

The best source for basic biographical data on prominent personages is now *American National Biography,* especially the full-text searchable online edition. People excluded from the *ANB* can sometimes be tracked down via older biographical reference standards like the *Dictionary of American Biography, Appleton's Encyclopedia* (which can be accessed for free on the web), or more specialized works like Craig Horle, Joseph S. Foster, et al., eds. *Lawmaking and Legislators in Pennsylvania: A Biographical Dictionary,* 3 vols. (Philadelphia: University of Pennsylvania Press, 1991, 1997, forthcoming).

INDEX